Transition and Turmoil in the Atlantic Alliance

Transition and Turmoil in the Atlantic Alliance

Edited by

Robert A. Levine

CRANE RUSSAK
A member of the Taylor & Francis Group
New York • Philadelphia • Washington, DC • London

USA	Publishing Office:	Taylor & Francis New York, Inc. 79 Madison Ave., New York, NY 10016-7892
	Sales Office:	Taylor & Francis Inc. 1900 Frost Road, Bristol, PA 19007-1598
UK		Taylor & Francis Ltd. 4 John St., London WC1N 2ET

TRANSITION AND TURMOIL IN THE ATLANTIC ALLIANCE

1 2 3 4 5 6 7 8 9 0   B R B R   9 8 7 6 5 4 3 2 1

This book was set in Times Roman by CRC Press. The editors were Andrew N. Bartlett and Corinne Naden; the production supervisor was Peggy M. Rote. Cover design by Debra Eubanks Riffe.
Printing and binding by Braun-Brumfield, Inc.

A CIP catalog record for this book is available from the British Library.

Library of Congress Cataloging-in-Publication Data

Transition and turmoil in the Atlantic alliance / edited by Robert A.
  Levine.
      p.   cm.
    Includes bibliographical references and index.
    1. North Atlantic Treaty Organization. 2. Europe—Military
  policy. 3. United States—Military policy. I. Levine, Robert A.
  UA646.3.T733   1991
  355′.031′091821—dc20   91-13220
                                                        CIP

ISBN 0-8448-1701-5 (case)
ISBN 0-8448-1702-3 (paper)

Contents

Preface   ix

Chapter 1   **Introduction**   1
                 Robert A. Levine

                 Flows   4
                 Timetables   8
                 Interactions   10
                 Notes   12

Chapter 2   **The United States**   13
                 Robert A. Levine

                 Variables   14
                 Canonical Scenario   18
                 Varying Scenarios   21
                 U.S.-Initiated Variations   27
                 Notes   29

Chapter 3   **A Unified Germany**   31
                 Ronald D. Asmus

                 Introduction   31
                 Consequences of Unification: The Statistics   32
                 The New Political Landscape   35
                 The New Economic Landscape   48
                 The New Foreign Policy Environment   60
                 Future German Armed Forces and Defense Planning   76
                 New Challenges and New Risks   84

| | | Germany's Triple Transition | 97 |
| | | Notes | 103 |

| **Chapter 4** | **France** | | **111** |

Gregory Flynn

	Shifting Context and Changing Assumptions	114
	Emerging Policy Context	118
	Future Policy Directions	126
	Conclusions	137
	Notes	137

| **Chapter 5** | **The United Kingdom** | **141** |

Phil Williams

	The Underlying Judgments and Assumptions	145
	Challenges to the Policy Framework	150
	Adjusting to Change	161
	Notes	166

| **Chapter 6** | **Italy** | **169** |

Ian Lesser

	Key Assumptions	170
	Italian Security Policy and the Alliance: Likely Scenarios	177
	Some Variations on the Likely Case	189
	Conclusions	191
	Notes	192

| **Chapter 7** | **The Low Countries** | **195** |

Richard A. Bitzinger

	Domestic Developments and the Security Consensus	195
	Depillarization and the Polarization of the Political Process	197
	Effect on the Traditional Security Consensus	201
	Recent Trends in Belgian and Dutch Defense Efforts	203
	Belgian and Dutch Security Policy Over the Near Term	209
	Conclusion	213
	Notes	215

Chapter 8 **Scandinavia** **217**
John Lund

Key Assumptions 218
Danish Security Policy: The Next Five Years 222
Specific Danish Issue Areas 225
Some Variations on the Likely Case 231
Conclusions About the Future of Danish Security
  Policy 234
Norwegian Security Policy: The Next Five Years 235
Specific Norwegian Issue Areas 241
Some Variations on the Likely Case 247
Conclusions About the Future of Norwegian Security
  Policy 251
Policy Recommendations for Scandinavian NATO 251
Notes 252

Chapter 9 **Conclusion** **255**
Robert A. Levine

The Key Players: Into the 1990s 255
Premises for U.S. Policy 262
General Recommendations for U.S. Policy 264
Note 267

Index 269

About the Contributors 283

Preface

This book originated as part of a 1988 RAND Corporation Project AIR FORCE study for the United States Air Forces, Europe, on alternative postures for Europe-based U.S. nuclear deterrent forces. A number of new issues had been raised by the negotiations of the previous year that had led to the signing of the INF treaty by (then) President Reagan and Chairman Gorbachev.

The study examined both military/deterrent uses for American nuclear weapons in Europe and political variables affecting alternative postures. It was clear from the start that the political variables—ranging from the desire of some Europeans for continued strong coupling of deterrence of a Soviet attack with U.S. nuclear might, to the antipathy of other Europeans toward any nuclear weapons, and including American views of these issues—should be at least as important as military considerations in any analysis of nuclear posture. The study therefore commissioned expert analyses of the NATO policies of the major members of the Alliance: the United States; the Federal Republic of Germany; France; the United Kingdom; Italy; the Low Countries; and Scandinavia. Most of the analysts involved in this effort were members of the RAND staff; two of them were consultants, including the only non-American among the authors, the British writer of the chapter on the United Kingdom.

In early 1989, it was decided that a compilation of the analyses would make a useful book. Remarkably, a review of the project after the revolutions of late 1989 and the onset of rapid German unification suggested that with the obvious exception of the chapter on Germany, the rest of the material had been written about fundamental policy roots and needed only updating to retain its utility.

The German chapter was wholly rewritten (based on a paper supported by RAND's Army Research Division) and the others were updated; the result is *Transition and Turmoil in the Atlantic Alliance,* a title that is even more appropriate at the time of publication than it was at the time of conception. The study consists of a brief introduction, seven chapters on the major NATO nations and regions, and a final chapter concerning the implications of the others for Europe's security future in general and for U.S. policy toward Europe in particular.

Robert A. Levine

Chapter 1

Introduction

Robert A. Levine

Life'd not be worth living if we didn't keep our inimies.—Mr. Dooley[1]

This book examines the European security policies of the West, as Europe, beginning in the East, is transforming itself with a rapidity unprecedented since 1945.

The political/military examination is based on two premises, one analytical and predictive, the other normative and prescriptive. The analytical premise is that the North Atlantic Treaty Organization (NATO), which has underwritten the security and freedom of Western Europe for the last 40 years, is under substantial internal strain. One can argue about the initial causes of that strain. A few years ago, some Europeans, particularly among the French, contended vigorously that it was caused initially by American policy[2]; subsequently, others, also including many French, pointed to the Federal Republic of Germany.[3] Some Germans, even before the fall of the Berlin Wall and the frictions attendant upon rapid reunification, bridled at perceived American and other NATO infringements on their sovereignty. Some Americans returned their allies' favors by blaming West European decadence.[4] My own analysis, set forth elsewhere, suggested that in spite of dubious moves from both sides of the Atlantic Alliance, particularly from the United States from 1977 through 1988, the growing intra-NATO strains since 1985 have been based largely on uncertain Alliance reactions to the unprecedentedly radical initiating actions of the Soviet Union under Mikhail Gorbachev, rather than on any first causes from within Western nations.[5] Now, what had begun in the Soviet Union itself has been magnified and accelerated in what were once known as the Soviet "satellites" of Eastern Europe. In particular, the disappearance of the "threat" from the Warsaw Pact has thrown into question the concept and to some extent the very existence of the Alliance.

1

Gorbachev broke the ice of 40 years of Soviet intractability, and the currents thus liberated have shifted and formed whirlpools and vortices. Hence the initial quotation from the turn-of-the-century Irish-American political wit. We were happy with Brezhnev and Gromyko as "inimies"; we are uncomfortable that Gorbachev and Shevardnadze might want to be our friends, thus leaving us bereft of our old "inimies."

Who started the process of change, however, is important only insofar as it affects what is now happening and is likely to happen in the future. Although the Alliance was formed to protect Western Europe against the Soviet Union and that remains the stated *raison d'être*, NATO policy has always been largely inwardly directed—toward maintaining the internal coherence of the Alliance in the face of perceived threats from the East.[6] Gorbachev's massive shifts in Soviet policy have changed the external pressures, but until very recently the problems and the debates have revolved mainly about NATO's internal adaptations to these external shifts.

Because of the unprecedented nature of the Eastern changes, however, the resulting strains within the West are also unprecedented. The institutional arrangements into which Western Europe and North America have structured themselves are challenged. This is true of the economic institutions; changes in Eastern Europe have suggested to some a need for reexamining the shaping of Western Europe's Economic Community, the EC. It is even more true of NATO, the basic security institution with which this book is concerned. Nobody challenges the continuing necessity for increased European economic integration; that need has been made even more acute by the Eastern changes. But the reduction of the security threat to the West,[7] brought about by apparent Soviet willingness to reduce unilaterally and negotiate away multilaterally its massive conventional military preponderance in Europe and by the newfound independence of the other members of the Warsaw Pact, clearly throws into question the future structure of NATO and perhaps even its near-term as well as its long-run existence.

The normative premise of the book is that Alliance survival is to be hoped for and worked for by the United States, at least for some years into the future until the peaceful transformation of Europe is much clearer than it is now. NATO has formed the foundation for West European security against military aggression and intimidation, for national independence and political freedom, and for economic prosperity through the last 40 years; since American security continues to be based in large measure on European stability, the well-being of the United States is also dependent upon the survival of NATO.

It may be argued that such reasoning has now become obsolete; even Secretary of Defense Richard Cheney has suggested that "It doesn't make a lot of sense to spend a lot of time worrying about the Polish army actively participating in an attack on Western Europe."[8] Indeed, with the unification of Germany, parts of the army of the former German Democratic Republic have been incorporated into the *Bundeswehr* of the Federal Republic.

In spite of this radical reduction of the military threat to the West, however, NATO remains important for three reasons. First, things change; although it seems highly unlikely that the Soviet Union will return to the military threats of Stalinism even if it should build an economy that can support both military might and consumer satisfaction, it is still within the realm of possibility that a future turn will revive some variety of Soviet-induced military/political danger to Western Europe. Second, and perhaps more important, the very shifts that have relegated a coordinated attack by the armies of the Warsaw Pact to a remote consideration outside the ken of real security planning conjure up potential new threats—e.g., the Balkanization of the Balkans and north—that make it undesirable for the West to simply declare peace throughout Europe and go about its business. And third, NATO remains much the most important transatlantic *political* link, not to be given up lightly until others are much firmer.

These contentions underlie the normative premise that NATO is still important for the United States and Western Europe. They also suggest, however, that it is the *existence* of NATO, rather than any specific political or military configuration, that remains the crux. The key to security has been the existence of a coherent Alliance of democratic nations, able to credibly threaten to open the Pandora's box of nuclear war by "coupling" conventional and nuclear weapons sited in Europe to U.S. strategic weapons that might ultimately be used against targets in the Soviet Union. Since 1967, the coupling strategy has been known as "Flexible Response," but what is essential is not such that specific strategy, but the credibility and deterrent effect of the coupling. The premise here is that the foundation of deterrent credibility is a politically sound and confident Alliance, not the details of any military posture.

This book is about the NATO policies of the member nations of the Alliance and their interactions. It contains seven chapters by separate authors: individual analyses of the underlying factors governing the policies of the five largest members—the United States, the Federal Republic of Germany, France, the United Kingdom, and Italy; and discussions of the Low Countries and the Scandinavian members. A concluding chapter discusses the ways in which these policies may affect the changing future of Europe and appropriate policy approaches for the United States. The seven national/regional chapters were all written well after the start of the Gorbachev "earthquake" and its initial aftershocks in Poland and Hungary, but before the immense sympathetic temblors in

East Germany, Czechoslovakia, Bulgaria, and Romania that portended the radical rearrangement of the Eastern landscape. The Eastern premises for these Western analyses were: optimism about gradual political improvement in the East; pessimism about economic improvement; expectation of prudent loosening of the bloc and the Warsaw Pact; but also, a perceived possibility of major crises and surprises in the East.

With the overturning of the hard-line communist regimes in East Germany, Bulgaria, Czechoslovakia, and Romania, the possibility of crises and surprises has become the fact. Now, events beginning in the German Democratic Republic have thrown into doubt not the fundamentals that determine the reactions of NATO's nations, but the applications of these fundamentals on new events, and the timetables on which these events will occur. The seven national chapters of this book analyze the fundamentals, the factors that will continue to govern the NATO policies of NATO's members. Much the largest of the chapters is the one on Germany. As discussed in the next pages, Germany is where the action now is. The United States remains the largest and still-dominant member of NATO, but Germany is the source of fears, hopes, and changes in the Alliance.

The remainder of this chapter takes up the past and potential flows of actions among the member nations as they form NATO policy, the timetables of the new European world we have entered, and a brief suggestion of how the flows, the timetables, and the national fundamentals may interact to determine alternative futures for NATO, for the West, and for Europe as a whole. The concluding chapter of the book examines more fully alternative future directions for Western security and related policies, based on the old positions and interactions as they approach the new timetables. The standpoint is an American one and the policy suggestions that stem from the analysis are for the United States.

FLOWS

Figure 1-1 provides a conceptual illustration of the way issues and decisions flowed through NATO until very recently. The initial impulse for Alliance decision making, at least in the most recent years, has come not from a member nation at all, but from the Soviet Union. Toward the end of 1989, this broadened: initiating impulses came not only from the Soviet Union itself, but from other members of the Warsaw Pact, and indeed, not only from the 1989 governments of these Pact nations but from their peoples.

The flow within NATO has been changing in parallel. Within the Alliance, the traditional prime mover has been the United States. Even before the October 1989 revolution in the GDR put Germany at the center of the stage, however,

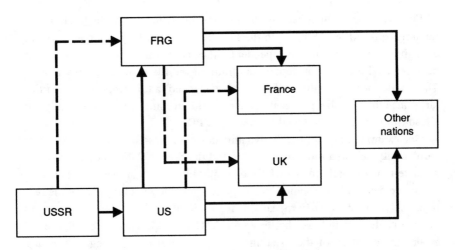

Figure 1-1 Flow of issues through the Alliance.

the Federal Republic had begun to take within-NATO initiatives. As in the case of the United States, these were stimulated primarily by internal political and other reactions to external Soviet stimuli, but they were also based in some measure on internal imperatives—the fading of memories of the Nazi era and the desire for full sovereignty and a political role based on present economic and military strength. The events of October and subsequent months accelerated this shift of the role of the FRG to initiator within the Alliance. The issue within the West increasingly revolved around the ongoing and potential changes in Central Europe, and these in turn focused on the most powerful West European nation, the FRG; the most powerful and crucial non-Soviet East European nation, the GDR; and potentially the most powerful nation in Central Europe—in all of Europe west of the Soviet Union—Germany taken as a whole.

Thus, whereas the first mover is the Soviet Union and the second has historically been the United States, the next mover, perhaps becoming the prime mover within NATO, is the Federal Republic. In large measure it is Germany that activates the fourth group consisting of the two other major NATO nations, France and Great Britain. Of the two, France is perhaps a more important independent influence on Alliance outcomes, not because it is inherently more influential than Britain, but because it is more independent and it is more concerned with the German role. The United Kingdom still tends to stick with and depend on the United States; in recent years under Prime Minister Thatcher, the British tended to be more American than the Americans, particularly in their suspicions of the Soviet Union and their adherence to classical "tough" NATO policies.

Finally, the other member nations are most likely to react to the big four, particularly to the United States and the Federal Republic. Italy is large and strong enough to have a potential independent influence, but thus far this potential has been realized more in the economic affairs of the EC than in security matters. The smaller northern nations of NATO have tended to follow Germany, particularly since the Socialist parties that are powerful in some of them frequently take a lead from the German Social Democrats (SPD).

One example of the pre-1989 dynamic lies in the reactions to the 1987 "zero-zero" treaty between the United States and the Soviet Union, abolishing intermediate-range missile forces (INF), over 500 kilometers in reach. Although the following description is somewhat simplified, not allowing for some of the reactions of Europeans *qua* Europeans or for some of the side interactions, it provides a useful example of the flow of NATO issues illustrated by Figure 1-1, before the overturn of the existing order in Central Europe began to change things around.

- The Soviet Union took the first step toward the INF Treaty, when Gorbachev reactivated the dormant and not-really-intended NATO proposal to swap Pershing II and cruise missiles for Soviet SS-20s.
- The United States reacted, accepting the Soviet acceptance and quickly negotiating the basis of the treaty.
- Europeans as a whole (a vastly oversimplified concept, which is only momentarily useful here) reacted with initial shock, then with grudging acceptance of the *fait accompli,* and then in many cases with some enthusiasm. At this point, the issue seemed to calm down.
- But the West Germans, many of whom had been part of the initial grumbling and then acceptance, in fact reacted more slowly. Resentment over the INF affair provided much of the stimulus for a seeming restructuring of German thought, which by 1989 resulted in German stubbornness with regard to U.S. pressures to "modernize" missiles with ranges under the treaty limits, and in German initiatives concerning negotiations over other theater-based nuclear weapons. This German reaction provides an example both of the new assertiveness mentioned above and of the role of that assertiveness in moving the Germans into a position of direct reaction to Soviet moves. The FRG policies on modernization and negotiations responded in part to irritation at being ignored by the United States in the INF negotiations, in part from the belief among large portions of the electorate at a time when an election was approaching that the Soviets were no longer a threat.[9]
- Britain remained constant, on the side of the United States (or vice versa), but the French, thoroughly worried about German direction, reacted in a

number of ways: first, panic over U.S. abandonment; then concern about German assertiveness; all of which was overlaid by an enigmatic calmness on the part of President Mitterrand.

- Of the smaller nations, the Netherlands stayed with the United States and the U.K.; the rest moved toward the FRG.

By early 1989, however, this had changed radically. The Federal Republic was becoming more of an in-Alliance initiator, largely because of its own internal imperatives: the fading of memories of the Nazi era, and the desire for full sovereignty and a political and military role based on present strength rather than "singularization" (special treatment based on past sins and defeats). The new West German assertiveness was manifest particularly in the fierce NATO debate over the siting of short-range nuclear forces (SNF), particularly the Follow-on to Lance (FOTL) missile, in the FRG. The U.S. and Britain wanted FOTL; the West Germans did not, and did want SNF negotiations with the Soviets; President Bush crafted a compromise putting the issue off until the end of the negotiations on Conventional Forces in Europe (CFE). In the event, FOTL disappeared in the wake of the revolutions and the moves toward German unification in later 1989 and 1990; in fact, the issue had been decided long before that, and the new missile system never would have been deployed.

In any case, revolutions and reunification changed the map of European decision making. Rather than by the directional arrows of Figure 1-1 by 1989 European decisions could be better depicted by Figure 1-2, as a Soviet/German/American triangle plus one box representing everything else, with arrows in various directions. The crucial 1989 decisions, in the 2 + 4 talks between the two Germanys and the four World War II victors, in the CFE negotiations, and most important, in the constant round of one-on-one meetings among the American, West German, and Soviet Foreign Ministers, had to do with the balance between

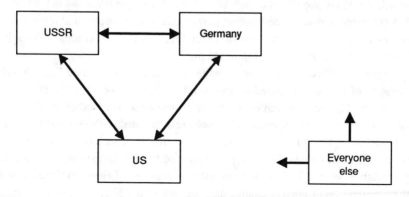

Figure 1-2   Flow of issues through NATO, late 1989–?

the security concerns of a newly unified Germany and those of tne Soviet Union, with the United States playing a major role in the balancing process. The other European nations, particularly France and Britain, remain important parts of the balance, but it is their responses rather than their initiatives that must be considered.

These changes, putting Germany at the fulcrum, are likely to govern the future responses of the Alliance to the changing signals from the East.

TIMETABLES

Both the decision flows discussed above and the national fundamentals analyzed in the central chapters of this book are essentially time-free structural concepts. Changes may take place, as exemplified by the shift in the role of Alliance prime mover from the United States to the Federal Republic and by the changes in the FRG itself as German unification shifts from a philosophical issue to one of policy. The flows and the fundamentals may act slowly as in the long debate over the meaning of "Flexible Response" that has gone on since the promulgation of the doctrine in 1967 until now; they may be faster, as in the year-and-a-half INF Treaty activity. Now, in any case, the same fundamentals have begun to form the basis for very rapid decision making, as has been the case with NATO's reactions to the sudden changes in the East.

What will govern future directions almost as much as national and Alliance structural factors will be the timetables on which decisions must be made or should be made. Politicians tend to make decisions on a "must" basis, but it has been argued that the West should get out ahead of the game, making decisions before they are forced upon us, in order to anticipate changes in the East and help guide them—to "take the initiative away from Gorbachev." The extent to which the West should take such initiatives is a major issue for debate within NATO, discussed in the concluding paragraphs of this chapter and more fully in the final chapter. Even the "must" timetable, however, is complex enough to impose major constraints on future alternatives.

Figure 1-3 illustrates the timing issue with six composite time lines showing the sorts of events, scheduled or unscheduled, that may occur in the first half of the 1990s. The most certain events are the ones at the near end of the time scale and the holding of elections, all of which are scheduled (although unlike American elections few of those in Europe have the precise day pinned down in advance). Later events, including outcomes of the scheduled elections, are less predictable because of both the normal uncertainties of time amplified now by the acceleration of current change and because of the likelihood that the earlier

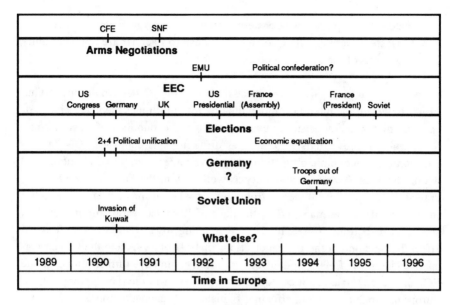

Figure 1-3. Time in Europe.

events on any one of the six linear sequences will affect the later events on the others. Analysis is frequently too compartmentalized to take proper account of such interactions.

Looking across any of the top four lines in Figure 1-3, the future viewed along any single one may seem reasonably predictable:

- *Arms negotiations* will proceed apace, with CFE signed in 1990, followed by nuclear negotiations that are likely to result in an agreement sometime in 1991. Further conventional reductions will be taken, whether on a nego- tiated or mutual unilateral basis.
- *The EC* will achieve its single European market by the end of 1992. Further economic integration, and political integration, will move forward, not without obstacles, but with some degree at least of confederation achieved during the 1990s.
- *Elections* will take place on schedule, certainly in the West, probably also in the Soviet Union. Although, as shown in Table 1-1, the chance for some change in security policy stemming from one of the major elections is sub- stantial, no individual election is likely to bring about a major change in the security policy of any one nation.
- *Germany* unified politically in 1990. Economic reconstruction of the East, although likely to be difficult, will take place and will be substantially com-

pleted (to the point where eastern Germany is not much worse off relative to western Germany than some of the western Laender are now) certainly by the end of the decade, probably sooner.

Even leaving aside the two lowest lines, for the Soviet Union and "What Else?" however, the interplay among the first four multiplies the uncertainties of any one of them. Suppose, for example, that the economics of East German reconstruction prove divisive as well as difficult. This could lead Germans to question other economic obligations they have undertaken, bring about discord within the West German community as well as with the East, accelerate withdrawal of U.S. nuclear weapons from Germany but at the cost of raising other suspicions of the Germans, affect the pace of European economic integration; and unleash political forces in the U.S. tending toward withdrawal. It could affect the outcome of the British elections in 1991 or 1992, and the French legislative elections of 1993, both of which in turn could have further effects on the EC, and so on. Or a chain could begin with a snag in the development of the European Monetary Union, affecting British and French election outcomes. Or too much "success" in European integration could be seen as an economic threat to the United States and induce changes in the U.S. security position in Europe.

All of these are games played by shuffling the regular deck. The Soviet Union and the "What Else?" lines add new wild cards. For the Soviets it can be said, first, that there is a substantial chance of a change of regime and some significant chance of a change in external policy by the old regime or a new one; and second, that a change in external policy certainly, and a change in regime quite possibly, would change most of the other outcomes on the other lines of the table.

And events on the "What Else?" sequence have been dramatically illustrated by the Iraqi attack on Kuwait, which is likely to affect every other time line on the chart, either directly through its political and security effects or indirectly via the price of oil. Yet the Kuwait invasion is just one actualized event out of a broad set of potential happenings: an Arab-Israeli war; achievement of a nuclear-weapons capability by some rogue state in the Middle East or elsewhere; Libyan use of long-range missiles with chemical warheads; or some unexpected new direction from Japan or China.

Und so weiter.

INTERACTIONS

The final chapter of this book examines the timetables, the structural flows, and the national fundamentals as they come together. To summarize some key points:

- The Soviet Union and the nations of the East are driving events; these events focus in Germany; the United States and the rest of NATO are reacting. This is not because of Western timidity or President Bush's "lack of vision." The vast changes taking place in the East—hoped and prayed for for 40 years in the West—are not under tight control even by the Soviet Union; Western influence is less yet, and the best that we can do is to help and react appropriately, and try to avoid disasters. This is particularly true for security matters; as discussed below, avoiding economic disasters may call for more active participation.
- The future, always uncertain, has become much more so with the changes in the Soviet Union and the other nations of Eastern Europe. Given such uncertainties, long-run planning and hopes should be secondary to desirable short-run directions. Again, substantial emphasis should be given to avoiding short-run disasters that will preclude favorable long-run futures.
- One short-run disaster would be the premature dissolution or major weakening of NATO. The Alliance remains crucial for all the reasons adduced above, and it is far too early to declare it obsolete.
- As events focus down on Central Europe, they necessarily focus on Germany as the powerful center of the area. For the United States and the other members of NATO (and of the EC as well), these changes do not imply slavishly following Germany; they do imply dealing with the Germans as equals in security as well as economic and political matters and understanding their perceived interests. Many of the sounds emanating from Germany are and will continue to be motivated by electoral competition— as in the United States and Britain in 1992 and France in 1993—and Germany's partners should understand this normal side effect of democracy on foreign policy.
- Outside the immediate security/NATO sphere, the Deepening/Broadening debate in The European Community (EC) ought to move off symbols and get down to cases. What are the implications of the immediate issue of admitting Austria (and probably not Turkey)? What, if anything, is the real conflict between deepening and broadening? Can the economic and political institutions of EC be strengthened, at the same time leaving the door open to full membership for nations such as Hungary, Czechoslovakia, and Poland when they qualify economically and politically?
- Finally, and closely related to the EC issues, the West, including the United States, should be concentrating on economic support to the East as the major security issue of the 1990s. If the uncertainty about the long-run future leads to stress on immediate directions and avoidance of disaster, the chief disaster looming on the near-term horizon is economic collapse of the

Eastern nations, including—particularly—the Soviet Union. Were this to happen, all other bets would be off.

The concluding chapter of the book richens and details these guidelines by bringing in the analyses of national fundamentals discussed in the next seven chapters.

NOTES

1. Peter Finley Dunne, *Mr. Dooley in Peace and War*, 1898.
2. See, e.g, Jimmy Goldsmith, "Le Levier de la Defénse," *L'Express*, February 17–March 5, 1987.
3. Alain Minc, *La Grande Illusion* (Paris: Bernard Grosset, 1989), provides a full-blown example.
4. See, e.g., Melvin Krauss, *How NATO Weakens the West* (New York: Simon and Schuster, 1986).
5. Robert A. Levine, *Still the Arms Debate* (Aldershot, Eng.: Dartmouth Publishing, 1990). Part III, "NATO: The Subjective Alliance."
6. Ibid. That is the reason for the subtitle "The Subjective Alliance."
7. The substantial nature of that threat in the last quarter-century is open to some debate, but it has most certainly been the central premise upon which Western security policy has been based.
8. Quoted in Anthony Lewis's column, "Abroad at Home," *New York Times*, November 23, 1989.
9. This is discussed more thoroughly in Chapter 3.

Chapter 2

The United States

Robert A. Levine

It's a complex fate; being an American, and one of the responsibilities it entails is fighting against a superstitious evaluation of Europe.—Henry James (1872)

Superstitious evaluations cross the Atlantic in both directions. The theme of this chapter is that the United States is stable. To Americans, this is manifest—we are steady even in the face of the frequently demonstrated instability of one or another of our partners. To many Europeans, however, American steadfastness has been less obvious, particularly in the Reagan years; one would not think that the word "Reykjavik" could be hissed, but it can.

In fact, there has been erraticism on both sides of the ocean, and it has echoed back and forth, frequently amplifying in the process. This chapter suggests that, whatever has been the case and the cause in the past, the United States is not likely to *initiate* a new sequence of recriminations.

For two reasons, past American irregularity, at least as perceived in Europe, is not a very good guide to the future:

- We changed presidents in 1989.
- The perceived erraticism of recent years has been misinterpreted and exaggerated. Much of it, including Reykjavik, did not originate with American policy, but rather was based on clumsy American reactions to apparent sudden changes in the nature of our opponent.[1] The United States was not alone in such reactions.

This chapter moves to the future, breaking the discussion into four major sections:

13

- A discussion of the variables likely to affect U.S. NATO policy in the course of the first term of the Bush administration. These are divided into "endogenous" variables—the intentions and beliefs brought to policy by the members of the administration (and the Congress); and variables "exogenous" to U.S. policy, stemming rather from the world in which the executive and legislative policy makers find themselves.
- A "canonical" scenario for U.S. policy, i.e., the scenario, assuming the exogenous variables move in the most expectable directions.
- A series of variations from canonical policies, depending on which exogenous variables move in unexpected directions.
- Possible endogenous (i.e., U.S.-initiated) variations.

VARIABLES

Endogenous Variables: The Bush Administration and the Congress

President Bush began his administration by appointing pragmatic centrists to key foreign and national security policy positions. Secretary of State James Baker and Deputy Lawrence Eagleburger, Secretary of Defense Richard Cheney and his policy undersecretary, Paul Wolfowitz, and National Security Advisor Brent Scowcroft, all fit comfortably into that category. But the category did not cover Reagan's appointees—Secretary of State Alexander Haig, Secretary of Defense Caspar Weinberger and his two chief Europeanists, Undersecretary Fred Iklé and Assistant Secretary Richard Perle, or National Security Advisor Richard Allen; nor does it really cover such long-range NATO philosophers as Henry Kissinger and Zbigniew Brzezinski. Indeed, the "pragmatic centrist" appellation fits Bush and did not fit Reagan, not at the beginning of his first term. Further, the crucial committee chairmen in the Congress, Senator Sam Nunn and Representative Les Aspin, are of this persuasion.

This guarantees a narrow range of policy *intentions* in the current administration and the Congress—not a narrow range of policies, because these will be directed in substantial measure by events that are not fully controllable, but a narrow range of desires. The key players are all Old Natonians. In the past they put the single major stress of U.S. security policy worldwide (outside of strategic deterrence) on the political and military health of the Alliance, stressing the maintenance of as much conventional military power as could be mustered, given fiscal and political problems. In addition, however, they recognized and were willing to satisfy, within political constraints, the European desire to cling to the security blanket of the coupled American nuclear deterrent. More recently, the reaction of all these players to the major changes in Europe has continued to emphasize the centrality of the Alliance and the American commitment.

With regard to the Soviet Union, their views cover a range that can be traced back to their institutional roles. Secretary of State Baker has taken Soviet internal reforms and attempts at external detente as real tendencies, to be encouraged by U.S. policy. Secretary of Defense Cheney has doubted their reality, basing these doubts primarily on uncertainty about Gorbachev's stability rather than his sincerity. This difference is not surprising; the Defense Department is cast in the role of hedging against the worst case.[2] The difference is not large, and the president has tended to go along with Baker without explicitly disagreeing with Cheney.

The changes in Europe have made Germany almost as central to U.S. policy on European security as the Soviet Union, and here the administration's objective has been unified and clear. The belief has been that the German/American tie is central to the stability of Europe, and the objective has been to keep the relationship comfortable by encouraging rapid reunification, and thus to keep a unified Germany in NATO and American troops in Germany. Indeed, the old shibboleth about the purposes of NATO—"To keep the Soviets out, the Americans in, and the Germans down"—has been transformed to keeping both the Americans and the Germans in while continuing to perform the now-apparently-much-easier task of keeping the Soviets out.

Washington's European orientation implies that the rest of the world, even Japan, and in the long run even the Middle East, will remain secondary in a security sense. This has two implications, which although not part of NATO policy (and thus not discussed in detail here) are important for NATO policy. First, as discussed below U.S. forces in Europe may well be drawn down, but they are unlikely to be drawn down in order to increase forces elsewhere in the world. Second, the president and his centrists want to deflate the importance of such controversy-producing areas as Nicaragua and to produce a foreign policy that is bipartisan not only in regard to Europe (where it really has been for a long time), but across the board.

Exogenous Variables: The Policy Drivers

Initial intentions drive policy initially, but by the time that external imperatives and constraints work their way, the policy outcomes may look very different from the intentions. For U.S. NATO policy, the prime external drivers are the Soviet Union and Germany, with economics an important third. In addition, Iraq's invasion of Kuwait suggests another possible future driver. "Out-of-area" contingencies may, alternatively, force U.S. consideration of the role of its

European presence in maintaining its other interests, or allow the United States and NATO to find new missions as the threat of Soviet aggression fades.

Each of these drivers is subject to wide potential variation. For the *Soviet Union*, the range of possible variation is very wide. Ironically, what is outside of that range is a return to the massive aggressive potential that was apparent to many Americans in the Brezhnev era. For one thing, Soviet military as well as economic power has deteriorated seriously since 1985; it is doubtful that the threat of the 1970s (aside from the nuclear threat, which remains but was never central to Soviet policy in Europe) can be maintained or restored. And, more generally, history does not reverse in that way. Rather than Brezhnev (or Stalin), the downside of the range falls into uncertainties, but dreadful ones. Should economic or ethnic chaos cause Gorbachev to fall and be replaced by a military or other right-wing (perhaps populist) dictatorship, or by well-armed anarchy, the lack of reasoned control over Soviet nuclear and other military forces could pose major but unpredictable dangers for the West. Less dangerous but still disappointing in terms of current hopes would be the political survival of Gorbachev, but under constraints from military and other interests that would redirect current movements toward disarmament and detente. The best part of the range would be the success of Soviet reform in turning around the economy while maintaining and improving internal democracy and external retreat.[3] If that is too much to hope for, then at least the long-run leveling off of the muddling through that marked Gorbachev's first five years might be achievable.

Potential *German* variation is less than for the Soviets. A united Germany is simply not going to return to its black past, or anywhere near that past. Nor will the inevitable strains of bringing the failed and poverty-stricken communist economy of East Germany into the wealthy and successful capitalist economy of West Germany approach the potential disaster that may lie ahead for the Soviet Union.

The relatively optimistic "most likely" prognosis for Germany does include substantial economic strains, however; the obsolescence, investment, environmental, ideological, social benefits, and expectations aspects of bringing together 40 years of differential development are only beginning to be recognized. But even given such internal economic strains, this prognosis still assumes continued active German inclusion in a European Community that deepens its political as well as its economic institutions throughout the 1990s, while perhaps also broadening them by bringing in new nations toward the end of the period. German national politics under these assumptions will still be dominated by a coalition led by the Christian Democrats (CDU), with the result for security structures being that Germany's ties to NATO as well as the Economic Community (EC) will remain strong, albeit with a sharply decreased number of German as well as allied troops. A significant number of U.S. and other allied troops will remain on German soil as well as at least a token number of American air-launched nuclear warheads on either bombs or possibly short-range missiles.

The major upside variation for Germany would be an easier economic transition than has been postulated. That would most likely reinforce the political and security trends of the above paragraph, although it might lead to some strain in Europe by also reinforcing already foreseen German economic dominance of the continent.

The potential variations in the political dimension may be more dangerous to U.S. interests, however. Some combination of a future Social Democratic (SPD) electoral victory and a general hardening of nationalism in the German electorate might take Germany out of NATO. That would be a major change leading to a major reevaluation of American policy; a similar but weaker movement focusing on the removal of American nuclear weapons from German soil would be easier to cope with and would lead to a lesser reevaluation. Perhaps most dangerous of all, however, although seemingly unlikely, would be German elections in which the minor parties of the Left (Greens) and the Right (Republicans) gained enough Bundestag seats to make difficult the formation of *any* middle-of-the-road government. That could result from really major difficulties in the economic reconstruction of the East.

Economically, the underlying assumption here is that economic constraints will in any case impose severe limits on U.S. NATO policy; the fiscal and foreign trade deficits exist, and they will constrain the most pro-NATO intentions even in the most economically successful near-term future. But such a successful future is not guaranteed. Potential variations exist along two interrelated dimensions. No convincing evidence has been presented that supply-side or any other economics have abolished the business cycle, and severe recession or severe inflation, American or worldwide, could make more difficult any NATO policies that involved substantial expenditure. The other dimension for economic variation that might constrain U.S. NATO policy would be growing autarchy (real or perceived by Americans) on the part of Western Europe, as EEC moves toward 1992. Burden sharing will be an issue in any case, and any such perceptions on the part of Americans can make it an issue that could eat the North Atlantic Alliance.

For *out-of-area* contingencies, the central assumption is that in spite of the invasion of Kuwait, U.S. European policy will remain centered on Europe; and that NATO itself will continue to focus on and plan its military posture around missions in Europe. The variations on this might move in one of two opposite directions. First, a perception among American decision makers or electorate of nonsupport by Alliance members of American efforts in the Middle East could lead to serious erosion of U.S. support for NATO. Or, on the other hand, the Kuwait experience could catalyze explicit Alliance acceptance of a new role in coping with out-of-area events. The later evolution might both strengthen NATO politically for the long run, by gradually substituting a new visible mission for one that seems to be growing obsolete, and reorient the Alliance military posture around contingencies quite different from the traditional Soviet aggression against the West.

In any case, what is suggested here is that it will be the exogenous variables—Soviet, German, economic, or out-of-area—that will drive U.S. NATO policy for the remaining years of the Bush administration much more than the intentions of the administration's own decision makers.

CANONICAL SCENARIO

Assumptions

This scenario is based on "no surprises" assumptions. That is, the United States' erstwhile opponent and its allies proceed along expectable courses, the developed world avoids major economic fluctuations, and out-of-area events remain an occasional distraction without becoming NATO's central focus.

More specific assumptions (some of which, of course, are interlinked with the projections for U.S. policy) are:

- The Soviet Union proceeds internally along Gorbachev's lines, with no breakthrough toward economic success or solution of ethnic problems, but also no economic collapse or revolt, or political turmoil leading to major repression. Most of the bloc countries proceed at their own rates toward liberalization and toward dissociation from the Warsaw Pact in ways not seen as threatening to the Soviets. Soviet military power begins a retreat to within Soviet borders on the scheduled timetable.
- A united Germany remains in NATO and in a satisfactorily progressing EC; and U.S. (and other allied) troops remain in Germany, albeit in numbers that are decreasing substantially. Air-deliverable U.S. nuclear warheads also remain in Germany. Western troops in the eastern portion of Germany are light, consisting of some combination of border guards and territorial forces. These troops and the local populations achieve a stable relationship with the phasing-out Soviet forces. NATO is committed to the defense of all Germany.

- U.S. troop numbers in Europe are reduced to 100,000 or less, possibly by agreement under successor rounds of CFE or under CSCE, but more likely "unilaterally" in the sense that they are not negotiated with the Soviets, who are reducing concomitantly unilaterally anyhow, but are coordinated with NATO allies, who are carrying out their own reductions. NATO's integrated command structure continues.
- The Iraqi invasion of Kuwait is resolved without changing basic Atlantic relationships.
- Sometime during the four-year period, a U.S. and world recession, no more severe than those of the early 1980s, occurs, but recovery at least begins and perhaps is completed within the period. Third World debt and other problems are not fully solved but neither do they throw the developed economies into a tailspin. The net result is no more pressure than current on the U.S. budget and the twin fiscal and trade deficits, but also no less.
- EC moves to consummation of major economic unification in 1992, although neither fully reaching its economic goals nor coming anywhere near the political goals of those who hope it will lead to a United States of Western Europe. Economic openings to the East increase, but not at a rate where they are a major factor in Western economies.
- Not only the Germans, but the other European members of NATO, too, refrain from embarking on radical political courses.
  —British elections in late 1991 or early 1992 return either Thatcher or a somewhat wetter Tory, but with little variation in foreign policy.
  —In France, no domestic threat arises to upset either Mitterrand or the minority Socialist government. In foreign and security policy, Mitterrand remains a relatively benign enigma, neither throwing up major obstacles to unilateral or negotiating moves desired by the rest of the Alliance, nor putting France out in front of negotiations or force improvements. France remains as now, *de jure* outside of NATO's integrated structure, *de facto* partially inside.
  —The smaller nations remain tied into Alliance policies, albeit not without grumbling. Danish or perhaps other erraticism is possible, but the Alliance remains militarily and politically robust to likely changes. Radical change in the low countries would be more serious, but is less likely and is not assumed in this scenario.

U.S. Policy

Under these canonical assumptions, U.S. NATO policy is also likely to be canonical. For the most part, the pragmatic centrists in charge will respond pragmatically to the neutral-to-benign conditions that have been listed.

- Budgetary and other political pressures will quickly force the United States
  to plan troop reductions to around the 100,000 level, although implementation of the reductions will be slow for reasons of pure military orderliness.
  Reductions may be negotiated with the Soviets or unilateral, but in either
  case they will be worked out with NATO allies, who will also be reducing
  concomitantly. The result will leave the American troops in Europe primarily as cadre for rapid reinforcement, within an overall NATO posture
  intended in reality to preserve the political coherence of the Alliance
  including Germany, but with a military rationale designed to deter and
  defend against a renewed Soviet threat. The savings inherent in the two-
  thirds cut from the 325,000 of the 1980s will suffice to fend off, if not satisfy, congressional burden sharers. The postulated threat around which
  these forces are planned will be slower and smaller than that for which
  NATO planned from the 1950s through the 1980s and will be met farther
  to the East—on the Polish–German border or perhaps even within Poland,
  rather than on the old "inter-German border." That threat will come from
  the Soviet Union alone rather than including any of the old Warsaw Pact
  allies. Nonetheless, NATO's planning assumptions will be based on the
  same general kind of coherent and deliberate military thrust as in the old
  days. Western defense will be partly mobile, partly territorial, and heavily
  dependent upon reinforcement, particularly from the United States.
- Although reducing the number of nuclear warheads in Germany by not
  replacing the Lance short-range missile when it deteriorates and by removing most or all nuclear artillery (both most probably as the result of SNF
  negotiations with the Soviet Union), the United States will try to replace airborne nuclear gravity bombs with air-to-ground missiles. If this founders on
  the rocks of German politics, the American fallback position will be based
  on retention of the gravity bombs on German as well as other allied soil.
- The United States will continue to center its NATO political policies on
  Germany, in order to keep the Germans satisfied and in the Alliance.
  Reminders from the other allies that they too must be considered will be
  heeded, however. European economic and political integration will be
  encouraged, but economic bargaining between the United States and EC
  will be hard.
- Under the canonical assumption of continuity in the USSR, the United
  States will continue to encourage Gorbachev, or a successor willing to follow similar external policies. If Soviet continuity includes continuing internal liberalization and economic reforms that show some promise, American encouragement may even include some very modest economic
  assistance. Similar assistance will also be extended to other eastern nations.

In sum, U.S. policy toward NATO, like the Alliance itself, will evolve in response to exogenous variables, but it will not reverse or undergo a revolution, not under the canonical assumptions.

VARYING SCENARIOS

The canonical scenario for U.S. policy involved a lot of assumptions, and the two surest statements are: they will not all come out in the ways postulated; and that nobody can tell in advance which ones will vary in which ways. This section varies the assumptions systematically and evaluates the potential effects on U.S. NATO policy. Five sets of variations are considered:

- Variations related to the Soviet Union. Such variations might be in the direction of slowing down or even mild reversal of the detente/disarmament thrust of the late 1980s, or they could take the form of a new set of radical changes within the USSR, which would throw external as well as internal policies into doubt.
- Variations related to other East European nations.
- Variations based on changes by Germany.
- Variations in assumptions concerning other allies.
- Variations based on economics, including both world economics and EEC policies.
- Variations based on out-of-area contingencies.

Variations in Soviet Assumptions

Slowdown or reversal of detente/disarmament policies. The slowdown or reversal could take place under Gorbachev if he were beset by internal opposition based on domestic failures or perception by the military and others of the failure of his external policies to bring relief from Western pressures; it could also take place under a successor regime.

The U.S. reaction to such a change in Soviet policies would be likely to take the form of a countervailing "toughening up." By 1990 the Bush administration was taking the reality of the Gorbachev changes very seriously and what was seen as the need to help shore up the Soviet regime against internal pressures. President Bush and his people, however, were bred in the long Brezhnev period of the Cold War. Any perception of a return to the Brezhnev style—even though, as noted, Soviet weakness seems to preclude a return to the strong militarily backed political aggressiveness of that era—would probably engender both an American return to negotiating with the primary aim of maintaining position in American and European public opinion, and a renewed emphasis on the military aspects of an Alliance that had increasingly been thought of as becoming "political."[4] What would be as unlikely as a Soviet return to the Brezhnev-style threat, however, would be a U.S./NATO return to the military posture with which the United States and the West coped with that threat through the mid-1980s. U.S. budget imperatives and politics would be unlikely to allow the rebuilding to 300,000–400,000 troops of a European force previously scheduled to be cut to 200,000 or less; the same pressures would presumably apply to allied armies. Since the threat would also be less, however, NATO would be capable of mounting a lower level deterrent/defense posture that would fill the political and military needs. The point, in any case, is that a reversion to traditional Soviet/Western tensions would be most likely to engender a traditional American response. That would be disappointing but not completely uncomfortable for at least some American planners. Some conservative NATO-nians of the type dominating the Bush administration would heave a sigh of relief because they would feel they were back in a world they were familiar with. Whether such a return to the old verities was really the case or not would depend on many other factors, including allied governments.

Radical Soviet change. More radical changes might come from a successor regime to Gorbachev. One possibility could be a military or militarily backed "conservative" government. Although the most likely external policies might be those described above as "slowdown or reversal"—and even continuation of external detente would be possible from such a regime (or, even more, from a potential liberal successor to Gorbachev—radically renewed aggressiveness from a strong military regime would also be possible. Even more dangerous, however, would be a contest for power in all or in parts of the Soviet Union involving military as well as purely political elements. The uncertainties in such a contest could last over a long period of time, and the results could verge on anarchy. The major implication for the West of such chaos would be the revival of a military threat from the East, a threat less definable and deterrable than that of the Stalin-through-Brezhnev age. It would in some ways be more frightening; although militarily weaker in most dimensions, it would still have a nuclear component that might be as potentially irresponsible as those feared from various Middle Eastern and Asian nations, but would be far stronger than those small country nuclear forces.

The obvious initial U.S. response to the development of nuclear "loose cannons" in the Soviet Union, or to a renewal of lesser aggressiveness, would be a pause in the activities that had been predicated upon peaceful and relatively stable Soviet external policies and extensive consultation with NATO allies. What would happen next is less obvious, because how to deal with such relatively random dangers is not at all obvious. Perhaps the major effect would be a drawing back together of the Alliance as the response to a renewed perception of a common threat. Under some circumstances of immediate and palpable military danger, the reversal might even bring about a reversal of the drawdown of U.S. and other allied forces, but it is not clear that that would be the response, or that it should be. Questions about the effects on the West of Soviet civil war or military adventurism: How many troops in what posture it might take to defend against these effects, or how to deter the irrational use of major nuclear weapons (irrational even as compared to the classical if theoretical use in defense of national survival or other concrete ends) have not yet been asked, let alone answered.

Variations in Assumptions about Other East European Nations

The canonical assumption was that the other members of what had been the Warsaw Pact leave the pact quietly in ways not seen by the Soviets as threatening their own security. One variation that would require decisions by the United States (and the rest of NATO) would be an appeal by a formerly Warsaw nation other than East Germany to join NATO or at least to be taken under its security umbrella. This seems unlikely; casual feelers by some Hungarians have not been taken up either by NATO or the Hungarian government. Under circumstances of renewed Soviet pressure consequent upon some of the possible changes postulated above, however, such moves could be made.

For the United States under the Bush administration at least, the response seems foreshadowed by the 1990 response to the Baltic republics' appeal for assistance in their attempts to secede from the Soviet Union—which was in turn consistent with 40 years of history in East Germany, Poland, Hungary, and Czechoslovakia: "Good luck, but we cannot take the risk of superpower confrontation in order to extend anything more than good wishes." True, that history, from East Berlin through Vilnius, could be interpreted as recognition of a Soviet sphere of influence, in which post-Warsaw Pact Eastern nations no longer belonged so that more active Western assistance could be extended to Poland, for example. It seems much more likely that the fear of confrontation rather than the ambiguous niceties of spheres of influence will govern, and the United States will continue to avoid any direct confrontation with the Soviet Union.

Variations in German Assumptions

For Germany, the canonical scenario assumed that a reelected CDU-led coalition would continue German membership in NATO, and continue also, albeit at sharply reduced levels, U.S. troop and airborne nuclear weapons presence in Germany. Variations from this scenario might occur along two dimensions. One measures potential German falloff from NATO: Germany might maintain a connection with NATO but ask U.S. and other allied forces to leave; they might leave the Alliance and ask the United States to keep forces in Germany under other arrangements; it might leave the Alliance unconditionally; it might allow the troops to stay while insisting that all nuclear weapons be removed; it might continue in NATO but insist on a radical restructuring, for example, an end to the integrated military command.

The other dimension concerns the reasons for any of these falloffs: they might stem from the electoral victory in the mid-1990s of an anti-NATO coalition, which would then demand at least full denuclearization and a substantially altered relationship with the Alliance, perhaps more; they might be caused by uncontrollable pressures by the population of eastern Germany to quickly rid their area of Soviet troops that had continued there by treaty; or they might come from a combination of factors, for example, electoral return for anti-NATO forces in a campaign revolving around the appropriate German response to Soviet hard-lining.

Combining the two dimensions produces a large number of variations; the U.S. response would depend on the particular combination. Likely to be acceptable, although not without some grumbling, would be a partial denuclearization—removal of short-range missiles and nuclear artillery, freezing of airborne weapons rather than substituting air-to-ground missiles for gravity bombs; full denuclearization might also be accepted, although not without a struggle. Revision of the command structure, for example, a European Supreme Commander (SACEUR) might also be acceptable, although complete termination of the integrated military command might be considered a near-equivalent to the termination of NATO.

Beyond this, however, U.S. reactions to more fundamental changes in NATO structure would depend on the way in which they came about. Certainly if Germany decided to leave the Alliance or to ask the United States to remove all forces from German soil, the United States would have no choice but to acquiesce. Assuming that such a German decision were based primarily on internal politics, the United States would be likely to explore alternative arrangements with the new government, but the German moves would bring about fundamental questioning of U.S. interests and the U.S. military presence in Europe. One possibility would be a renewed Atlantic alliance without Germany, and with a U.S. troop presence continuing elsewhere on the continent (or in Britain). Such a new structure would be looked at, perhaps appropriately, as being designed to keep *both* the Soviets and the Germans out.

At some point, speculation becomes infinite and of little value. The central point is that more than moderate variations by the Germans from the canonical pro-NATO scenario would bring about severe repercussions in the United States.

Variations in Assumptions about Other Allies

The major allies under consideration are France and Great Britain; as noted in Chapter 1, the others including Italy tend to be followers rather than leaders within NATO. French variations are likely to be subtle, as with all things French; these subtleties are thoroughly discussed in Chapter 4 and are not covered here. For the United Kingdom, the major potential change has already come with the replacement of the Thatcher government by that of John Major. British NATO policy is likely to vary little; British policy with regard to the EC has become friendlier and more flexible, something that will call forth no American response.

Indeed, about the only allied variation that might require American changes or reconsiderations would be the return of a Labour government and the adoption of that government of a substantially anti-Alliance or anti-U.S. policy, which is unlikely from an electable government. Within the realm of mild Labour variations, for example, cutbacks on the U.S. presence, some of them might irritate the small-c conservatives of the Bush administration, but they would be coped with. Even an unlikely Labour move toward getting all American nuclear weapons out of Britain, although it could provide the *coup de grace* to the "special relationship," would have a lesser effect on the U.S. position in NATO as a whole, *unless* it were coupled with similar moves on the part of an SPD-led government in Germany. That combination could be deadly for the U.S. position and for NATO itself.

What it comes to, then, is that for the United States, or at least for the Bush administration, the crucial European security relationship is with Germany; all else revolves around that. And indeed, with the minor and unlikely exceptions of a radical British government taking unilateral anti-Alliance steps, or one or more of the nations newly liberated from the Warsaw Pact trying too hard for NATO protection or even membership, the major potential political/security variations from the optimistic canonical scenario center on the Soviet/German/U.S. triad.

Economic Variations

Severe U.S. or worldwide recession or inflation. The canonical scenario assumed that we have not yet solved the business cycle and there will be some kind of recession in the next four years, but that such a recession would be mild enough to avoid major effects on U.S. NATO policy. One assumption behind the variation discussed here could be a severe recession with resultant severe U.S. economic policies. That is not too likely, although by no means impossible, but the same sort of effects could be achieved by American overreaction to a milder recession.

Such overreaction might be the result of a degree and type of economic malfeasance that hopefully will be avoided. The 1982 Reagan recession caused neither direct negative reactions on U.S. NATO policy nor increased protectionism on either side of the Atlantic. What it did cause, however, was an increased U.S. deficit because of drops in tax revenues. Now we have Gramm-Rudman. Although Gramm-Rudman does have a sort of safety valve in case of recession, it may be politically difficult to invoke it and say: "We can allow the deficit to go up this year because tax collections are down." And, even though trying to reduce the deficit by either raising taxes or cutting spending is the worst possible policy in a recession (at least in the mind of an unreconstructed Keynesian economist like the author), it might happen. If it did happen, pressure for cuts in the U.S. contribution to NATO might possibly lead to even greater drawdowns than postulated above. This train of events seems unlikely, however. Even if the economic pressures did move in that direction, they would more likely add to the pressure for cuts that seem quite possible anyhow than to increase the size of the cuts.

What is perhaps no more likely but might have harsher effects on the Alliance would be accelerated U.S. or world inflation. This might proceed from an oil shortage or from other causes. The shortages and price increases were much the main cause of the bad economics of the 1970s, and although they seem less likely now, it would be quite foolish to assume their impossibility. In the United States, accelerated inflation would reduce the budget deficit (albeit less than would have been the case before tax indexing) and, in the converse case to recession, would thus reduce Gramm-Rudman pressure but call for reduced expenditures according to proper economic policy. One cannot count on proper economic policies that might put pressure on contributions to the Alliance, but one never knows.

In any case, if recession or inflation were quite severe, or if they were combined with U.S. perceptions of European protectionism, the effects (on NATO) could be worse, as described in the next variant.

EC protectionism. It seems unlikely at this time that EC will be so obtuse as to make 1992 the occasion for raising the walls of Fortress Europe. It is unlikely, but (1) it is not impossible, and (2) it is possible that marginal moves toward protectionism—or insufficient moves away from protectionism—might be overperceived by the United States.

This is not an essay on international trade, so the details of potential bad (or good) economic policy on either side of the Atlantic are not examined. The crucial point, however, is that *substantial American perceptions of West European unfairness through EC probably present a major—and largely unrecognized— danger to the Alliance.* Perceptions like these, added to the other pressures on NATO and the U.S. commitment, could lead to a full reevaluation of the American position and a consequent withdrawal of the U.S. military presence in Europe.

Out-of-area variations. Out-of-area variations might occur in two opposite directions. On the one side, American decision makers and/or publics might perceive, in Kuwait or in some subsequent crisis, that the European allies were "not pulling their weight." The response would be similar to the response to the not unrelated event of EEC protectionism: a full reevaluation of the American position and a consequent withdrawal of the U.S. military presence in Europe.

On the other hand, Kuwait or a subsequent similar crisis could cause NATO to decide that it has a mission in out-of-area contingencies. Explicit recognition of such a mission could revivify the Alliance and the U.S. ties, answering the question, "Why do we continue an Alliance and a troop presence designed to cope with Soviet threat that has disappeared?" This sort of danger to the Alliance, from boredom, is discussed next.

U.S.-INITIATED VARIATIONS

Two potential pressures are possible here:

- The budget.
- A general American "malaise" about our security commitment to Europe, combining new perceptions with traditional isolationism: "What business do we have there when the Soviet threat we went there to contain 40 years ago has disappeared?"

Both exist and both create strong pressures. Neither is likely to induce U.S. reductions or withdrawals beyond those included in the canonical scenario.

Before the arms control breakthroughs of 1989–1990, it seemed quite possible that budgetary pressures would force a U.S.-induced sequence of competitive force reductions within the Alliance. The growing federal deficit was compounded mainly of "uncontrollable" spending increases in domestic areas such as health, massive mistakes, and malfeasances leading to the "bailout" of Savings and Loan institutions, and the massive tax reductions of the early Reagan administration. It was not caused by defense spending; defense has been reduced in recent years as the deficit grew. Nonetheless, defense spending presented and presents even more in the 1990s a tempting—and justified—target for savings to help reduce the deficit. The Soviet threat *has* been reduced far below what it was believed to be a decade earlier. The need for defense against this central threat *should* be much lower than it was. And since the major locus of that threat (aside from the possibility of strategic exchange) has been Europe and it is the Soviet threat in Europe in particular that has been reduced, Europe is where much of the cut should be taken.

Much of the pressure on the defense budget would have existed even without the changes in Europe, and cutting overseas expenditures could have become a crucial issue. But now, the canonical scenario and practically every variation *already* include reductions of two-thirds or more of U.S. forces in Europe. These reductions will take place over time and will bring about concomitant budget savings—savings likely to be large enough to satisfy the most eager defense-budget-cutter, unless the cutter is also motivated by a deep desire to end the American commitment to Europe.

Such a deep desire does exist and has certainly grown stronger as the need for the commitment is seen to be decreasing in response to the decreased Soviet threat in Europe. A neutrally worded poll would be likely to show more Americans opposed to the U.S. commitment to Europe than favoring it. Yet the Congress of the United States, a body of democratically elected statespeople highly responsive to the views of their constituents, consistently continues to back that commitment. The specter of Representative Patricia Schroeder haunts many Europeans, but not many other members of the House or Senate follow her. Why? The likely answer is that aside from the budget issues that are likely to be neutralized by ongoing reductions, the question is of very little importance to most Americans. A ranking of salience of public issues would put the United States NATO commitment somewhere in the one-digit range in percent of the electorate that was interested. Opposition to the commitment is not a strongly felt feeling reflected in an active movement; it is more properly described as a lack of interest. "So what" rather than "Get out!"

Under such conditions, Americans are willing to follow their leaders, and American leaders are willing and able to lead. So long as the president and his foreign policy and defense advisors consider the NATO commitment essential to U.S. security, so long as the congressional leaders who are listened to by their colleagues on this subject agree, and so long as the budget pressures can be responded to without abrogating the commitment, *the United States is unlikely to initiate changes that threaten the Atlantic Alliance.*

The world is changing very fast, and NATO will surely change drastically over the next five years. Perhaps it will even go out of business. The United States will necessarily be a major player in such changes. But they will *originate* in the Soviet Union or in Germany, or perhaps in other parts of Europe. They will not start from the western shores of the Atlantic.

NOTES

1. This is discussed in more detail in Robert A. Levine, *NATO, the Subjective Alliance: The Debate Over the Future*, Rand Report R-3607-FF/CC/RC, April 1988, particularly Chapter VII.

2. Paradoxically, that is why Secretary of State Shultz was the "Third World" hawk in the Reagan administration, Secretary of Defense Weinberger the dove. For Weinberger, the worst case would be losing the political backing of the American people and the war, as in Vietnam.

3. That internal Soviet success might lead to renewed and much more effective aggressiveness is feared by some, but any such possibility is so long in the future that it need not be considered here.

4. The meaning of a "more political" NATO has never been very clear. For many years *before* the onset of Gorbachev, the Alliance was, as I wrote in 1988, "a subjective one, engaged to a substantial degree in analyzing itself . . . [The] military as well as the political shape of the Alliance is based more on national and Alliance politics than on imminent military threats." (*NATO, the Subjective Alliance: The Debate Over the Future.*)

Chapter 3

A Unified Germany

Ronald D. Asmus

INTRODUCTION

German unification marks a watershed in postwar European history. A byproduct of the collapse of communist rule in Eastern Europe, the overcoming of Germany's division may also bring about the end of Europe's division some 45 years following the conclusion of the Second World War. A unified Germany will play a key role in shaping the future political, economic, and military landscape in Europe.

The purpose of this chapter is to look beyond the tumultuous events of the unification process in an effort to address the longer-term ramifications of German unification. What, for example, will be the political and economic outcome of the merger of the two German states? Similarly, how will a unified Germany respond to the radically altered foreign and security policy environment in which it finds itself? What degree of continuity or change will characterize future German domestic and foreign policy? Will Germany's agenda change, and, if so, how? Will the past style and instruments of German foreign policy be adequate to meet the new challenges that will confront a unified Germany?

Such questions are crucial in light of Germany's central position and in view of its growing importance in shaping the future course of European politics. The central theme of this study is that the collapse of communism has transformed Germany into the lead actor on the European stage. As a divided country and a front-line state exposed to massive Soviet power, the Federal Republic of Germany (FRG) enjoyed a sheltered existence for much of the postwar period. Unification and the collapse of Soviet influence to the East will enhance German political and economic influence in the region but will also impose new responsibilities and burdens on German policy makers.

Accordingly, the key questions addressed in this study center on how such changes will affect German perceptions of their own interests, roles, and commitments in Europe and beyond, including their relationship with the United States. The FRG has been one of the closest allies of the United States throughout the postwar period. As a result, the course that Germany takes will be a key factor determining not only the future political landscape of Europe but the American role in European affairs as well.

CONSEQUENCES OF UNIFICATION: THE STATISTICS

A central aspect of unification, and one that must be stressed, is that the newly created German union was by no means a marriage of two equal and powerful partners. Rather, it more closely resembled the adoption of a weaker Eastern sibling by its stronger Western counterpart. A comparison of the basic statistics of the two German states, shown in Table 3-1, amply illustrates this point. As this table shows, the German Democratic Republic (GDR) was a small to medium-sized country from a European perspective; at the end of 1989, its population was about one-quarter and its GNP some 10 to 15 percent of that of the FRG. Its productivity level varied greatly across industrial sectors but in overall terms was estimated to have been roughly 40 percent of that of the FRG. Hence, even if the former GDR were eventually to attain the productivity level of the FRG, its absorption would amount to little more than the addition to the FRG of a country roughly the size of one of the larger West German *Laender*, such as North Rhine-Westphalia.

This unified state also differs from the Germany of prewar vintage with regard to its composition. The territory of a unified Germany, for example, will include only two-thirds of the area of the former German Reich. Until the end of the First World War, this Reich, with 541,000 square kilometers, was the largest nation in Europe and second only to Russia on the continent. By contrast, a unified Germany in 1990 will span some 357,000 square kilometers, placing it in fifth place in Europe behind France, Spain, and Sweden, and only slightly ahead of countries such as Finland, Norway, and Poland.

The relative weight of a unified Germany becomes clearer when it is placed outside the context of Europe. The population of a unified Germany, for instance, is less than one-third of that of the United States and three-quarters of that of Japan. Similarly, the size of the economy of a unified Germany will be only one-quarter of the United States and 60 percent of Japan. Although Germany is one of the world's leading export countries, its dominance in this realm appears less formidable if one treats the European Community (EC) market as a

Basic statistics	West	East
Area sq km '000	249	108
Population 1950	50.0 m	18.4 m
Population 1988	61.7 m	16.7 m
Of which working age 15-65	42.8 m	11.2 m
Pensioners 65	9.4 m	2.2 m
Pensioners as % of population	15.2%	13.2%
Life expectancy 1988		
Males	70 yrs	69 yrs
Females	77yrs	75 yrs
Fertility rate* 1987	1.3	1.7
Workforce 1988 (including armed forces)	29.7 m	8.6 m
Employment (as % of population)	48.1	51.5
Males	60.7	55.1
Females	37.0	48.3
Percent employed in agriculture	5	12
Industry	41	48
Services	54	40
Gross domestic product $ bn	1200	155
1988 per person $	19,500	9300

*Number of children a woman will bear in her lifetime

SOURCES: Commerzbank, Deutsche Bank, OECD

Table 3-1
The two German states compared

domestic market for German goods, since over half of Germany's exports are to EC countries. Similarly, Germany is highly vulnerable to changes in the world economy and is heavily dependent on imports from around the world—up to 100 percent in some key sectors.

Germany also suffers from a critical demographic problem. The contrast between the population and demographic trends of prewar Germany and Germany today, for example, is striking. Three decades ago, Germany had a population of some 60 million, placing it nearly 50 percent ahead of either France or Great Britain and exceeded only by Russia with 90 million. Together with the Austro-Hungarian Empire, then, the German-speaking area of Europe was by far the most populous on the continent—equaling that of France, Great Britain, and Italy combined. By contrast, the newly reunified Germany has a population of 79 million, including some five million foreigners. Moreover, both halves of Germany suffer from a declining birth rate. Hence the population of Germany is expected to decline by some five million per decade—so that within 30 years, the number of Germans in a unified Germany will be roughly that of the population of the FRG today and will be only slightly ahead of France, Britain, or Italy.

There has, of course, been considerable emigration of ethnic Germans from the East into the FRG in recent years; in all, approximately 1.2 million people, some 700,000 of whom were East Germans or ethnic Germans from Poland, Romania, or the USSR, left the Soviet bloc in 1989. Such flows will not, however, reverse the demographic trends of a unified Germany. As a result, Germany will continue to import foreign labor and will increasingly become a multicultural society with all the advantages and problems inherent in that process. Some estimates suggest that a unified Germany may have to import labor on the scale of some 500,000 annually by the end of the decade.[1]

This process of emigration that has been taking place since the mid-1950s will be augmented by labor flows resulting from the implementation of the European Single Act of 1992 and the elimination of internal barriers against intra-EC immigration as well as by substantial migration pressures from the newly democratizing countries in Eastern Europe—pressures driven by the significantly higher birth rates in those countries and by Germany's relative affluence and extensive social welfare system.[2] Emigration pressures emanating from the USSR may be even greater, however; Soviet officials have estimated that the liberalization of Soviet travel restrictions, combined with ongoing economic reform in the USSR, could lead some seven to eight million Soviet citizens to apply for emigration within the first year after the regulations are introduced.[3] While such problems will confront the EC as a whole, Germany's advanced welfare system, its historic ties with the region, and the border it shares with the new democracies of the East make it a likely destination for those seeking jobs and prosperity in the West.

Although such statistics do not alter the centrality of a unified Germany's role in Europe, they do underscore the fact that the Germany of today is far different from its predecessors in both its size and its composition. Above all, Germany is far more dependent on its neighbors for everything from labor to export markets. And while German resources and influence will doubtless increase as a product of unification, the collapse of Soviet power, and the enormous changes taking place in Europe, Germany will remain a country that is closely linked to its European neighbors and vulnerable to changes or pressures emanating elsewhere in Europe. Such trends will inevitably affect the manner in which Germans define themselves, their problems, and their preferred policy options, as will be discussed later.

THE NEW POLITICAL LANDSCAPE

One key issue concerning the future of a unified Germany pivots on the question of how the political fabric of Germany might change as a result of unification. German unification has taken place through the implementation of Article 23 of the West German constitution, a measure that granted the former states of the German Reich the right to accede to the FRG—and the invocation of which has ensured that established postwar West German institutions will provide the political and legal basis for a future unified German state. Such a move did not merely represent a vote of confidence in postwar West German democracy, however; it was also a measure aimed at providing a strong guarantee to Germany's neighbors that the future German state would continue along the democratic path that West Germany has followed since 1945.

The decision to unify via Article 23 was one of the early watersheds in the unification process. Despite the initial opposition of sections of the German Left in both states to the venue of Article 23, a consensus quickly emerged that this was both the safest and the most certain way to minimize the uncertainties of the unification process.[4] In the spring of 1990, following the GDR election, Bonn moved to secure East German support for unifying through the venue of Article 23. Bonn's decision to adopt a 1:1 exchange rate for the East German mark in connection with monetary union was part of a broader package of compromises whereby the GDR government simultaneously agreed to adopt West German law.

Bonn's willingness to absorb the additional costs and economic risks of such an exchange rate in return for a commitment to unification on West German terms was but one of several examples of its willingness to assume considerable short-term financial costs in an effort to guarantee the continuity of structures that have proved so successful for West German democracy in the postwar period. A second example of this pattern, and one that will be discussed later, was Bonn's willingness to absorb considerable costs with regard to aid for the USSR in an effort to convince Moscow to accede to ongoing German membership in

NATO. Here, too, Bonn was willing to pay for the maintenance of the external structures that have proved successful for the FRG.

At the same time, the new Germany will be more than merely an enlarged FRG. Indeed, one of the most interesting aspects of unification will lie in the manner in which the reintegration of a nation divided for 40 years by ideology will work out in practice and how that process will affect the future political fabric of Germany. Perhaps the most immediate impact of the collapse of the Berlin Wall on West German politics has been the reversal in the political fortunes of the two major parties in the FRG, the Christian Democratic Union/Christian Social Union (CDU/CSU) and the Social Democratic Party (SPD). Before November 1989, the CDU/CSU appeared to be in a stage of political decline. It had performed poorly in a series of local and state elections, losing power in Schleswig-Holstein, West Berlin, and Lower Saxony. On the national level, too, there were signs of strain and erosion in the CDU/CSU-Free Democratic Party (FDP) coalition after eight years of governance. And despite the strong performance of the West German economy, Helmut Kohl's popularity had reached a record low in public opinion polls, leading to growing speculation over a possible change of government in Bonn and a return to power of the SPD.

The unification process has led to a remarkable reversal in the CDU's political fortunes in several important respects (see Figure 3-1). First, Chancellor Kohl's early advocacy of rapid unification, together with his handling of the diplomatic aspects of German unity vis-à-vis both the Western allies and the Soviet Union, has transformed him in the public's view from a provincial politician to a senior statesman, therby giving his popularity a significant boost. Kohl's political genius lay in the fact that he was among the first to recognize the opportunities that the collapse of communism in the GDR offered for his country, his party, and his role in history. Recognizing the extent to which Germans in the GDR were alienated from their system and state, Kohl perceived that the measured reform and lengthy period of confederation advocated by many East German intellectuals did not represent the sentiments or needs of GDR society as a whole. Indeed, while the notion of an indigenous GDR model may have enjoyed support among East German intellectuals, little enthusiasm for yet another "socialist" experiment emanated from the average "man in the street," who increasingly saw unification as the quickest and best guarantee of Western standards of freedom and affluence. Ignoring the advice of experts and his own intellectuals, the average East German took to the streets in growing numbers to demand that Bonn fulfill its commitment to German unity so that East Germans could reap the same benefits their West German brethren had long enjoyed.[5]

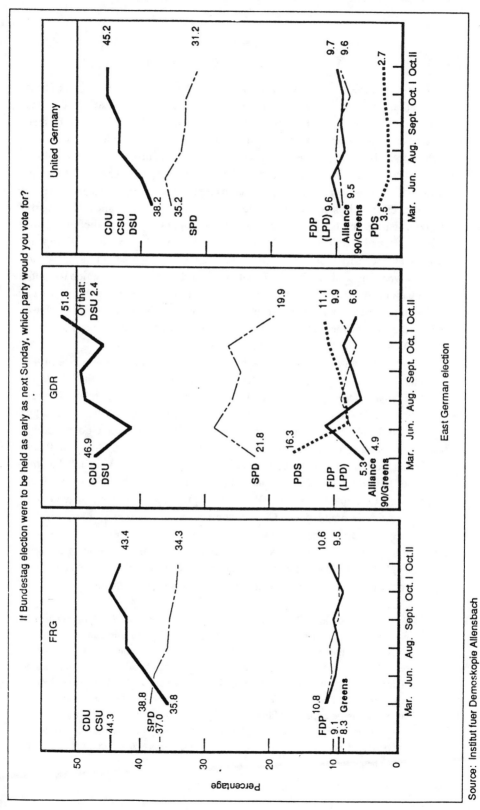

If Bundestag election were to be held as early as next Sunday, which party would you vote for?

FRG

CDU
CSU
44.3 — 43.4

SPD
37.0 — 38.8 — 34.3 — 35.8

FDP 10.8 — 10.6
9.1 — 9.5
8.3 — Greens

Mar. Jun. Aug. Sept. Oct. I Oct.II

GDR

CDU 46.9
DSU — 51.8   Of that: DSU 2.4

SPD
21.8 — 19.9

PDS 16.3 — 11.1

FDP
(LPD) — 9.9
5.3 — 6.6

Alliance 4.9
90/Greens

Mar. Jun. Aug. Sept. Oct. I Oct.II

East German election

United Germany

CDU
CSU
DSU
38.2 — 45.2

SPD
35.2 — 31.2

FDP
(LPD) 9.6 — 9.7
Alliance 9.5 — 9.6
90/Greens

PDS 3.5 — 2.7

Mar. Jun. Aug. Sept. Oct. I Oct.II

Percentage — 50, 40, 30, 20, 10, 0

Source: Institut fuer Demoskopie Allensbach

Figure 3-1 Strength of Political Parties.

Kohl's personal credibility was also greatly enhanced by the emergence of the unification issue. As the chancellor remarked in an interview in early 1989, long before the changes in the East had become manifest, no chancellor since Konrad Adenauer had spoken so often in public of the German commitment to unity.[6] Although Kohl's emphasis on unity was attacked by his liberal critics throughout the 1980s as anachronistic and out of touch with the times, the course of history vindicated Kohl as he stepped forward to claim credit for achieving German unity.[7]

Chancellor Kohl's active role in the unification process also allowed his party to refurbish its foreign policy credentials. Throughout much of the 1980s, the CDU/CSU had found itself on the defensive on many key issues of European foreign and security policy, divided among itself on many touchy issues, such as nuclear weapons, and lacking the talent and expertise it needed to guide the public debate on security issues.[8] The Christian Democrats were widely perceived as lagging on many core questions of foreign policy—above all toward the East, where the tone of the public debate was set either by veteran Foreign Minister Hans-Dietrich Genscher or by the SPD opposition.

With the collapse of communism in the GDR and the rapid emergence of the unification issue, however, the CDU's stubborn advocacy of unity suddenly appeared in a different political light. Kohl's active participation in the unification process also allowed him to portray himself as a statesman and to claim credit for unification. Kohl's central role in the process even permitted him to outmaneuver his own popular foreign minister, Hans-Dietrich Genscher, in claiming credit for achieving German unity; historically, Genscher may have been vindicated by the events of the fall of 1989, but it was Kohl who emerged as the primary political benefactor.[9] Combined with the CDU's solid reputation as the party of economic competence, this enabled the CDU to pursue an aggressive strategy toward redefining the political agenda in German politics and to present itself as the champion of German unity and solid economic growth. In an interview in early February, Volker Ruehe, the new general secretary of the CDU, sketched out his party's political strategy for the forthcoming months when he stated,

> And what about the SPD's commitment to unification? No one has forgotten that it was only a couple of months ago that the SPD called unification an illusion, that Willy Brandt termed the goal of unification one of the great lies of the Federal Republic, and that Egon Bahr went so far as to term our advocacy of unification environmental pollution. And the close ties between the SPD and the SED [Socialist Unity Party] were also a fact. Moreover, in economic affairs the Union clearly has more competence. In addition, I believe that many people want a degree of continuity in government policy at a time when so many other things are changing. Our policies have made us so strong in economic terms that we are now in a position to help others.[10]

Such factors, Ruehe continued, would constitute considerable handicaps for the SPD in the East and could translate into a comparative political advantage for the CDU. According to Ruehe,

> The SPD in the GDR has three Achilles' heels that one doesn't even have to point to because the population in the GDR is fully aware of them. First, the SPD has a good many former SED members in its ranks, a fact that many people don't exactly find positive. Second, [the SPD] suffers from a lack of credibility with regard to its commitment to achieving German unity in years past. One hasn't forgotten that the SPD was willing to abandon a single German citizenship and wanted to close the Salzgitter Center for monitoring human rights violations. The third and most important point is the fact that economic and social issues are the core issues in the GDR, and the Social Democrats in the Federal Republic and in the GDR are both weak in their commitment to a market economy. In the programs of both parties one finds calls for great state involvement in and control of the economy.[11]

These factors help explain the strong performance of the Alliance for Germany—a coalition of conservative parties in the GDR forged with the help of the West German CDU—in the March 1990 elections in the GDR, as well as the subsequent performance of the CDU in Eastern Germany. (See Table 3-2.) In the spring of 1990, for example, Chancellor Kohl was able to effect a shift in the East German electorate of over 20 percent in favor of the Alliance for Germany through a set of aggressive and well-organized campaign rallies.[12] In the longer term, however, it is clear that Kohl and the CDU seek to capitalize on strong anticommunist sentiments and on the clear desire for rapid economic growth and consumption in the GDR in their efforts to fashion a new political base for the CDU in the East. Anticommunism and prosperity were in fact two key elements that Konrad Adenauer used in the 1950s to forge the CDU's initial political base and to turn that party into the largest political party in the FRG. West German conservatives have made it clear that they will seek to make patriotism and economic competence the key themes in German politics.

At the same time, the CDU will also undergo significant changes as a result of unification. In addition to gaining some 20 percent in its membership through its unification in both parts of Germany, for example, the CDU may have to change its programmatic profile. The West German CDU's strong liberal and Catholic wing, rooted in the west and southwest, will now be counterbalanced by a more northern and largely Protestant wing that will increase in strength through the addition of Christian Democrats from the largely Protestant former GDR. Former East German Prime Minister Lothar de Maiziere, Kohl's sole deputy as party leader in a unified CDU, has repeatedly emphasized that a unified CDU must pay greater heed to social and ecological issues and that the

States	PDS	SPD	Fed. of Free Democrats (Lib)	Other	CDU	German Social Union
Berlin	30.0	35.0	3.0	11.4	18.4	2.2
Mecklenburg	22.4	23.9	3.6	11.4	36.4	2.3
Brandenburg	18.4	28.9	4.8	10.2	34.0	3.7
Sachsen-Anhalt	14.0	23.6	7.7	7.6	44.7	2.4
Thueringen	11.2	17.4	8.2	2.4	53.0	5.6
Sachsen	13.3	15.1	9.1	3.5	43.6	13.2
Election results	16.3	21.8	9.4	3.5	40.9	6.3

Table 3-2
The results of the GDR elections of March 1990 (percentage of popular vote)

party must become more of a bridge to the East in foreign policy. In the words of the CDU's secretary general, Volker Ruehe, "The party will be more northern, eastern, [and] Protestant, and also younger."[13]

Those factors that have played to the CDU's comparative advantage have simultaneously been key handicaps for the SPD. There is little doubt, for example, that the rapid collapse of the SED regime and the groundswell of popular sentiment for rapid unification took the SPD by surprise. And although the SPD undoubtedly enjoyed excellent contacts in the GDR and Eastern Europe, such contacts were largely focused either on the ruling communist regimes or on small groups of dissident intellectuals—groups that were often Social Democratic in orientation but that, in retrospect, turned out to be unrepresentative of the sentiments of these societies as a whole.

The SPD was also wedded to its own concept of *Ostpolitik*—one that was designed to effect change in the East through small steps and through gradual reforms implemented from above. Theirs was a vision that eschewed unification as a short-term goal, calling instead for looser forms of German unity based on an improved inter-German relationship that would ultimately lead to some form of confederation. It is only against this backdrop that one can understand why the SPD found itself on the psychological and political defensive following the crumbling of the Berlin Wall and the consequent surge of sentiments for unification. Although Willy Brandt quickly pushed for a *volte-face* in party policy by embracing the goal of unification in late 1989, considerable reticence nonetheless remained evident in party ranks—and this hesitancy to embrace the need for rapid unification was ruthlessly exploited by Chancellor Kohl.

A second blow to the SPD came from the discovery that it did not have a natural constituency in the GDR. Past conventional wisdom had held that the SPD would be very strong in the GDR; those parts of Germany constituting the GDR, for example, were Social Democratic strongholds before the war. In addition, Brandt's *Ostpolitik* had seemingly been popular in the 1970s, and many of the leading figures in the GDR opposition openly sympathized with the SPD. Yet such factors turned out to be of limited value in GDR politics in the free-for-all that followed the opening of the inter-German border. Historic Social Democratic strongholds such as Saxony and Thuringia voted overwhelmingly for conservative parties as voters proved to be motivated more by anticommunism and consumerism than by prewar party allegiances.

The SPD's dilemma has been reflected in the fortunes of the party's candidate for chancellor, Oskar LaFontaine. LaFontaine very much represents a new generation of postwar West German Social Democratic politicians—one that is often termed Brandt's "grandchildren." A product of the radical activism of the 1960s, LaFontaine is a remarkably gifted speaker to whom Willy Brandt once referred in jest as a "successful combination of Napoleon and Mussolini." LaFontaine has always been a divisive figure in the SPD—one who has enjoyed the reputation of a skilled tactician who is willing to challenge conventional wisdom and constituencies within the SPD in an effort to reach out to broader portions of the electorate either on the left or in the center, depending on the issue.[14] Yet the issues LaFontaine addressed were largely those of a postindustrial society (e.g., the advanced welfare state, ecology, and disarmament).

LaFontaine also favored transnational integration and often criticized the CDU's unification policy as an outdated attempt to resurrect the nation-state at a time when it should be transcended. Prior to the crumbling of the Wall, for example, LaFontaine had advocated that steps be taken toward recognizing an East German citizenship and had repeatedly criticized the CDU's ongoing commitment to unification. In the immediate aftermath of the collapse of the Wall, LaFontaine criticized Kohl and the CDU for pushing the unification issue, increasingly raised the question of the potential costs of unification to the West German taxpayer, and even went so far as to oppose the first state treaty governing monetary union in July 1990. Although such arguments struck a resonant chord in West German public opinion, LaFontaine's own party became increasingly uneasy about the impact of his strategy in the GDR and of the danger of being portrayed by the CDU as the party opposing German unity. Ultimately, the injuries LaFontaine suffered as a result of an unsuccessful assassination attempt in the late summer of 1990 weakened him, leaving the party struggling for leadership at a key time before the crucial phase of the election campaign was launched and reopening old differences over the party's future course and direction.

LaFontaine's strategy clearly pivoted on blaming the CDU-led government in Bonn for the economic problems that have arisen in the GDR. By contrast, the coalition insists that such problems are the residual effect of 40 years of SED economic mismanagement. And while the prospect of further economic turmoil in the former GDR is very real, at least in the immediate term, it is not clear who would reap benefits from such a development. Although the opposition Social Democrats will clearly seek to ascribe responsibility for such problems to Kohl, the SPD does not enjoy a reputation as the party that can best handle economic matters. It will therefore be of interest to see which party or parties portray themselves as best suited to deal with economic problems in the future.

Whether such problems represent a short-term crisis in the SPD or a longer-term strategic dilemma is still not clear. Many Social Democrats candidly admit that they cannot compete with the CDU given a political agenda dominated by issues such as the national question, patriotism, or economic competence. At the same time, the Social Democrats insist that the postunification political agenda will shift toward issues of social justice and job security, areas in which the SPD is strong. Yet despite the SPD's poor start in the East, politics in the former GDR remain very much in a state of flux. At the same time, many Social Democrats have been forced to concede that they overestimated the strength of social democracy in postcommunist Central Europe while simultaneously underestimating both the depth of anticommunist sentiments and the manner in which 40 years of communism would discredit the tradition of social democracy in the region.[15]

The SPD, too, will change as a result of unification, as it will also inherit a sister party organization from the East that differs in many ways from the West German SPD. Peter Glotz, SPD parliamentarian and editor of the party's theoretical monthly, *Die neue Gesellschaft*, has suggested that through unification the SPD will acquire a wing composed of members who are far more traditional and in many ways reminiscent of the pre-Godesberg SPD of the 1950s in West Germany (e.g., members whose commitment to state intervention and skepticism toward the market are greater and who are less Atlanticist and more European in their political orientation). When the SPD met in late September for its own unification congress, a number of party leaders were forced to concede that they had some way to go before the two branches of one of the oldest parties in German history were reunited.[16]

The impact of unification may be even greater, however, on the smaller parties within a reunified Germany. The West German liberal Free Democratic Party (FDP), for example, tripled its membership through its merger with the East German Federation of Free Democrats of the GDR, itself composed of two former East German bloc parties. In the West, the FDP's constituency has increasingly become a mixture of young affluent entrepreneurs and liberals—a constituency whose size is uncertain in the GDR. This has led to some concern that the FDP's own identity, based on liberal positions on social issues, a liberal foreign policy, and a strong commitment to market principles in economics, may be diluted and might thus revert to its more national vintage of the early postwar period. Moreover, much of the FDP's political staying power in the past decade has been tied to the enormous political popularity of Foreign Minister Hans-Dietrich Genscher, who remains the single most popular politician in Germany today. Although currently it is almost impossible to imagine German politics without Genscher, the foreign minister's health has been failing in recent years, and in the longer term the prospects of the FDP without the active leadership of the veteran foreign minister appear somewhat less certain.

The future of political parties on the far Left is even more uncertain. Although the radical environmentalist Green party had become a hallmark of West German radical politics, they now find themselves in competition with a number of left-wing groups from the former GDR. Although an electoral alliance was formed between the Greens and the former East German party Alliance 90, the real competition on the Left has been waged between such alternative leftist groups and the new reform communist party from the former GDR, the Party of Democratic Socialism (PDS); both are competing for the vote to the left of the SPD, and both have thus far remained bitter political foes, a dispute rooted in the Greens' strong opposition to the SED regime and to "real socialism" as it was practiced in Eastern Europe. Led by the dynamic figure of Gregor Gysi, the PDS initially seemed to have a chance to survive all-German elections in December 1990—but the electoral prospects of the PDS suffered a critical blow in October 1990, when federal authorities entered PDS party headquarters without a warrant to arrest several party officials for making illegal money transfers to Soviet bank accounts. One former SED official arrested at that time subsequently confirmed that this money was being transferred to prepare the party to go underground in case the party lost in the forthcoming elections. This served only to confirm suspicions that the PDS's reformist credtentials were merely a democratic facade and that the party remained dominated by old Stalinist functionaries from the former SED regime.[17]

The future success of political parties in an all-German framework will in the final analysis rest on how well these parties adjust to the new themes and political agenda of a unified Germany. In this context, one must ask what impact the merger of the two states will have on German political culture and politics. A new German republic will continue to be pro-Western, liberal, and capitalist— yet it may also become more traditionally German and Eastern-oriented as the former GDR is merged with West Germany. It is often forgotten that the real revolution in the postwar period, in terms of political attitudes and political culture, took place in the West rather than in the East.

Indeed, one of the ironies of 40 years of communist rule in the GDR is that it has preserved many aspects of traditional German society—aspects that have long since faded in West Germany under the pressures of modernization and Westernization. Germans in the GDR, for example, were not allowed to participate in any of the processes that played pivotal roles in shaping West German democracy—except through the lens of West German television and the Western media. Moreover, no real integration in the East paralleled the positive forces of the EC and the Atlantic Alliance. Instead, both the Council for Mutual Economic Assistance (CMEA) and the Warsaw Pact were essentially instruments through which the USSR exerted its hegemony through a series of bilateral relationships.

As a result of this relative isolation, the countries of Eastern Europe—including Poland, Hungary, and Czechoslovakia as well as the eastern portion of Germany—have had little opportunity to transcend old nationalisms. Observers of the GDR, for example, have long noted the ostensibly greater "Germanness" of the GDR—a trait that was glorified in the early 1980s by a number of prominent German journalists and intellectuals, who presented the GDR as a country that was less brash, harsh, and hectic, and hence more traditionally German, than the ostensibly "Americanized" FRG. The GDR was often viewed as a sort of *Heimatmuseum*—a place to go to see the traditional German values and customs that had been preserved.[18]

Some Western observers attempted to portray such attributes as a potential sign of strength and legitimacy for the SED regime. In reality, however, it reflected only the alien nature of the communist system and the resistance of German political culture to Soviet cultural and political penetration. Moreover, the passivity of Germans in the GDR turned out not to be a sign of support for the regime but merely apathy—clearly the lull before the storm. When the East German communist leadership met to celebrate the GDR's 40th anniversary in October 1989, few would have anticipated that within six weeks they would be toppled and that one year later the socialist German state would have officially disappeared. Perhaps nowhere in Eastern Europe was the collapse of communism so quick, decisive, and unexpected, and nowhere was the transformation of a society more dramatic. As the East German writer Stefan Heym noted in November 1989,

It was as if someone had thrown open the windows, after all the years of spiritual, economic, and political stagnation, the years of phrase-washing and bureaucratic caprice, of official blindness and deafness. What a change! ... Someone wrote me (and the man is right): In these last weeks we overcame our speechlessness and we are now learning how to walk in an upright manner. And that, friends, in Germany where previously every revolution had failed and where the people had always been subservient—under the Emperor, under the Nazis, and later too.[19]

Politics in the former GDR thus remain in a state of flux. Party organization remains shallow. Moreover, the effects of 40 years of socialism are likely to persist for some time to come. As many Germans have noted in recent months, it was only after the Wall came down that many Germans in both East and West realized how much they had grown apart over the past four decades. As elsewhere in Eastern Europe, for example, East Germans had developed traits characteristic of the legendary Good Soldier Schweik in order to survive under a communist dictatorship, and they now found themselves confronted with the need to survive in a competitive capitalist environment. As Manfred Stolpe, a leading lay official in the East German Evangelical Church subsequently elected as head of the state of Brandenburg in the former GDR, put it,

East German citizens were not raised to think independently or creatively. There was and still is a certain passiveness, a defense posture which was needed to survive under East German conditions. It was part of the art of survival; it meant not being the first one to report and to go forward but rather to wait and see in which direction things were going to go. It is characteristic of East German citizens that they are very reserved. When they now meet West Germans who have learned to present themselves, an inferiority complex is created.[20]

In the words of one West German expert, it was almost as if the political culture in the GDR had been frozen in time at a stage that characterized the FRG during the immediate postwar period:

For the citizens of the GDR the institutions that had until now determined the parameters of their lives have simply dissolved. What seems to have emerged is a certain continuity with the political culture and the traditional bourgeois values of prewar Germany. As a result, one has the paradoxical impression that what is seen in the Federal Republic as the end of the postwar period looks very much like the start of the postwar period in the GDR. For years to come we are going to be faced with significantly different regional structures of political culture and values [in the two former German states].[21]

The lesson to be drawn from these observations is that the Germans in the GDR are still on an important learning curve with regard to Western-style democracy, the competition of a capitalist economy, and the positive values of Europe and multilateral integration—and although the slope of this curve is undoubtedly high given the successful example of postwar West Germany, full assimilation will nonetheless take time. One should not forget that several decades elapsed before democracy became firmly rooted in West Germany and before the German political class developed confidence in its own institutions. And although West Germans were justifiably proud of their economic accomplishments even in the 1950s and 1960s, it was not until the 1970s that a strong attachment to and sense of satisfaction with postwar political institutions in the FRG really emerged. In the case of the former GDR, the process will undoubtedly be more rapid, but it could easily take a generation for the Germans in the GDR to fully absorb the political lessons that their Western counterparts have learned in the course of four decades. As Chancellor Kohl has noted,

> More difficult than finding a solution to the economic problems . . . will be the task of overcoming the grave consequences for the psyche of the population of the GDR resulting from four decades of communist dictatorship. Here we confront problems for which there are no patent prescriptions. We, who have had the luxury to live in freedom in the Western part of Germany for many decades, must perceive the completely different experience of our countrymen in the GDR. We must attempt to understand how decades of repression have affected their thinking and perception.
>
> We must realize that the last free elections before March 18, 1990, were held 58 years ago, in November 1932. Those who were able to cast a vote then, are now 79 years or older. For all those who are younger, the election on March 18 was a unique experience up to that time.[22]

Finally, what will be the impact of unification on German nationalism? The collapse of the Wall was followed by a surge of national pride and by manifestations of patriotism that took many observers by surprise, rekindling fears of a new German nationalism. The euphoria that swept the country following the collapse of the Wall in many ways represented the pent-up release of a divided nation that had been struggling for four decades to define itself in terms of a national identity. Yet the unification of Germany will do more than to finally bring an end to the painful realities of German partition; it will also allow Germany to rid itself of the identity crisis that has continually plagued it as a divided nation. Germans no longer need to agonize over questions as to whether their identity is East or West German or all German; it is now simply German.[23] Asked in an interview about the prospects of German nationalism, Chancellor

Kohl stressed that unification might allow the Germans to find a new equilibrium in terms of their national identity as well:

> I think it is now possible and perhaps even probable that the Germans will find that type of inner equilibrium that is so characteristic of other European nations. Heretofore we Germans have had a hard time with this for understandable reasons. Unity has opened the possibility of creating a natural form of patriotism, [and] one that is of course necessary in the long run for a nation's sense of itself—an enlightened patriotism that is committed to the values of freedom and whose goal is not a German-dominated Europe but rather a European Germany.
>
> Such a form of patriotism means that we Germans accept ourselves as we were and are—with all of our strengths and weaknesses and with our history in all of its various parts. A sincere and honest acknowledgement of one's own historical roots is the basis and at the same time the precondition for going beyond the solution of our national question and remaining open for a true partnership in the spirit of Europe.[24]

Foreign Minister Hans-Dietrich Genscher has been more outspoken. Speaking before the United Nations, Genscher claimed that his country in the postwar period had been one of the most willing to abandon national sovereignty in order to nurture the process of political and economic integration and to build a Western collective security alliance. A unified Germany, he suggested, would follow a "policy of the good example" and demonstrate its own commitment to defusing nationalism in Europe by remaining in the forefront of those willing to give up their national sovereignty in pursuit of a broader European unity.[25]

Whether Germany succeeds in finding what Chancellor Kohl has termed its "inner equilibrium" will have implications for all of Europe. Should Genscher's prediction hold true—namely, that Germany will continue to be a driving force favoring the transcendence of national sovereignty and embracing multilateral integration—Germany could play a key role not only in promoting political and economic union in the West but also in helping overcome nascent nationalism to the East. Alternatively, should the wave of national euphoria released by the collapse of communism spill over into Germany and lead to rising national sentiment, the process of European integration might be slowed if not halted.

In the final analysis, the prospects for the political reconstruction of Eastern Germany are positive, and there is every reason to believe that democracy will quickly take root in the former GDR. Indeed, the preconditions for democracy are better in the former GDR than anywhere else in East-Central Europe. At the same time, it is equally clear that the need to reconstruct the former GDR in political and economic terms will absorb a good deal of Germany's energy and capital. Moreover, unification will inevitably add a new element of uncertainty to German politics. Nearly 20 percent of the parliamentarians in a new all-German parliament will come from the former GDR, and they will undoubtedly question many aspects of West German political life that have long been established practice or conventional wisdom. New alliances and coalitions will thus form both within the existing parties and across the political spectrum. The end result is likely to be a Germany that is democratic and Western yet quite different in character from the FRG that we have known for the past four decades.

THE NEW ECONOMIC LANDSCAPE

Perhaps nowhere is Germany's central role in shaping the future map of a post-Cold War Europe more evident than in the field of economics. How well Germany handles the challenge of economic reconstruction will have a major impact on ensuring the stability of Central Europe. Although in the short term West German resources directed toward the GDR will not be available for investments in Spain, Portugal, Eastern Europe, or the USSR, a booming German economy will in the longer term serve as a primary source of growth for the entire region. Similarly, the manner in which Germany elects to finance its economic reconstruction (i.e., through borrowing or tax increases) could have a critical effect on capital flows and interest rates both throughout the region and globally. Finally, Germany's voice will be a critical one in debates over the future shape and speed of economic and monetary integration as well as in core European-American economic issues, such as monetary stabilization, trade liberalization, and the promotion of viable economic reform in the East.

The economic opportunities and challenges arising from unification must, however, be placed within the proper time frame. Unification will offer Germany tremendous economic opportunities by creating new production options resulting from simple economies of scale and a significantly expanded internal market; the addition of territory and population will increase German economic strength, augment its share of the European industrial product, and open potentially enormous opportunities for business. Similarly, the influx of significant amounts of private capital and massive public support, coupled with a strong demand for investment and consumer goods in Eastern Germany, will translate into increased economic output, a technologically upgraded industrial base, and growth in an all-German GNP that may approach some 5 percent annually by the end of the decade. Moreover, the collapse of Soviet influence and the shift to Western-style market economies in Eastern Europe have set the stage for expanded economic ties between Germany and the countries of the European Free Trade Association (EFTA) and Eastern Europe. Coupled with the stimulus provided by the Single European Act of 1992 and by the deepening of economic integration in Western

Europe, such factors have led many commentators to speculate about the possibility of a second German economic miracle of the postwar period.

Yet at the same time, unification will in the short run impose an extraordinary burden on the German economy, as the capital costs for modernizing the former GDR will be nothing short of staggering. One estimate suggests that the West German government and private sources will have to provide some 500 to 600 billion deutsche marks (DM) to modernize East German industry, transportation, and housing—and if one adds roads, agriculture, and environmental cleanup to the equation, the estimates of East German capital needs will easily top one trillion marks.[26] Moreover, West German sources will initially have to provide much of this capital, at least until East German production begins to generate its own capital. The dilemma facing German policy makers today is that there is a link between these two phases: in short, policies that might ease the initial shock of the transition to a free-market economy might simultaneously jeopardize long-run prosperity. Conversely, excessive short-run disruptions could jeopardize the political and economic stability that is required for a stable process of reintegration and unification.

The success with which Germany confronts these conflicting challenges will hinge in part on how successfully it overcomes the hurdles of economic reconstruction in the GDR. The magnitude of such challenges, however, cannot be underestimated. At the same time, the West German economy could hardly be better positioned to meet its current challenge—for unification has coincided with an economic upswing in the West German economy that has been evident since mid-1987. Moreover, the better-than-expected overall economic performance of the FRG in recent years has been bolstered by a judicious combination of interest and exchange-rate policies, fiscal consolidation, and strong foreign demand for German investment goods.[27]

The economic impact of unification, in other words, is being superimposed on an economy that is already operating at high speed and close to capacity. In 1989, for example, real GNP in the FRG, spurred by strong exports and business investment, grew by 4 percent—the fastest rate recorded in the post-1982 upswing. Inflation there has nonetheless remained moderate, and economic buoyancy has allowed for the first significant inroads to be made in unemployment since the Kohl government came to power. This booming economy allowed the FRG to absorb much of the massive immigration from the GDR and elsewhere in Eastern Europe, above all from Poland, that took place in 1989—a wave of immigration that in fact provided mobile labor made necessary by the labor rigidities of the West German economy.

The surprising strength of the West German economy has been matched, however, by a growing awareness of the economic weaknesses of the GDR, once officially ranked as the 12th largest economy in the world. The collapse of communism and the opening of the GDR has allowed Western experts to get their first comprehensive look at the industrial and resource base of the former economic showcase of the communist world, and the results have been sobering. West German studies conducted in the mid-1980s, for example, placed East German labor productivity at one-half that of the FRG[28]—but more recent studies show the average productivity in the former GDR to be as low as one-third that of the FRG.[29] Similarly, with regard to the GDR's industrial base, GDR Economics Minister Gerhard Pohl claimed in the spring of 1990 that his ministry had reviewed some 3,000 firms and had found that some 30 percent were competitive on the world market, with another 50 percent capable of becoming competitive with modernization.[30] Yet subsequent studies have suggested that such numbers are overly optimistic. In fact, some 21 percent of the GDR's industrial stock is now estimated to be over 20 years old, with 52 percent between 5 and 20 years old. While some 27 percent is less than five years old, official estimates now suggest that much of this equipment is already technologically obsolete.[31]

A brief glance at the telecommunications sector highlights some of the problems facing the two German states. Western experts have suggested that the East German telecommunications system is at the level West Germany attained in the 1950s. Not only are most telephone lines worn out, but digital switching, the pivotal technology of modern telecommunications, is virtually unknown; instead, the East German system is based on electromechanical switching, with nearly one-quarter of the local switching centers having been engineered in the 1920s and 1930s. The GDR has only about 11 phone lines for every 100 inhabitants, compared with 46 in the FRG; prior to the collapse of the Wall, over 1.2 million applications for a telephone were pending.[32]

The collapse of the Berlin Wall and the surge of sentiment favoring unification led to a proliferation of studies dealing with economic unification between the two German states. Most notably, the West German government asked the five leading economic institutes in the FRG to examine the issue. The German Council of Economic Experts subsequently produced a comprehensive analysis, as did many leading West German banks, and a consensus was quickly reached on several key points. First, it was agreed that monetary union was by far the most important and urgent measure to be addressed. This economic measure, more than any other, was regarded as a symbolic step toward unity in that the dispute over a single German currency in 1948 had triggered the Berlin blockade, culminating in the effective division of Germany. Second, concurrence was reached that economic unification had to take place quickly; otherwise, different persons and enterprises would act under different rules. The economic chaos that would result, in the words of one German institute, would be akin to allowing driving on the right-hand side and driving on the left-hand side in the same city. The growing fragility of the East German economy and the ongoing flow of refugees from the GDR to the West only accentuated the political imperative of a quick merger to stabilize the deteriorating economic situation in the East.[33]

Third, it was agreed that the unification of Germany was to be a friendly takeover. East Germany would adopt the laws, regulations, and processes of the West German capitalist economy, and East German enterprises would have to function within a competitive environment. In return, Bonn was to absorb the lion's share of the early transition costs and would agree to a highly favorable exchange rate for monetary union. In part, this stance reflected Bonn's long-standing position that West Germans had a moral commitment to help those Germans who had had the misfortune of having been on the wrong side of the border at the time of Germany's division. Yet at the same time, it also reflected the realization that major economic discrepancies in different parts of Germany could beget considerable political turmoil.

A consensus also emerged on the broad outlines of a four-phase plan for economic unification. The first phase, implemented with the signing of the first state treaty and the start of monetary union, foresaw the implementation of West German economic laws and regulations, the initiation of price reform, reductions in subsidies, wage adjustments, and the like. The second phase, which commenced after the start of monetary union on July 1, 1990, was to focus on the privatization of state enterprises, the establishment of a commercial banking system, the revamping of the social security system, and the sanitizing of any monetary overhang left from monetary union. During the third phase, scheduled for 1991, foreign trade would be freed from earlier agreements and obligations. A fourth and final phase, described as an "adjustment period," was scheduled to last up to a decade and would be characterized by the use of appropriate monetary, fiscal, employment, and social policies to bring the former GDR up to the level of the Western sections of a unified Germany.

Such plans were clearly ambitious but perhaps unrealistic. At the same time, they highlighted the overall thrust of West Germany's economic strategy. As the unification process has unfolded, however, Bonn has had to come to grips with several new problems. First, it soon became clear that Bonn would have to inject large infusions of West German capital into East Germany simply to prevent the East German economy, budget, and social system from collapsing outright. In early 1990, Bonn announced the creation of a German Unity Fund, a government-backed instrument to raise bonds of 95 billion DM over the following five years. This fund was designed to cover two-thirds of the East German budget deficit up to the end of 1994, thereby establishing a solid financial base for the GDR and later for an all-German government.[34] By late summer, however, Bonn was being called upon to deliver additional billions to help plug new gaps emerging in the East German budget and social security system as East German tax revenues failed to meet their targeted goals.

Second, it became clear that West German investment in the GDR was not proceeding as smoothly as Bonn had initially hoped. Although West German managers flocked to look at potential deals in the GDR, letters of intent were far more common than signed deals. The initial pattern of investment has been that service industries have moved quickly to establish a presence while manufacturers have continued to hold back. In part this has simply reflected the growing realization of just how formidable the problems in the GDR really were. In addition, many of the GDR's reported advantages (e.g., its role as a gateway to markets to the East) apply primarily to specific industrial sectors and hinge on the future political and economic evolution of these countries. Many West German manufacturers, then, saw the addition of the GDR as introducing a market no larger than that of one large West German state, such as Hessen or North Rhine-Westphalia—and many did not feel obliged to equip every large state with a production plant.

Finally, the very speed with which economic union has been effected has caused a number of crucial questions to be settled in principle only, with the details left to be worked out later—an approach that has underestimated the difficulties inherent in resolving such details, especially given the new and relatively inexperienced political leadership in East Berlin.[35] Perhaps the best example of this trend has lain in the issue of property and privatization. Successive waves of collectivization over the years in the GDR have left behind a maze of claims that must now be untangled. Yet an estimated one million claims by West Germans have raised significant fears among East Germans that they might lose their apartments or weekend homes, or that the country will be quickly bought out by the capital-rich West Germans. The two German governments have thus attempted to tread a narrow path between the principle that private property is vital for the reconstruction of the GDR (and that all property in the GDR will therefore be returned to its previous owner) and a sense of social and political justice for the East Germans thus affected.[36] Responsibility for the privatization of state-owned East German firms now lies in the hands of a newly created state trusteeship, or holding company (*Treuhandanstalt*), which is charged with the task of selling off some 8,300 East German companies as quickly as possible.

By the end of 1990, key tools of German government policy were in place. They consisted, first and foremost, of general financial assistance and credits funneled through the European Recovery Program (ERP) and investment loans provided by the Bank for Reconstruction and Development. These were flanked in turn by liquidity assistance provided by the Treuhand until former East German firms were privatized. By virtue of unification, former GDR firms also became eligible for the same export promotion assistance enjoyed by West German firms as well as EC-sponsored economic support programs. The spring of 1990 saw a series of compromises within the EC according to which the EC supported the integration of the GDR into the community; subsequent negotiations produced an agreement regulating the amount of EC assistance for which the GDR would qualify.[37]

In addition, the second state treaty of September 1990 transformed the five states of the former GDR into a regional-aid zone with a total of 45 billion DM earmarked through 1993 for regional-aid measures. Investments in the GDR can be subsidized up to 33 percent if they meet certain criteria. Up to 90 percent of infrastructure investments by local communities will be covered as well, with an additional 10 billion DM set aside for housing assistance. Bonn also moved to take additional steps to ensure that potential investors received needed guarantees concerning property disputes to facilitate the raising of capital and investment. Such measures are crucial in terms of creating new jobs—jobs that will be needed in light of the fact that economists estimate that up to 40 percent of East German companies could go bankrupt in the first year, that 2.5 to 3 million East Germans may be unemployed at some stage of the transition to a market economy, and that one of every two former East Germans may eventually have to change jobs.[38] Unemployment and dislocation problems could have enormous political repercussions if they are not handled carefully and with some degree of compassion.[39]

Bonn's policy of shock therapy was, of course, not without its risks or costs; as economic and monetary union unleashed considerable short-term disruptions, it quickly became evident that many had underestimated the difficulties inherent in disentangling the administrative structures in the GDR and in ensuring the inflow of capital needed to turn around Eastern Germany's economy. East German industrial input, for example, fell some 12 percent during the first seven months of 1990, and some 42 percent compared with the year before. Overall industrial production for 1990 is expected to fall approximately 20 percent, and sharp decreases in industrial and agricultural production could translate into a drop in GNP for 1990 for the former GDR of 10 to 15 percent.[40]

Initial growth projections for the German economy as a result of unification were quite robust. In the spring of 1990, for example, the German Institute of Economic Research estimated that economic and monetary union would add 1 percent to German GNP in 1991 and another 1.5 percent by 1993.[41] Similarly, the West German Deutsche Bank predicted a growth rate for the territory of the FRG through the end of the decade of 3 percent per annum; coupled with a projected per-annum growth rate for the territory of the GDR of some 7.5 percent, this would amount to an estimated growth of some 4 percent for a unified Germany through the end of the decade.

By the fall of 1990, many of the initially optimistic projections for economic growth in the former GDR and for Germany as a whole had become less so. In a report issued in late October 1990, for example, Germany's five leading economic research institutes predicted that economic growth for Germany in 1991 would approach 2.5 percent, compared with some 4 percent for West Germany in 1990.[42] Although the government as well as a number of leading West German banks immediately rejected such projections as too low, rising oil prices resulting from the Gulf crisis, together with other risks to the world economy stemming from an American recession, could dampen economic growth.[43]

Unemployment is also expected to worsen considerably before it gets better. Following the start of monetary union in July, unemployment in July and August rose to some 360,000, and an additional 1.44 million East Germans became so-called short-time employees. Many of the latter would in fact be unemployed were it not for an assistance program that allows firms to keep such workers on the payroll, with the government absorbing the preponderance of the costs. Many of these firms, however, may go bankrupt as soon as liquidity assistance expires in the course of 1991, as is currently scheduled. Although no one knows exactly how much hidden unemployment exists in Eastern Germany, some estimates have placed the figure as high as 15 percent of the work force. Large-scale layoffs are expected in the electronics sector, light industry, and consumer industries. Unemployment is expected to reach 700,000 to 800,000 by the end of 1990 and to peak in the first half of 1991 with a figure that could go as high as 1.4 million jobless and 1.8 million short-time workers.

Many economists nonetheless suggest that the collapse of the economy of the former GDR will bottom out by early 1991 and that strong signs of economic recovery will become evident by the middle of the year. The combination of strong private consumption resulting from pent-up demand, financial aid from the West, and investment in areas such as construction, machinery, and equipment could facilitate a turnaround in the economy in the former GDR sometime in mid-1991.

It is important to remember, however, that such challenges remain those of a transition. Should Germany succeed in overcoming its short-term problems, it can tap into considerable growth potential. The mid- and long-term prospects for the GDR are impressive, for the GDR has advantages that no other Eastern European country has. Unlike Poland or Hungary, for example, it does not have to start out with a large hard-currency debt; nor does it have to introduce monetary and fiscal stabilization programs to create a convertible currency. Similarly, the former GDR was from the outset fully integrated into Western capital markets. Although the East German infrastructure needs are enormous, it is difficult to imagine spending more than a fraction of this per annum, the result being the likely prospect of a sustained program of public sector priming the economy for many years.

Although West German industry has thus far been slow to invest in the former GDR, many of the obstacles hindering investment are being removed as the German government implements additional incentives and guarantees. A poll of West German industrial leaders conducted in late September 1990 revealed that although a mere 3 percent of West German firms polled had already started production in Eastern Germany, one-quarter of all firms planned to invest.[44] The best guarantee for East German economic recovery continues to lie in the West German government's political commitment. Indeed, whatever problems may arise in the short term, Bonn has already invested so much prestige and capital in the GDR that it can hardly afford to let this experiment fail. Furthermore, Bonn knows that the quicker and stronger the East German "takeoff" is, the lower its longer-term costs will be for the West German budget and taxpayer. Similarly, if firms in the GDR are to be given a chance to stay in business in the new and highly competitive environment of a unified Germany, it is essential that a decentralized wage-bargaining approach be adopted, particularly during the transitional phase of adaptation and adjustment. Hence the Organization for Economic Cooperation and Development (OECD) has singled out wage development in the GDR as the key to ensuring strong economic growth in the future.

Although the question of who bears the costs of unity could become a divisive one in West German politics, OECD estimates place the costs of German unity for the FRG at 1.5 to 2.0 percent of the GNP, a burden that the West German economy can easily accommodate. By the end of the 1990s, the gap between Eastern and Western Germany could thus be reduced to a scale equivalent to that which currently separates the more affluent southern states of the former FRG from the poorer states in the north.[45] Germany's ability to achieve this goal will, of course, pivot on the policy decisions that it makes in the short and medium term. Ironically, it is the most draconian scenario—one entailing the rapid elimination of the many layers of bloated East German bureaucracy, the quick shedding of inefficient enterprises burdened by overemployment, and the concentration of new financial means into investment in the most modern industries as opposed to the propping up of inefficient industries—that would guarantee the most rapid economic growth. Yet such a goal must be carefully balanced against an array of additional policy objectives, such as smooth adjustment, minimizing refugees, protecting Germany's currency, and reassuring both East and West of Germany's ability to handle such complex and difficult problems.

How quickly and effectively Germany manages to meet the challenges inherent in economic unification could have major ramifications for the rest of Europe and beyond. Among some of the less developed countries of the EC, above all Portugal and Spain, concerns have been raised that German investment will be redirected toward the East in general and toward the GDR in particular.[46] Moreover, in Western Europe concern remains that German preoccupation with the reconstruction of the GDR will come at the expense of the EC and the future of European integration. The Bonn government has repeatedly sought to counter this impression by insisting that unification can and must be used as a catalyst to spur European unity and by pushing for an acceleration of steps toward monetary and political union (issues that will be discussed at greater length later in this chapter).

The manner in which Germany handles the challenges of economic unification will nonetheless affect its neighbors in a number of ways. First, Germany's influence in Europe will be bolstered by the removal of economic barriers within the EC by the end of 1992. Yet 1992 will also force painful changes within Germany, as it will open or break up a variety of arrangements that have previously protected uncompetitive sectors of the German economy. According to the Kiel Institute of World Economy, only about one-half of the West German economy is currently free of state regulations and subsidies, and West German state subsidies have risen steadily throughout the 1980s to total 120 million DM annually. The GDR, in addition, was completely in the hands of the state. Should the political costs of a quick transition prove high, Germany might be tempted to continue to subsidize uncompetitive sectors of industry in the former GDR against its own longer-term economic interests.

A rapid and successful transition in the eastern part of Germany is also needed to ensure that Bonn does not lose political momentum in its efforts to forge greater European economic and monetary union. A standard claim among German politicians is that German unification will accelerate the process of European union as well, and one of the first and most crucial cases testing this thesis will be the decision concerning the pace and nature of monetary union. On all of these issues, Germany's voice will be crucial. The DM, after all, is the world's second largest reserve currency, second only to the U.S. dollar. It is both the core of the Euopean monetary system and the keystone of European financial developments. Indeed, both the nature of the European Central Bank and the policies it advances may well be modeled on the German Bundesbank. These developments are critical to an understanding of future German leadership in Europe.

Germany's handling of economic reconstruction in the GDR will also have major implications for its neighbors further east. In Eastern Europe, concerns have been voiced that German investment in the GDR will leave little capital for the rest of that region of Europe. At the same time, Eastern Europe has clearly pinned its hopes on Germany to support its desire for closer contact with the EC. Similarly, a growing German economy offers the best guarantee of export-driven growth for the countries of the region. In the words of the Polish Finance Minister Leszek Balcerowicz,

> What happens in Germany is not only important for the Germans but for other countries as well, above all Poland. On the one hand there are certain dangers for the Polish economy but there are also opportunities. . . . We fear, for example, that new trade barriers will be erected on the Oder-Neisse border [by the EC]. We want to participate in the investment boom in the GDR. In order to do this we must have a chance to export our skills, for example in the construction industry. It is a question of whether a Germany fixated on itself exploits its interests without paying attention to the old and new structures emerging around it or whether Germany continues to be a leading advocate of trade liberalization.[47]

German politicians have repeatedly emphasized the special role that countries such as Hungary and Poland played in the collapse of communism and the unification process. As a result, they contend that Germany has a special moral and political responsibility to assist such countries in their reform efforts. At the same time, little doubt remains that Germany sees this area as one of tremendous opportunity. In the words of West German Economics Minister Haussmann:

> The market of the former CMEA countries is the largest market potential in the world. In the short term, growth rates will be limited because of currency problems and transition costs. But we shouldn't forget that the GDR is by far the largest trading partner of the USSR. . . . This means that a unified Germany will automatically become the largest trading partner of the USSR. In terms of absolute growth rates there is not a single region in the world, apart from the developing countries, that has such a pent-up demand for consumer and investment goods. What is needed in the 1990s is to complement the market reforms in these countries with flanking measures—I don't mean credits but economic know-how, management training, etc.—so that the countries of Eastern Europe can use our assistance to put themselves in a situation where they can participate in the international division of labor.[48]

Finally, the manner in which the Germans handle the economic aspects of unification will affect the United States in two important ways—the first resulting from shifts in international money tied to unification. The economic consequences of rebuilding the GDR in the early 1990s, and of rebuilding Eastern

Europe later in the decade, may well constitute the third great financial shock the world economy has sustained since the end of the Vietnam War. The first such shock was OPEC's decision to quadruple oil prices in 1973–1974; the second was the Reagan administration's economic program of the early 1980s, which turned the United States into the world's largest borrower while Japan and Germany emerged as significant leaders. Each set into motion upheavals in global capital flows, currency values, and trade patterns that dominated the world's economy for nearly a decade.

The cost of rebuilding the GDR and other Eastern Bloc economies could well lead to a redirection of capital flows akin to those induced by the OPEC oil shocks of the 1970s and by Reaganomics in the 1980s. Indeed, rapidly increasing expenditures for German unification have already pushed the unified German government budget deficit up to 100 billion DM for 1990, or 3.3 percent of the GDP—compared with a deficit of only 21 billion DM, or 0.9 percent of the GDP for 1989. Some estimates suggest that the deficit may rise as high as 125 billion DM in 1991—more than five times the level of 1989. Yet excess German savings and a current account surplus of some $60 billion in 1989 suggest that Germany will in fact be able to finance much of its reconstruction costs without having to become an external borrower as the United States did in the early 1980s. At the same time, Germany's capital needs have already led to pressures for increases in interest rates, the magnitude of which will rest on how Germany finances unification—through raising taxes, increased public borrowing, or some combination of the two.

The consequences of this trend are very sobering for the United States. By 1990, some 12 percent of the roughly $3 trillion U.S. federal debt was held by non-U.S. investors. Although Germany did not play as direct a role in financing America's external deficit as did Japan, nearly $100 billion of U.S. assets were purchased during the late 1980s by British banks attracting funds from Frankfurt.[49] Because the U.S. economy is dependent on foreign capital, such changes in capital flows away from the United States and toward Central Europe suggest that long-term interest rates in the United States are unlikely to decline significantly, the budget deficit reduction plan notwithstanding. This is hardly a recipe for economic relief for a U.S. economy in a recession.

The second crucial area in which unification will affect American economic interests lies in the EC. Germany's growing economic weight, together with the central position it occupies in the EC, means that Germany will play a pivotal role in shaping the outcome of EC positions in European–American negotiations on an array of core issues, such as trade liberalization. At the same time, the EC market is perhaps the most important one for U.S. exporters and investors; the United States and the EC exchanged over $160 billion in trade in 1988, with the

American trade balance improving dramatically in recent years. U.S. corporate investment in EC countries has grown considerably as U.S. firms position themselves to take advantage of EC plans to eliminate internal market barriers by 1992. Similarly, the EC continues to increase its lead as the primary direct investor in the United States.

A number of trends, however, may point the EC toward becoming a more inward-looking community than the proponents of 1992 contend will be the case. Germany's importance to the United States lies in its role as the leading economic and financial power in the EC and in the role it can play in supporting a liberal German economic policy within the EC, within Europe, and globally. This role was explicitly recognized by Helmut Kohl in his commencement speech at Harvard University in the spring of 1990:

> Open borders . . . imply that the Europe of the future must not seal itself off by protectionist measures. Only free world trade generates prosperity. This is in the enlightened self-interest of everyone. And it would be a disservice to the partnership between Europe and America if, in the economic sphere, our relations were marked by unfair competition and short-sighted egoism. Germany can do much to ensure that the EC remains America's strongest partner in efforts to strengthen an open international trading system. More than ever before, German leadership must be engaged to bolster open European markets within an open world economy, underpinned by an efficient and effective international monetary system.[50]

Should Germany succeed in meeting these challenges, it is not difficult to imagine a unified Germany reemerging as the dominant country in a pan-European trading and financial bloc stretching from Portugal to Moscow. In Eastern Europe, the German economic presence is already strong and is likely to become stronger. Between 1985 and 1989, for example, West Germany's share of the industrialized countries' total exports to Eastern Europe rose from 17 to 21 percent—and the FRG is the region's leading supplier in areas such as textiles as well as capital goods. Moreover, in 1989, some 60 percent of Poland's imports from Western Euope came from the FRG; the figures for Czechoslovakia, Bulgaria, Hungary are 57, 52, and 50 percent, respectively. And in 1989, the FRG cornered some 30 percent of the entire Eastern European market, compared with 7 percent for Italy and 6.5 percent for France.[51] Such trends may culminate in Germany's reassumption of the economic primacy it enjoyed in the region before traditional trade and investment patterns were destroyed during the Second World War and in the postwar period. Indeed, leading West German politicians have already sketched out the vision, in the words of Helmut Kohl, of a "pan-European economic space from the Atlantic to the Urals with over 500 million people."[52]

THE NEW FOREIGN POLICY ENVIRONMENT

German unification both coincides with and is a product of far-reaching changes in the environment in which German foreign and security policy has been formulated over the past 40 years. The collapse of communism and the pending withdrawal of Soviet military power to Europe's periphery holds the promise of liberating Bonn from the strategic dilemma of being a front-line state exposed to overwhelming Soviet military power. Such shifts will inevitably reduce the FRG's previously heavy dependency on the West—above all the United States—for its military security in Central Europe. Moreover, growing German power, coupled with the changing political landscape in Central and Eastern Europe as well as in the USSR itself, will present new challenges for future German foreign policy in the East.

The key question for the future is how German foreign policy priorities will be readjusted against the backdrop of this new Central European political mosaic. Three major challenges confront German foreign policy makers, and the answers they provide to these challenges will help determine the future map of Europe.

The first challenge facing Germany rests on the need to decide how German and European security can best be guaranteed in the future. Specifically, how will German leaders provide the Alliance with a sustainable political rationale as well as a cohesive strategic mission at a time when the Soviet threat has diminished and the survivability of the USSR as a state seems increasingly doubtful? Will German leaders simply opt for a continuation of the key Alliance structures that have provided them with security in the past, drawing down force levels in NATO, for example, while retaining the basic structures? Or will they ultimately opt to transform such structures into a more European defense alliance in a much looser cooperative relationship with the United States?

The second challenge facing German leaders lies in the future of European integration. It has practically become second nature for German politicians to insist that German unification will accelerate the unification of Europe as well. The extent to which this proves true, however, remains to be determined, for the construction of European unity is a task that will take years if not decades. At the same time, Germany will play a critical role in resolving a number of key European issues, including the future pace and contours of further monetary and political integration following the implementation of the European Single Act. Should the EC strive to develop a coherent foreign and security policy? And how do such questions tie into changes already taking place or planned for existing structures such as NATO?

The third and final challenge lies in reconciling such issues with the need to assist the new democracies in the East. Should the EC seek to broaden by bringing these countries into the stable structures of Western integration as quickly as feasible, even at the risk of diluting the cohesion of the community? Or, alternative, should the EC, while offering looser associations with Eastern Europe, concentrate on deepening political and economic integration to increase its cohesion and strength, thereby giving the postcommunist countries of Eastern Europe a strong and viable partner with which to cooperate? Such questions are among the key issues that will help define the future political, economic, and military map of Europe. Germany's voice in shaping the answers to these questions will be critical owing both to its central geographical position and to its political and economic weight.

Any attempt to address this question should first note that the far-reaching changes that have taken place in East-Central Europe have not negated the strategic thrust of previous West German foreign and security policy thinking. To the contrary, future historians will undoubtedly debate the causes of the collapse of communism in East-Central Europe for years to come. And although it was Soviet policy—above all the decision not to intervene in Eastern Europe— that facilitated the ultimate collapse of communism in the summer and fall of 1989, it has become clear that the West's strength and cohesion also played a pivotal role in bringing about the recent dramatic changes in Soviet policy. This was true not only because the West did in fact serve as a magnet for the East by discrediting communism and underscoring the fact that there was an alternative to it, but also because the unified Western position on German unification in NATO left the Soviets little option but to acquiesce in this regard. Thus, although German debate is often colored with gratitude toward Soviet policy and Gorbachev's role in the unification process, little doubt remains that the FRG's previous foreign policy course, together with its strong Western ties, added a crucial element to this success story.

If Germany's principal Western connection has not been called into question, however, important debates have emerged over how the three pillars of West German foreign policy—NATO, the EC, and the CSCE process—should be refashioned in accordance with the changing political and security environment. The one lesson to be learned from the course of events of 1989 and 1990 is that the West Germans displayed little inclination to deviate from their Western orientation or to cast aside their Western ties in return for neutrality. At the same time, there already are signs that the Germans will seek to transform these institutions into optimal venues for pursuing Germany's own agenda in a changing world. Each offers a forum through which Germany can deal with its three most important interlocutors—the United States through NATO, France through the EC, and the USSR through the CSCE—and German influence in all three is likely to increase as a result of unification.

Germany's future foreign policy interests and priorities can be seen in the way in which the Germans have already moved to reshape these institutions. The question of Germany's future role in NATO, for example, has been at the core of the emerging debate over German foreign policy. At first glance, there are four compelling reasons a future reunified Germany should seek to remain in the Western Atlantic Alliance. First, barring the complete disintegration of the Soviet state, the USSR will remain the dominant land power on the European continent. Thus, even if Soviet forces are removed from East-Central Europe, the possibility remains that a future Soviet government might seek to use its residual military forces or to reconstitute a force that is capable of pursuing limited strategic objectives vis-à-vis Europe.

Second, the fact that the USSR will remain a nuclear power provides an even stronger incentive for a non-nuclear, reunified Germany to remain within the Alliance as well as to continue to seek an extended nuclear guarantee from its nuclear-armed Western allies.

Third, a close security relationship with the West has always been seen by the Germans as a form of insurance that would safeguard the stability of German democracy. For the founding fathers of the FRG, entry into NATO was motivated by the belief that their country's foreign policy posture would determine both the domestic order and the orientation of the new Germany. Although the days are long gone when NATO and the American presence were seen as a guarantee for West German democracy, a clear recognition remains that Germany's prosperity and freedom have been closely linked to its membership in a Western collective defense alliance.

Finally, the alternatives to Germany's participation in NATO are neither attractive nor cost-free. Although neutrality might at first glance appear attractive to some, it is potentially the most destabilizing scenario—for while Germany would be the most powerful state on the continent, there could be no iron-clad guarantee that it would remain neutral. This would inevitably lead Germany's neighbors to vie for the loyalties of the German state, thereby tilting the balance of power on the continent. Alternatively, a neutral Germany could transform the alliances into anti-German formations designed to guard against the resurgence of German power. Finally, neutrality would not resolve the question of nuclear guarantees and might in the long run tempt a future German state to acquire its own nuclear forces.

This helps explain why there has been little enthusiasm, either in Germany or elsewhere, for Germany to revert to the balancing act it once played between the East and the West. The concept of neutrality has been discredited throughout the postwar period in West Germany, in large part by an influential school of historiography that has argued that the temptations of lying in the center of Europe and of attempting to play a balancing role constituted one of the principal reasons German history took such a disastrous course.[53] Neutrality has also been widely perceived as leading almost inevitably to discrimination against Germany or to attempts to form anti-German coalitions in efforts to contain that country. Whether this stance will change with the passing of generations and as perceptions of threat and neutrality alter is an important question that will be addressed later. Suffice it to say that it would currently take an intellectual revolution to relegitimize neutrality as a foreign policy option among the current German political elite.

Factors such as these helped sustain the FRG through one of the most tumultuous phases in postwar diplomacy without altering its domestic consensus on foreign policy issues. It is, in fact, remarkable how well the consensus on German membership in NATO remained intact throughout the rush toward unity, especially in light of the often acrimonious debates of the early 1980s and in view of the doubts expressed in many Alliance circles over an ostensible waning of German fidelity to NATO. In large part, this endurance resulted from the skill of the current Bonn coalition—above all Chancellor Kohl and Foreign Minister Genscher—first in managing the German domestic debate on security issues in a tumultuous unification year and second in convincing the Soviet Union, through the joint efforts of Washington and Bonn, that acceptance of German membership in NATO was in the Soviets' interests as well. Delivering a speech in late May in which he again rejected the option of German neutrality or any agreement that sought to dilute Germany's Western ties, Chancellor Helmut Kohl pointed to Germany's checkered past and drew the following conclusion:

> The first and most important lesson of history is that peace, stability, and security in Europe were always assured when Germany—the country in the center—could live with its neighbors in secure relations, with regulated compromise, and with mutually beneficial exchange. In contrast, when Germany chose or when criminal nationalists evoked some special German path, or when it was forced into isolation by its former enemies after a lost war, then the result was always conflict, instability, and insecurity for all of Europe. This painful history only permits one conclusion: there cannot be a second Versailles. It is therefore impossible for a unified Germany to even think about neutrality, demilitarization, or nonalignment.[54]

Strong German support for NATO has in fact been a cornerstone of the current coalition since Helmut Kohl came to power at the height of the stormy INF debate in the fall of 1982.[55] The Chancellor has stated repeatedly that NATO can claim credit for having brought about German unity and that it must continue to play an important role in organizing European security in the future. Recalling the basic geopolitical arguments of Konrad Adenauer, Kohl has repeatedly claimed that only the United States can balance the USSR as the traditional dominant land power on the Eurasian continent. In Kohl's words, "A trans-Atlantic security union is of existential significance for Germans and Europe. Only it can create true balance in Europe. A look at the map underlines this!"[56]

At the same time, German leaders have played a crucial behind-the-scenes role in pushing for the changes in NATO that culminated in the London declaration in July. Speaking in late May, Chancellor Kohl stated: "The Alliance will have to rethink its strategy and structure. For our defensive Alliance is not an end in itself but rather a reflection of the political situation. If this changes, then the Alliance must change as well. The Alliance of tomorrow with a unified Germany will therefore be a different one than the Alliance we know today."[57] Bonn's push for far-reaching changes in both nuclear and conventional strategy obviously reflected a desire to address Soviet security concerns during the "2 + 4" negotiations on a unified Germany's security arrangements—but it was also linked to the obvious fact that unification would render conventional NATO military strategy and doctrine anachronistic. An equally important motivation for German leaders, however, lay in the realization that NATO's traditional rationale was rapidly eroding in the face of a diminishing threat and that a new legitimization was needed for the Alliance lest NATO be deemed irrelevant in the public eye.

Finally, the strong support of Kohl and the CDU for NATO is reflected in their firm rejection of institutions such as the CSCE or notions of collective security as alternatives to the Western Alliance. In numerous public statements, the chancellor strongly supported an expanded and institutionalized CSCE process but emphasized at the same time that the CSCE must be seen as a complement to, and not as a substitute for, NATO. Speaking in Budapest in July 1990, German Defense Minister Gerhard Stoltenberg laid down this position in no uncertain terms:

> The issue today, and for the foreseeable future, is not to conjure up a completely new European security system. Rather, it is to create a cooperative collaboration of different but nonetheless complementary security structures. Such an approach offers great advantages, above all with regard to preserving stability. In our opinion such new structures could develop arising primarily from the CSCE process and in parallel to the proven structures of the Western alliance and the European Community.
>
> Let me, nonetheless, make one thing clear in this context: We do not think that pan-European security structures, be they within a CSCE framework, or in some other form, can become the sole pillar of European security in the foreseeable future. Without the political security foundation of the Western alliance with its balance of power function that continues to be important, any overarching security system would be doomed to failure. General collective security systems in which

everybody is allied to everybody in principle and thus has no particularly close ties to anyone have always proven themselves to be unstable in the course of history, for the strong and ruthless will always have the advantage over the weaker states. One has but to think of the League of Nations between the two World Wars.

It would also be a step back in historical terms if we were to give up the Western alliance and the resulting level of voluntary integration in favor of a pan-European collective security system. Instead it is important to see the Atlantic Alliance and the CSCE process as linked in a complementary relationship.[58]

The CSCE nonetheless remains an important policy instrument in the perception of German conservatives. A primary motivation for German support for the CSCE process in the 1970s and 1980s resided in the belief that the CSCE represented not only the best available means of institutionalizing detente in Europe but also an effective vehicle for the transmission of Western ideas—concepts that would promote internal liberalization in the East, isolate the GDR, and eventually facilitate a resolution of the German Question. With unification accomplished, the CSCE process remains important as a venue for consolidating reform in Eastern Europe, as it provides the institutional framework that allows Germany to play an active role in managing change in Eastern Europe in a multilateral guise while also offering a forum through which the new democracies of Eastern Europe can develop their own concepts on future European security. Above all, however, the CSCE process is the forum through which the USSR can be engaged without allowing it to become the dominant power on the continent.

If there is a long-run alternative to the Atlantic Alliance in the minds of West German conservatives, it is European integration—a notion that has always lain at the core of conservative German foreign policy. Prior to the crumbling of the Berlin Wall and the subsequent emergence of the unification issue, for example, Helmut Kohl proudly stated that the greatest foreign policy accomplishment of his chancellorship had been the progress that had been made toward European integration. In the past, however, any discussion over the EC's assumption of a major foreign and security policy role seemed wildly optimistic; the overwhelming Soviet military power confronting Western Europe translated into a strong dependency on a large American military presence, and the progress toward European integration that would breed a new consensus on foreign and security policy issues was lacking. As a result, European unity was deemed significant largely for its ability to amplify Europe's voice in the Alliance and for its bargaining weight vis-à-vis the United States—not for its potential to supplant the American role.

Two factors have altered this equation or have at least demonstrated the potential to do so. The first is the considerable progress that has been reached toward achieving greater political and economic cohesion in the EC and toward the goal of developing a foreign policy profile. The second is the collapse of any immediate Soviet threat and, consequently, the reduced need for military security in Europe. In short, the dramatic reduction in the Soviet threat, coupled with the Single European Act and with progress toward monetary and political union, have changed the terms of this political debate. Such developments, for example, have opened up the long-term possibility that a political union in Europe might ultimately assume primary responsibility for its own security. German conservatives nonetheless remain guarded in their discussion of the EC as a long-term alternative to NATO. Developments in the East remain in flux, the future of integration in the EC is also uncertain, and talk of supplanting the American role or presence could become counterproductive—catalyzing, it is feared, a premature American withdrawal from Europe well before the EC has reached any degree of cohesion on security matters.

Although little doubt persists that German conservatives aspire in the long run to a far more cohesive and autonomous Europe in a restructured transatlantic relationship—one in which the American presence is significantly reduced and perhaps ultimately eliminated—a number of difficult short-term questions remain.[59] First, many Germans have been among the most vocal proponents of the so-called broadening of the EC to include some institutionalized relationship with the new democracies of Eastern Europe; German leaders have repeatedly stated that they have an obligation to assist the new democracies of Eastern Europe by virtue of the latter's role in bringing about the downfall of communism and German unification. Moreover, German leaders are keenly aware that should these countries fail to adapt to Western democracy and market economies, the ramifications for Germany could be tremendous. Although political and economic instability in Eastern Europe will impact all of Western Europe, Germany will be affected most acutely owing to its proximity. Images of mass migration or some type of new *Voelkerwanderung* sparked by political and economic collapse in the East are understandably visions of horror for German leaders, who know that such problems would immediately spill over into their own society.[60]

A rapid broadening of the EC would, however, run the risk of slowing or even halting attempts to deepen political and economic integration within the EC. Bonn must therefore strike a balance between simultaneously deepening and broadening the European alliance. Skepticism voiced in the wake of unification over Bonn's commitment to integration has led Chancellor Kohl to try to reconcile conflicting goals and to convince key allies, such as France, that Germany's commitment to European unity has not faltered. The chancellor has repeatedly stated publicly, for example, that his country's commitment to stabilizing the East will not affect its political commitment to the deepening of West European integration and that any broadening will not be allowed to threaten the cohesion of the EC. According to Kohl,

> Only a European community strengthened internally can be a driving force in the pan-European process. Europe does not end at the Oder and Neisse rivers. The people in Poland, Czechoslovakia, Hungary and the other countries of Central and Southeast Europe require a European perspective. The same applies to the EFTA countries, with which we enjoy close co-operation. We wish to create with them a European economic area, which could become a model for the whole of Europe to grow together.
>
> It must not, however, simply be a matter of admitting as many countries as possible into the EC. Such a strong-arm act would not leave the Community unscathed. The fatal result would be that the EC would be reduced to the level of an elevated free trade zone: precisely what was not—and is not—our aim in unifying Europe. Hence those who want the *political* unification of Europe must restrict accession to the Community, for the foreseeable future, to those countries which are prepared and able to create the European Union without reservations.[61]

Such broad political commitments notwithstanding, the real difficulty ahead will lie in forging the details of future integration and in reconciling the competing interests of deepening integration in the EC and keeping that community open so as to deal with the aspirations of other countries in Europe—and ultimately transforming it into a pan-European institution. The chancellor's national security advisor, Horst Teltschik, has noted that the growing interest of non-EC members in Western Europe, combined with increasing interest in Eastern Europe resulting from the revolutions of 1989 and the EC's past successes in assisting countries such as Spain and Portugal in their transition from an authoritarian system to democracy, makes it inevitable that the EC become a pan-European institution. No consensus has been reached in the EC, however, with respect to how this should be accomplished, with which groups of countries, at what cost, and with what kinds of tradeoffs. In Telschik's words,

> The European Community must become the point of departure for pan-European solutions. Yet, what answers will the EC or its individual members provide for these questions? In general terms we say that we must create a pan-European peace order with structures that transcend the alliance. But how is it to be shaped? President Mitterrand speaks of a "European confederation." The core would consist of the EC which would then form a confederation with the other European states. But the EC would remain a privileged community in this concept. The members of EFTA and the countries of Central Europe are placed in the same category and are kept excluded from the Community. Whether the USSR and the

USA are included in such a confederation is also unclear. Nonetheless this French concept leaves open many options.

It is true that all twelve EC members agree that the Community should not be broadened until the end of 1992. The completion of the internal market, economic and monetary union, and political union all have priority. The realization of these goals within the agreed upon timeframe will be difficult enough. Yet, we must ask ourselves if the EC can really deny the EFTA countries entry if these countries ask for it and meet the criteria? Austria has already applied for membership. Switzerland, Norway, Sweden, and Finland have already introduced policies that are bringing them into line with the criteria for membership. Leading political and economic circles in three countries are already questioning whether it is in their interests to be pursuing policies corresponding to those of the EC while remaining outside the Community.

The situation in the countries of Central and Southeastern Europe is different. It would be premature to put them in the same category as the EFTA countries. They should become associated with the EC as closely as possible. In the long term, however, full membership for them should also be allowed. It is precisely a united Germany that must be the spokesman for these neighbors to the East. The result could be a Europe from the Atlantic to the Bug, a Europe of free democratic countries with the same economic system and currency, a Europe of fatherlands that culminates in a united Europe with Federal structures.[62]

It would certainly be a mistake to assume that Foreign Minister Genscher does not share the geopolitical concerns and arguments that underlie the thinking of the chancellor and the CDU/CSU—or the desire to ensure a future American role in European security affairs. Moreover, Genscher clearly shares Chancellor Kohl's commitment to the priority of European integration and to Germany's special responsibility to assist the new democracies of Eastern Europe. At the same time, the overall tenor of Genscher's foreign policy approach has always differed from that of Kohl and the CDU in several subtle yet important respects.

In many ways, Genscher has come to incorporate many of the shifts that have taken place in mainstream German foreign policy thinking in the past two decades, which helps explain why he continues to be the most popular politician in Germany. Essentially, the staunch Atlanticist of the mid-1970s became the symbol of detente and arms control as a special German national necessity and responsibility in the early 1980s. While Genscher has continued to advocate a close transatlantic relationship and an American presence in Europe, his increasing support of Franco-German cooperation has reflected a conviction that the existing degree of West European dependence on the United States is politically unhealthy for both sides and that Europe must take steps to assume greater control over its own destiny.

Genscher has always perceived East-West relations in highly flexible and dynamic terms. He has become a master at maximizing his and his country's latitude in order to best exploit changing East-West trends to his advantage. Over the past years, for example, the FRG's foreign minister has repeatedly emphasized that the bipolar order is coming to an end and that changes in East-West affairs offer Europe a unique opportunity to assert itself in a more independent fashion. Genscher's early enthusiasm for Gorbachev must therefore be seen in the context of the veteran foreign minister who was the first senior Western statesman to recognize the potential for change in Gorbachev's reform and to publicly call upon the West to take Gorbachev at his word. This reflected Genscher's belief that Gorbachev's reforms, if successful, could represent a unique historical opportunity to initiate a transition to a new cooperative system of European security based on a reformed USSR, on restructured alliances, and on a looser and more balanced U.S.–European relationship.

It is important to stress that these ideas and concepts were essentially articulated by Genscher and the German Foreign Office well before the revolutions of 1989 took place in East-Central Europe. The events of the last year only confirmed Genscher's conviction that changes in the USSR and Central Europe, along with German unification, offer Europe a unique opportunity to build a new, stable, and cooperative order. In his public statements, Genscher has repeatedly underlined the special responsibility that the Germans bear to become the driving force behind European unity so as to ensure that Europe does not revert to an age of disruptive nationalisms—and such that unification remains a positive force in European politics.

Genscher has repeatedly referred to six central building blocks for a new European security order. In the spring of 1990, Genscher publicly sketched out a new vision of Europe based on these elements. They include the following:

The deepening of integration in the EC leading to political union;

The restructuring of transatlantic relations between a unified Europe and the United States;

The stabilization of the reform process in the countries of East-Central Europe and the USSR;

The expansion and institutionalization of the CSCE process and its transformation from a series of conferences to an "Institution of European Security and Stability"; and

The adaptation of a security policy to the new situation in Europe and the creation of cooperative security through disarmament and the transformation of the alliances into political instruments.[63]

Genscher also suggested a loose game plan that would include the sequence in which these new building blocks for a European peace order should be assembled—one in which German unification would be followed by the deepening of integration in the EC. At the same time, the EC would be impelled to include the reforming countries of Eastern Europe, leading to the creation of a common European space from the Atlantic to the Urals as a common democratic, legal, economic, ecological, and security entity. In the meantime, the CSCE process would have to be expanded and institutionalized if it was to be transformed into the type of durable collective security organization that could function as a safety net in times of crisis. During this transition, the Atlantic Alliance would function as a form of reinsurance against setbacks in new processes of pan-European integration and as a caucus for keeping the United States actively involved in European security affairs. Nonetheless, growing European integration would ultimately create the preconditions for a restructuring of American –European relations into a much looser and balanced alliance.

Genscher is clearly loath to speak of any broad blueprint, and hence one will seek in vain for any detailed German "grand design" for Europe in his many speeches and policy statements. As the foreign minister himself remarked in an interview in the fall of 1990, the secret of success of "Genscherism" lay in remaining cognizant of one's long-term goals and in maintaining the flexibility to pursue these goals and to seek to push events in the proper direction.[64]

The abovementioned principles can therefore serve as a general guide both to Genscher's longer-term goals and to his thinking toward the future evolution of institutions such as NATO, the EC, and the CSCE. Genscher has clearly opposed efforts to turn NATO into an institution for power projection outside Europe, preferring instead to turn it into a more cooperative structure—one that can work together with an expanded and institutionalized CSCE. While willing to accept future Bundeswehr participation in UN-sponsored missions the foreign minister has, however, firmly rejected any talk of German force projection or attempts to develop a new rationale for NATO as a forum for coordinating broader Western strategic and military thinking on a more global scale. Such fears appear rooted in Genscher's own views on how a country with Germany's past should define its role in the European and international arena, on his opinions with respect to the tools that should or should not be included in Germany's diplomatic arsenal, and on his fears that any steps in this direction would be exploited politically by the German Right.

It is nonetheless clear that Genscher sees Germany as having a crucial role to play in the building of a new Europe. In his words, "This historical task means the beautiful fulfillment of the Germans' European mission."[65] The strengthening of the EC and the CSCE are, in Genscher's thinking, the means to achieve this goal. The foreign minister repeatedly refers to the EC as the "anchor of stability" in Europe and as an institution that must increasingly assume responsibility for integrating the new democracies of Eastern Europe as well. At the same time, Genscher has always insisted that the reconstruction of Eastern Europe must be a joint task for the West as a whole.[66] Similarly, he has singled out the CSCE as the key "pillar" for a new European security system that includes the USSR.

One of the great ironies of the revolutions of 1989 in East and Central Europe and of the German unification process is how these events took the SPD by surprise and allowed it to capture little of the credit for the changes now taking place in Central Europe—despite the fact that the SPD initiated Bonn's policy of *Ostpolitik* from the late 1960s to 1970s while playing a crucial role in building Bonn's close ties with the East. The fact that the SPD, which has prided itself for its ability to conceptualize change in East-West affairs in Europe, was unable to capitalize on these dramatic changes was linked in part to the fact that it happened to be in the political opposition when the political avalanche swept through the region. It was also, however, tied to what appears to have been some basic conceptual errors in Social Democratic thinking on how change in the East was likely to occur and what its outcome would be.

Social Democratic *Ostpolitik* from the outset was predicated on three assumptions. The first was that change in Eastern Europe could occur only in small steps—and only if implemented from above via reform-minded communist leaderships. As a result, Social Democratic policy concentrated on building ties with reform communists in the region, including the SED regime in the GDR. The second assumption underlying Social Democratic thinking was that Bonn's traditional stance in favor of unification had become an impediment to change in the East. While the SPD was by no means resigned to the status quo in the GDR, it increasingly came to reject unification, instead embracing calls for some looser form of confederation between the two German states. Third, the SPD believed that changes in security policy and arms control could and should be actively used as instruments of political engineering to create the type of foreign policy environment that would serve as a handmaiden for internal change. Throughout the early 1980s, the party passed one resolution after another calling for internal reform in Eastern Europe coupled with an eventual transition to a collective security system that transcended both alliances.

The thrust of Social Democratic thinking was to pursue policies that would render the inter-German border more porous and eventually irrelevant and, subsequently, to transcend the nation-state by creating new pan-European institutions. As a result, the SPD was politically and psychologically unprepared for the rapid turn of events that swept the GDR and Eastern Europe in the fall of

1989—for change in Eastern Europe came not in small steps but rather as a sudden political earthquake. Moreover, many of the center-left intellectual dissident groups that the SPD had cultivated over the years were swept aside in the tumultuous events that took place in these countries. Finally, the SPD's ambivalence on the goal of unification came back to haunt it amid the surge of unification sentiment in the GDR. Sensing the growing danger facing his party on this issue, Willy Brandt initiated a *volte-face* on the German Question in late 1989 by embracing the unification of the two states. A number of prominent SPD intellectuals, however, continued to oppose unification for many months to come.[67]

Finally, the rapid disintegration of communist rule, coupled with growing calls from the new democratic elites in several Eastern European countries for withdrawal from the Warsaw Pact, undercut many of the old Social Democratic arguments about both alliances serving as instruments of stability to manage a transition to a new security system. Faced with the *de facto* disintegration of the Warsaw Pact and the almost insurmountable obstacles impeding the creation of a new pan-European security system in the short term, Social Democrats had little choice but to embrace the position that a unified Germany should remain in NATO pending the creation of a new pan-European security system while insisting that the Alliance undertake a major review of its nuclear and conventional strategies.[68] Even on this issue, however, the SPD soon found itself overtaken by events for in the early summer of 1990, the ruling coalition in Bonn itself took the lead in pushing for far-reaching changes in Alliance strategy in its run-up to the NATO London summit.

Social Democratic thinking on future European security is in a state of considerable flux as old concepts are being reexamined, salvaged, and adapted to a new order. Although foreign and security policy has traditionally been an area that the SPD has considered to be its strength, for the moment it appears to have lost its edge even in this respect to Foreign Minister Genscher and perhaps even to the CDU, which has sought to reassert its voice in the German foreign policy debate. At the same time, several key components of the SPD's foreign policy thinking are likely to remain constant. For example, a strong undercurrent of opinion in the SPD still clings to the position of dissolving both blocs and sees the Western Alliance's role solely in terms of managing a transition to a new security system. More than any other German party, it is the SPD that advocates that NATO is ill-prepared to master the tasks of common security in Europe and that a quick transition to a new pan-European security system is needed. In the words of one SPD parliamentarian,

> It may be true that NATO and the Warsaw Pact are useful, indeed irreplaceable tools for managing the transition from the East-West conflict to a new European

security structure. But their task has become one of bankruptcy managers, the significance of which no one denies, but whose tenure is of limited duration. A new collective European security structure must and will develop around Germany and, equally important, it will coincide with a pan-European economic space which extends far beyond an eastern expansion of the European Community.

Germany does not want to become neutral or to become a wanderer between two worlds [in the East and in the West]. It wants to assume its traditional broker role with the East while remaining part of a Western community of values and a member of the European Community and without succumbing to the temptation of some third way. That this has become possible is the result of the policy of Mikhail Gorbachev. By abolishing the blocs and by bringing Western modernity into the Soviet Union, [the USSR] will find in Germany a natural and historical partner without Germany being compelled to give up its Western ties or to choose between East and West. It is for this reason that the German people, more than anyone else, have an interest in the success of the current policy in the Soviet Union.[69]

The SPD also remains strongly committed to European integration. In his keynote address at the SPD's unity congress in late September 1990, Oskar LaFontaine laid out his concept of a "two-speed Europe," that is, a Europe in which the dual process of deepening West European integration could be wedded with an expansion of cooperation with Eastern Europe.[70] In the words of Karsten Voigt,

> The goal of the SPD is a United States of Europe. The European Community should be developed into a United States of Europe. East European democracies should be allowed to join. For economic reasons a full membership of the East European states is only realistic in the longer-term. Until then we should strive for other forms of cooperation such as a closer association. The European Community should also seek to establish a closer harmonization of the foreign and security policy of its members. Responsibility for defense matters, however, should not be given to the EC in the immediate future as this would only prevent the inclusion of the neutrals and the former Warsaw Pact countries.[71]

The SPD's vision is clearly one of a unified European Left growing in its strength as a result of the overcoming of the division of Europe. Just as the SPD is striving for a new post-Cold War constituency in German domestic politics, so does it hope to knit together a new Europe-wide coalition based on democratic socialism and centered on the themes of social justice, ecology, and disarmament. As many Social Democrats themselves point out, the key question for the future is whether processes such as European integration in the western half of Europe and the dramatic changes that have taken place in Eastern Europe will work to the benefit of the European Left or conservative forces. One of the many ironies that

Social Democrats themselves are forced to concede is that the realization of a longstanding goal—that of overcoming the division of Europe—caught the SPD off guard and may unleash new forces of nationalism that will ultimately play into the hands of their opponents. In the words of Peter Glotz, member of parliament and editor of the SPD's theoretical monthly *Die neue Gesellschaft,*

> It would be foolish for the European Left to assume that the explosive developments in East-Central Europe will automatically play into our hands. Reform communists in the 1960s in Czechoslovakia still believed, for example, in convergence; the future of Europe was socialism with a human face which would be pushed by reform communists in the East and social democrats in the West. Not much has remained of this theory. A considerable portion of the new political groups in Eastern Europe are inclined to reject any type of socialism, even democratic; in the United States and in Western Europe conservatives are convinced that the "victory of the West" has proven not only Marxism-Leninism to be a failure but democratic socialism as well. We cannot ignore the danger that the democratization of Eastern Europe, which most surely represents progress as it will lead to greater self-determination and progress in the sense of the European enlightenment, may paradoxically lead to a strengthening of the European Right. The European Left will have to fight to prevent this.[72]

In surveying the German foreign policy debate one year after the collapse of the Berlin Wall, one is struck by three facts. The first is how well Germany's foreign policy consensus has held up despite the tumultuous events of the unification process. Many observers' fears of a possible backlash against the Western Alliance or the emergence of an agonizing debate over potential trade-offs between European integration and German unity have thus far failed to materialize. In part this has reflected the political skill of the German elite in ensuring that the question was never posed in the negotiations over German unity, together with efforts on the part of key Western powers to convince the Soviets not to exploit such potential weaknesses. Yet it also reflects the fruits of 40 years of successful policies along with a keen awareness among West Germans that Western integration not only brought them prosperity and security but ultimately contributed to the failure of communism in the East. The example of a successful West exerted a powerful magnet effect on the peoples of Eastern Europe. Throughout the unification process, public opinion polls showed that while West Germans strongly supported unity, they were unwilling to sacrifice their Western ties in order to achieve it. Finally, the fact that unification took place on West German terms in foreign as well as domestic policy was an initial vote of confidence by the Germans in the East for the FRG's postwar orientation and institutions.

The second trend concerns German foreign policy goals. Unification has altered not only the German domestic landscape but the terrain of the foreign policy debate as well. Specifically, Germany is no longer a divided front-line state whose room to maneuver was narrowly restricted by the military presence of the USSR and by the need for an American counterweight; instead, it is now an ascendant power in a more integrated Europe in which the influence of the two superpowers is rapidly receding. And while the longer-term consequences of Germany's changing domestic landscape on foreign policy remain to be determined, the radical changes that have taken place in Germany's foreign and security policy environment have already altered the parameters of the foreign policy debate.

In short, German foreign policy goals are no longer centered on the need to shelter and defend an exposed and vulnerable medium-sized actor in Europe. Rather, they revolve around the desire to use growing German weight and influence to play a proactive role in constructing a new Europe. Although the goal of a new pan-Europe has always been at the heart of the foreign policy programs of all major German parties, it previously represented only an abstract, long-term aspiration. Now, however, the current political agenda includes the possibility of creating a new Europe—one that stretches from Portugal to Poland and in which Germany plays a principal leadership role on the basis of its political and economic weight and its crucial strategic position in Europe's center. This new Europe will continue to be closely linked to the United States but will also be increasingly capable of acting as an autonomous actor on the world stage. Germany's response to this new context has not been to reject or to abandon the institutions on which the FRG has relied in the past; rather, it has sought to recast such institutions in a fashion that will allow it to use them toward these goals.

The third trend concerns the initial signs of Germany's maturation as a major European power. The German elite's handling of the unification process has lent a major boost to German self-confidence. Similarly, the collapse of Soviet power in the region and the likely diminution of American influence and presence in the region have created a power vacuum in the heart of Europe—a vacuum that Germany is predestined to fill. Moreover, 40 years after the war, Germans increasingly feel that they have earned their democratic credentials and are now increasingly willing to set aside previous self-imposed restrictions on their room to maneuver. Having accomplished unification and having regained their national self-confidence, Germans are proving increasingly willing to assume a more active role in Europe and beyond.

At the same time, ambivalence and internal divisions remain within the German political class over just how far and how fast Germany should move toward embracing a more active role and what types of policy instruments it should emphasize. Among some German leaders, centered in the CDU and the Bundeswehr leadership, there is a growing sense that a unified Germany is simply too big and powerful to indulge in geopolitical abstinence and that German resources and leadership are badly needed to fill the vacuum left by the collapse of Soviet power in Eastern Europe and by the pending reduction in American influence in Western Europe. Proponents of this school clearly believe that a healthy sense of geopolitics is now needed to maintain elite and public support for NATO, a continuing Alliance with the United States, and elite and public support for defense spending and the armed forces.

The recent crisis in the Persian Gulf has provided a major impetus for a debate that was already under way over Germany's future geopolitical role and responsibility in Europe and the world. Although Chancellor Kohl was unable to push through his initial plan for a more overt German role in supporting the United States in the Persian Gulf, the debate marked a watershed of sorts in German domestic politics as a new consensus emerged that the time had come to revise Bonn's constitution to allow the use of German armed forces in future crises outside the central front.[73]

This issue nonetheless has the potential to become a divisive one in German domestic politics. Issues of power, the use of military force, and geopolitics remain sensitive themes that have been taboo through much of the postwar period in light of Germany's past and the excesses perpetrated under National Socialism. Many Germans remain reluctant to adopt such a role for fear that it will still evoke resentment among their neighbors or residual mistrust in their own ability to manage such a role. At the same time, Germany is rapidly being thrust into a major leadership role as a result of the changes in and around it.

FUTURE GERMAN ARMED FORCES
AND DEFENSE PLANNING

The need to restructure future German armed forces has been a key element that has prompted Germany to rethink its future foreign and security policy goals and options. In part this was because specific issues, above all the future size of the Bundeswehr, rapidly became central to discussions over the regulation of the security arrangements for a future unified Germany. At an early stage in the process, German politicians sought to ensure that the future size and composition of German armed forces would not become a politically volatile issue and that such decisions would not be left to the whims of international negotiations.

Such thinking was also linked, however, to the realization among German politicians that the rapidly diminishing Soviet threat in the East—and the concomitantly dramatic fall in threat perceptions among the German public—automatically raised key questions about the very purpose and future role of German armed forces. Questions concerning the future purpose, size, composition, and missions of German forces could not be considered in a narrow military or national context, however; the need to think about the reorganization and eventual integration of former East German forces into an all-German structure inevitably posed broader questions concerning the restructuring of the Bundeswehr as a future all-German force.

More important, the need to think about the defense of a future unified Germany immediately touched on core aspects of NATO strategy and the missions of German armed forces. As a result, discussions over the future of German armed forces increasingly became a mirror in which one could read many of the emerging trends in thinking over the future of German foreign policy, its place and role in the Alliance, and the broader purposes to which the instruments of German foreign policy should be applied both in and outside Europe.

The need to confront such core issues early on has propelled Bonn into the forefront of intra-alliance debates over the future. This was also a debate in which the CDU and the ministry of defense have tried to take the lead in an attempt to capitalize on the success of Chancellor Kohl and to regain the initiative on foreign and security policy thinking that in years past has often been dominated by Foreign Minister Genscher or by the Social Democratic opposition. Addressing a forum of high-ranking German military officers in March 1990, CDU General Secretary Volker Ruehe matched his praise for the role of the German armed forces in contributing to unification with a clear call for far-reaching changes in German and allied strategy:

> We would never have reached this threshold of a new age if the alliance and the Bundeswehr had not provided for our external security. Our soldiers can be proud of their contribution to forty years of peace and freedom, forty years of prosperity, and forty years of European rapprochement and German–American friendship.
>
> Looking back is not enough, however. We need phantasy and a sense of responsibility in order to develop a convincing program for our future security. Our people consist neither of peaceniks nor militarists. We have a society that is well-informed and capable of formulating its own views. Only some 13–15 percent of our population sees a threat from the East; but more than half of them see peace threatened in and from the Third World. Whoever takes a sober view of the situation will reach two conclusions. First, the Soviet Union will remain a world power in the area of nuclear weapons and sea power, and it will also be the strongest land power on the European continent. Second, Europe will not be able to become an island of peace in the conflict-ridden world, the dissipation of the East–West conflict and positive arms control results notwithstanding. . . .

It is important to define the tasks, scope, and structures of future German armed forces now. Only in this way can we integrate Germany in a future European security landscape and only in this way can we influence the future of arms control according to our political and strategic needs. We must move very quickly to replace the concept of integrated forward defense close to the border for we cannot organize NATO's defense in the middle of Germany. Nuclear deterrence will also have to be given a new content.[74]

Ruehe outlined five criteria to justify a future all-German military of some 400,000. First, according to Ruehe, Germany had to be represented in a future European security structure in a manner commensurate with its political and economic weight and geopolitical position. Second, Germany had to take into account the historically based fears of its neighbors; therefore, German armed forces should not be larger than those of either France or Poland. Third, Germany would continue to need allies and partners, as it was not self-sufficient in economic terms but rather highly dependent on open world markets and on unimpeded access to raw materials and energy sources. Fourth, Germany had to have sufficient forces to contribute to Alliance defense needs and to assume the national defense responsibilities of territorial forces, above all in the GDR. Finally, German forces had to remain affordable and structured in a fashion that corresponded with the arms control process in Vienna.

In the spring of 1990, Bonn played an important behind-the-scenes role in pushing for a reformulation of official NATO strategy—a role that culminated both in the London Declaration issued at the NATO summit in early July 1990 and in the concept of "flexible reconstitution." This strategic review encompassed the three components of NATO's military strategy MC 14/3—direct defense, deliberate escalation, and general nuclear exchange. Speaking before senior military officers in mid-June, Defense Minister Gerhard Stoltenberg publicly sketched out the broad outlines of Bonn's thinking on future Alliance political and military strategy. Given the achievement of German unity and the withdrawal of Soviet forces from East-Central Europe, the minister claimed that the Alliance had fulfilled its goals as defined in NATO's Harmel Report from 1967 and now needed to redefine its future mission and goals in accordance with changed strategic realities.

Stoltenberg also called for significant revisions in Alliance strategy. Specifically, he called for a shift away from a strategy based on deterrence, flexible response, and deliberate escalation toward a new posture predicated on the concept of stabilization and reassurance. Although Bonn officials had been urging a shift away from deterrence as the core of NATO nuclear strategy, arguing that deterrence implied a confrontational stance that was no longer appropriate in a new cooperative European security regime, Stoltenberg's remarks were the first high-level public pronouncements suggesting that NATO officially adopt a stance making nuclear forces the weapons of last resort. More specifically, German officials now urged that all short-range systems be removed from German soil and advocated future reliance on nuclear weapons consisting solely of air-based forces and some mix of dual-capability aircraft, stand-off missiles, or American sea-launched cruise missiles. According to Stoltenberg,

> With regard to nuclear strategic options, there will be a shift in the relative weights of options and capabilities. If in the past we placed an emphasis on a ladder of deterrent options, in the future the emphasis will be less on deterrence of a specific enemy and more on serving as a form of insurance and as a factor of stability in a mutually agreed upon system of mutual security in Europe. In this context NATO will be able to change its concept of deterrence to one of reinsurance. Following the successful conclusion of the current Vienna negotiations, we will be able to start follow-on negotiations on SNF on this basis aimed at achieving a mutual minimum of nuclear weapons in Europe according to the principle of sufficiency.[75]

Noting the progress toward unification and the impending withdrawal of Soviet troops from the GDR and the rest of Eastern Europe, the minister noted that such changes also meant that NATO's conventional strategies based on the traditional NATO "layer cake" approach also needed to be revised:

> Under these conditions NATO should replace the operational concept of forward defense with a concept of defense at the borders which will allow us to react accordingly to all possible forms of future military risk. It is crucial in this context that our defense concept is oriented toward a broad spectrum of potential military risks. . . .
>
> It is already clear that the previous form of a linear North-South oriented operational concept of conventional defense must be replaced. A flexible form of concentrating mobile forces wherever they will be needed in crisis will be implemented in its place. The ability for a step-by-step reconstitution of our defense potential will increase considerably in importance in connection with significantly reduced armed forces and a lengthier warning time in Europe.

German defense officials have nonetheless emphasized several elements of continuity in German defense planning. The abandonment of flexible response and the shift toward a greater emphasis on stand-off weapons, they insist, imply neither the denuclearization of Germany nor a return to massive retaliation as the basis for NATO's nuclear strategy, for such changes will take place in a Europe marked by conventional parity and in which the risk of military conflict with the USSR has seriously diminished. Similarly, the abandonment of NATO's traditional layer-cake approach and forward defense in the traditional sense does not mean that Germany will not be defended forward in the former GDR or at its new eastern border.[76] Bonn's willingness to consider transitional solutions in which the former GDR receives a special status notwithstanding, German defense officials have always made it clear that a unified Germany will be defended as a single entity, above all as the decision has been made to eventually move the capital to Berlin. Finally, although allied forces in a unified Germany will be reduced, and despite the fact that foreign troops will not be deployed in the former GDR, Bonn defense officials have made it clear that their goal is to retain integrated forces in an echelon defense in which German forces assume primary responsibility for the initial phase of defense and the residual allied troops function as an operational reserve.[77]

The basic contours of such changes in Alliance policy were officially embraced several weeks later at the London Summit in July 1990, and were reflected in the London Declaration as official Alliance policy.[78] Shortly thereafter, these changes also set the backdrop for negotiating the final aspects of an agreement on the security status of a unified Germany between Kohl and Gorbachev. The main components include agreements that,

A unified Germany can choose to be a member of any alliance on the basis of the principles of the CSCE process.

A bilateral treaty between a unified Germany and the USSR regulates the withdrawal of Soviet troops from the territory of the GDR by 1994. Western troops will remain stationed in Berlin on a bilateral basis pending the removal of all Soviet troops from German soil.

Articles 5 and 6 of the NATO treaty take effect for the territory of the former GDR upon unification. At the same time, no NATO troops will be deployed on the territory of the former GDR pending the removal of Soviet troops.

German troops not integrated into the NATO command (i.e., territorial troops) will be deployed in the former GDR upon unification during the transition. Following the departure of Soviet troops, Bundeswehr troops can be deployed throughout a unified Germany, albeit without nuclear delivery systems in the former GDR. Foreign troops will not be deployed in the former GDR.

The future peacetime size of the Bundeswehr will be set at 370,000 at the time of the successful conclusion of the negotiations on conventional forces in Europe (CFE).[79]

A unified Germany renounces nuclear, biological, and chemical weapons and remains a signatory of the NPT (non-proliferation treaty).

With the final agreement negotiated between Kohl and Gorbachev, the overall parameters for future German force planning have been clearly set both for a transition period in which Soviet troops are withdrawing from the GDR and for the time period thereafter. At the same time, future German views on strategy and force planning will be closely tied to future threat assessments and assumptions. The conclusion of an agreement on the security provisions for a unified Germany, the Soviet-German agreement of September 1990, a CFE agreement, the withdrawal of Soviet troops from Eastern Europe, the democratization of Eastern Europe, and progress toward democracy in the USSR have radically altered past threat assessments.

As a result, German force planners have been forced to contemplate a wider variety of potential threats and to differentiate between their likelihood and their danger—both for the purposes of planning and public debate. The most dangerous threat to German and Central European security in the immediate future continues to lie in residual Soviet strategic capabilities, both nuclear and conventional. At the same time, the likelihood of this residual Soviet threat is debatable and will become increasingly so if centrifugal tendencies in the USSR persist. It will therefore be increasingly difficult to justify NATO solely in terms of the threat to the central front, especially at a time when the West is itself engaged in efforts to assist reform in the Soviet Union. Western political and military strategy would be seen as out of sync and working at cross purposes. This is especially true in the case of Germany, where the interest in bringing the USSR into Europe is pronounced and where the threat in past decades has been largely defined in ideological terms.

German defense planning must therefore incorporate two additional categories of risk, both rooted in regional conflict: conflict resulting from intra-ethnic or other strife both in Eastern Europe and on NATO's southern flank. These could include complex scenarios in which the conflict is neither initiated nor controllable by either NATO or the Soviet Union. Such scenarios, although they do not represent the classic East–West confrontation for which NATO has prepared in the past, may be far more realistic in the future than any direct conflict with the USSR. It is therefore in both German and allied interests that the debate over future Alliance strategy and force planning be broadened to include a wider set of contingencies lying outside the central front. A redefinition of NATO's strategy in the direction of the concept of "defense at the borders," outlined in the London Declaration of July 1990, could, for example, mean that German forces would plan and prepare to take part in a multinational NATO framework in defense operations not only in Central Europe but also on the northern and southern flanks of the NATO region.

Such changes will also place new demands and requirements on the structure and type of German armed forces for the future. The importance of operational mobility will grow, reinforcing a trend already evident as a result of the arms control process and the thinnning out of the potential battlefield. Germany will need rapid reaction forces for initial defensive operations close to the borders— forces that must be flexible and available with little or no mobilization to give the German leadership maximum political flexibility in a potential crisis. They, in turn, will have to be complemented by additional screening forces as well as by air-mobile and mechanized operational reserves for counterconcentration. In the words of one high-ranking Ministry of Defense planner,

> In preparing a defense concept for the future, one must cover residual and new risks. Defense at the borders calls for a high degree of flexibility, an optimum of warning time, and an appropriate mixture of quick reaction and mobilizable forces.
>
> The fact that Germany has to orient her defense concept toward several categories of risk means a major shift in strategic thinking away from planning at the intra-German border toward possible contributions in other regions. The defense concept for the future must serve both the most likely and the most dangerous case. In terms of the future orientation of the German forces, this means that part of the German forces must be available for initial operations on the basis of a quick reaction capability with almost no need for mobilization, thereby maximizing flexibility in response to a potential crisis. . . .
>
> Other elements, designed to ensure the buildup of the armed forces, may be cadred to differing degrees to be available for follow-on operations. In addition, the forces for initial and follow-on operations must be capable of acting as national or multinational maneuver forces for the defense in centers of main effort, as screening forces, and as air mobile or mechanized operational reserves for counter concentration.[80]

Leading German officials have already pointed to five characteristics that will be important for German armed forces in the future: 1) growing significance for command, control, communications, and intelligence (C3I); 2) a need for maximum operational flexibility and mobility; 3) a strong defense system based on extended barriers operations and firepower; 4) a responsive air defense; and 5) the growing importance of reinforcement capabilities and the protection of sea lines of communication.[81]

All of these factors point in the direction of a broadening of the political, economic, and military context in which future German security needs are debated. The need for such a debate lies not only in the desire to preserve the vitality of the alliance and German public support for NATO membership. Additional pressures for a broader understanding of German security and for new forms of German participation will also arise in conjunction with economic and budgetary trends and questions of future procurement policy. Arms control and falling defense budgets will lead to smaller quantities of major weapons systems and greater pressure to coordinate arms development and production—a process that has already been given impetus by the 1992 European Single Act.[82] The Europeanization of the arms industry will increase pressures in Germany to loosen the country's traditional restrictive arms export regulations. This may, however, lead to growing tension in view of political pressures to be more restrictive on proliferation issues—above all in light of criticism of German export practices in the wake of the Persian Gulf crisis.

European integration will also have a pivotal effect on the old and often contentious issues of burden sharing and role specialization. In the past, such progress has been blocked or has remained limited because countries were reluctant, in the final analysis, to cede national sovereignty and to become dependent on another country's defense capabilities. While progress in this realm is likely to remain limited until European unification has been furthered, political union and the emergence of a more coherent European strategic identity do hold out the possibility of cutting the Gordian knot that has blocked progress in the past. In conjunction with trends in procurement, this could provide a major impetus toward a new understanding of burden sharing and role specialization for Germany both in Europe and in the transatlantic relationship.

Such issues will set the backdrop for a new and crucial debate not only over the role of German armed forces but also over the overall strategy and purpose of future German foreign and security policy. German officials have emphasized their desire to see the Alliance produce a document that would provide the political guidance to enable Bonn to manage its public debate while simultaneously allowing for German and other allied force planning for at least the immediate future. Such a document would transcend both the political goals of the Alliance as outlined in the Harmel Report of 1967 and the various components of NATO strategy as outlined in MC 14/3.

While Central Europe will remain a focal point of German attention for the foreseeable future, the German debate must be both broadened and widened. This will inevitably raise touchy political questions, including a possible rethinking of constitutional provisions limiting the use of German armed forces outside the country. Similarly, the issue of German export controls and Germany's behavior in this regard will increasingly be seen as a test case of Germany's new global responsibilities. Yet it is in this broader context that German elite and public support for the Alliance can best be consolidated. And it is in this context that a new Germany will be able to shed many of its past self-imposed restrictions on security thinking and assume a new and more mature role in a European global, as opposed to national, context.

NEW CHALLENGES AND NEW RISKS

The challenge inherent in German foreign policy today lies in the necessity to balance the need to maintain and deepen integration in Western Europe, the need to rapidly support the political and economic reconstruction of the East, and the need both to consolidate a new transatlantic relationship as a necessary geopolitical backup or insurance during the transition to a new European order and to transform that relationship into a new and ultimately more balanced global partnership.

German leaders know that a race is currently being waged between integration in Western Europe and disintegration in Eastern Europe; hence, they also know that they must forge a set of policies that facilitate the deepening of the EC while simultaneously keeping it open as a safety net to deal with the problems produced by the collapse of communism in Eastern Europe and the potential disintegration of the USSR. It is also understood, however, that a second race is taking place as well—a race to create a new transatlantic bargain with the United States that would ensure active American participation in European affairs before the erosion of NATO's structure assumes critical proportions.

Four dangers face German policy makers in their attempt to meet these challenges. The first lies in the residual uncertainties of German domestic politics in the wake of unification. The successful political and economic integration of the former GDR will be a time-consuming process that will absorb Germany's attention and resources, especially at the outset. Moreover, the Germans from the GDR must learn to appreciate the benefits of Western integration and to become Europeanized if they are to ensure that Germany does not experience a resurgence of nationalism at a time when there will be growing pressures for it to cede sovereignty to multilateral Western institutions. The danger lies in the prospect that Germany will become preoccupied with its own internal woes at a time when the country is confronted with a full foreign policy agenda. Although the current German preoccupation with domestic issues may be understandable, it also harbors risks, as it could lead to a deceleration of precisely those processes that the Germans have underlined as key to building a new Europe.

The second danger is that Germany will not effect its political and economic integration into the EC as quickly or comprehensively as it hopes. Clearly numerous factors and issues are at stake in the debate over the future of the EC, but a key issue among them is the future of Franco–German relations—a factor that both Paris and Bonn have long viewed as the motor behind EC integration. Yet despite Bonn's rhetoric that German unification has furthered European unification as well, the reality of Franco–German relations during the past year has served as a sober reminder both of the complex problems inherent in integration and of the residual uncertainties concerning Germany's weight and of the reluctance on the part of Germany's neighbors to tie themselves closely to a country whose future politics and policies are still somewhat uncertain.

The details of Franco–German relations over the past year are beyond the scope of this study. Suffice it to say that they offer an object lesson in the manner in which political elites can maintain a dialogue on practically a daily basis while still misunderstanding each other's motives and intent. Specifically, initial irritations in Paris over a lack of consultation were compounded by German irritation over French overtures toward Moscow in the fall of 1989 and, more recently, by France's decision to withdraw French troops from Germany despite Chancellor Kohl's publicly expressed desire that such troops remain. The key question for the future is whether such differences can now be buried such that agreement can be reached on the proper course and timetable for European political integration and for the establishment of a future foreign and security policy role for the EC.

From Germany's perspective, France is hesitating precisely at a time when a new impetus from Franco–German relations is sorely needed. France, according to Horst Teltschik," . . . must now decide to what degree it is willing to work in an alliance with Germany in the Community."[83] In Paris, however, lingering doubts and suspicions remain over Germany's commitment to integration in the wake of unification. Moreover, while the French political elite clearly remains committed to European unification, realizing that it offers the best guarantee that Germany will remain integrated in the West, unification has created the potential for the EC to fall increasingly under German influence—a prospect that makes it all the more difficult for France to contemplate abandoning further elements of its national sovereignty. Finally, the fear of a German preoccupation with the East and German–Soviet rapprochement persists in some influential French circles.[84]

The third danger facing German policy makers is the possibility that they might be overwhelmed by the problems of political and economic reconstruction further east. Several powerful factors combine to leave Germany little alternative but to become actively involved in reform and change in Eastern Europe. First, Bonn has always felt a special moral responsibility toward Eastern Europe in light of Germany's historic role in the region; this motivation was at the core of Bonn's *Ostpolitik* in the early 1970s. Moreover, the key role that events in Poland and Hungary played in the eventual collapse of the GDR has strengthened Germany's sense of gratitude as well as its willingness to bolster the reform processes in these countries.[85] Second, no Western country is more attuned to the consequences of the failure of reform efforts in the East than Germany. German leaders are profoundly concerned about the possibility that political and economic turmoil in the East might spill over into Germany in the form either of a new flood of refugees or of renewed nationalism—both factors that could have a direct bearing on Germany's own domestic fabric. Ultimately, Germany cannot afford not to become involved in the East, for its own domestic stability and security requirements are intimately intertwined with the fate of reform and democracy in this region.

Germany's engagement in the region is also being driven by indigenous demand. Although it would be premature to conclude that anti-German feeling resulting from the Second World War has faded entirely, significant changes have occurred as a result of Bonn's own efforts toward rapprochement and generational change. Indeed, many of the newly democratic regimes of the former Warsaw Pact look toward Bonn as their primary Western spokesman and see Germany as their gateway to the West. Moreover, much of Eastern Europe looks toward Germany, a prosperous and democratic country with an extensive welfare state, as an example of how to rebuild a devastated country as well as a former dictatorship. As many of these countries turn West for political, economic, and educational assistance, they are increasingly focusing their demands on Germany as they discover that the Germans first and foremost have the political will and the resources to help them.

German political leaders repeatedly insist that they lack the resources to play this role themselves, especially in light of the enormous short-term economic and financial burdens placed on them as a result of unification. Moreover, for a political elite whose formative experiences have been gathered working through Western multilateral institutions, the notion of Germany assuming primary responsibility for managing change in Eastern Europe on its own is still an alien one. For this reason, Germany will continue to advocate a joint Western policy approach toward addressing the problems of this region.

Germany's dilemma lies in the possibility that problems in the East could emerge well before Western institutions such as the EC or the CSCE are capable of dealing with the political, economic, and security problems in the region. A Germany faced with growing instability on its Eastern flank and finding its calls for joint Western assistance for the region rebuffed could become increasingly tempted to adopt a go-it-alone approach in the region and to develop its own bilateral working arrangements with individual countries, including the USSR.

A related danger lies in the problems inherent in trying to manage a modus operandi with a disintegrating USSR. All of the dangers mentioned above with regard to Eastern Europe loom larger if one looks beyond the immediate horizon to contemplate scenarios involving the disintegration and possible breakup of the USSR. Should the USSR continue to disintegrate, the West—specifically the EC and Germany—will inevitably act as a pole or magnet that will exert a powerful pull westward—above all for the western republics of the Soviet state. Although conventional wisdom once suggested that German atrocities in the Second World War had left a strong anti-German sentiment in their wake in the western sections of the USSR, there are indications that the cultural and political predisposition of the newly emerging elites in the western republics of the USSR may be far less hostile toward Germany than is commonly assumed. Whether the Western magnet will be an increasingly cohesive EC that has opened itself to the East or simply Germany, however, will depend on the time frame in which such events unfold, on how successful the EC has been in broadening toward the East, and on the policies key Western countries might pursue toward such newly autonomous or independent entities.

Although the various scenarios for the future breakup of the USSR and the consequences thereof are seemingly endless, such a development would place an inordinate strain on German attention, resources, and diplomacy—for it would lead inevitably to the creation of a power vacuum in the East that would result in turn in a critical restructuring of political and economic influence in the region. This would place enormous pressure on the West, above all Germany, to find some new modus operandi with the newly emerging independent or autonomous elites of the region. The West and Germany would also be compelled to reach some sort of mutual understanding with the USSR in order to try to manage this process of chaotic change.

The prospect of a zone of politically and economically unstable and weak states starting on Germany's eastern border is a potential nightmare for any German policy maker—especially were that zone to extend eastward to include the western fringes of a disintegrating USSR. Despite strong historical, political, and economic interests in the region, the current German political elite has little interest in assuming the primary or sole responsibility for managing the enormous problems and challenges left in the wake of the collapse of communist rule in Europe. At the same time, the power vacuum that is emerging in the area will inevitably exert a strong pull on Germany toward the East—especially if the elites of this region call for German political, capital, and commercial resources, and rewewed cultural and educational ties. This has little to do with some mythical *Drang nach Osten* but rather would result from a *Zwang nach Osten*—or the imperative to become more involved in the East to prevent instability on the eastern flank from spilling over into Germany itself.

This helps explain the clear tone of concern that one can detect among some German policy makers as they contemplate both the unwillingness of many of their Western European neighbors in the EC to quickly broaden the community and the potential for instability on their eastern flank. The risk is that the inability or unwillingness of the West to develop a multilateral and coordinated approach to the region might result both in a political backlash and in growing social and economic instability in Eastern Europe, the consequences of which would directly affect the domestic fabric of Germany through such venues as increased migration from the East or a rise in national sentiment.

Such factors will also have a critical impact on Germany's attitudes toward its Western commitments. A Germany that is unsuccessful in harnessing Western institutions such as the EC or the CSCE to address mounting political and economic turmoil on its eastern flank, and one that feels increasingly compelled to act on its own in the region, could quickly find itself faced with the type of agonizing reappraisal of its relations with its Western neighbors that it has thus far sought to avoid. The pressures on Bonn to act in a unilateral or bilateral fashion, and in a manner contrary to its clear preference and own best interests, will grow considerably.

Although Germans are currently loath to draw a direct link between Western support for its policies toward the East and future commitments toward the EC or NATO, there is an implicit connection between the two. A Germany that finds little support or enthusiasm among its Western partners for dealing with issues in the East that directly affect vital German interests could be compelled to rethink its relative priorities. Such a sequence of events could also lead Germany to question the effectiveness of its past multilateral approach and to dilute its commitment and contribution to NATO, the EC, or both.

Such scenarios quickly bring us to the fourth danger facing German policy makers—namely, a premature attenuation of the transatlantic bond resulting from changing trends in German public opinion merging with American neoisolationism to produce a premature American withdrawal from European security affairs. The latter would place an enormous burden on the EC to assume a major security policy role precisely at a time when it is confronted with a delicate balancing act between deepening and broadening its scope. Although many German policy makers do want the EC to develop a security policy role, they see this as an incremental role that should gradually evolve to complement NATO and perhaps to replace it in the longer term. Any attempt to burden the EC with multiple new roles could lead to the political paralysis of that Alliance.

At first glance, German–American relations would appear to be better than ever. Early and firm American support for German unity has been gratefully acknowledged by German leaders—and not only is the standing of the Bush administration in German public opinion high, but much of the radical chic anti-Americanism of the early 1980s has dissipated. Hence the threat to the American presence in Germany does not lie in some sudden surge in anti-American sentiments or in vocal calls for an immediate troop withdrawal. Rather, it lies in the possibility that the American presence will, in the medium or long term, come to be seen as unnecessary, irrelevant, and a growing irritant.

Public opinion polls have shown that West German support for NATO membership has remained strong and fairly constant throughout the unification process. When asked in the spring of 1990 whether they would prefer a total withdrawal of American troops from Europe or retaining some troops "to maintain stability," the percentage of West Germans who opted for a residual American presence was still some 62 percent. At the same time, the percentage of those who view NATO as essential to their country's security has fallen, reflecting a trend evident throughout Western Europe.[86] Similarly, there is a strong public preference for the EC to assume a greater role in security policy over the longer term.[87]

Such polls point to a strong desire on the part of the German public to remain part of a collective Western defensive alliance as opposed to striving for neutrality. This should not, however, be interpreted as suggesting that little if anything has changed in the German public mindset. There have in fact been significant shifts in German public opinion—above all on the question of the American presence, which is tied to the collapse of Western perceptions of the Soviet threat. The percentage of West Germans concerned about a threat from the East has fallen from some 65 percent in early 1980, following the Soviet invasion of Afghanistan, to a mere 14 percent in the summer of 1989 (see Figure 3-2).

The full magnitude of the shift in German public opinion on such issues can be seen in polling data compiled by the Allensbach Institute in West Germany through the use of so-called trend questions (i.e., questions posed over a lengthy period of time in an attempt to capture longer-term shifts in overall trends in the public mood). If one compares the years 1970 and 1990, one can see a near-reversal in German attitudes on the need for an American troop presence as a guarantee for German security. When asked in the 1970s whether German security could be guaranteed without American forces, one-half of respondents replied that this was not the case. Following the onset of Gorbachev's reform policies in the mid-1980s, however, West Germans were roughly split on the question—and by the spring of 1990, after the revolutions in Eastern Europe of the previous fall, a clear majority no longer believed that American troops were needed (see Table 3-3).

Since the early 1960s, Allensbach has also attempted to determine how Germans would react were they to read in the newspaper that the United States was withdrawing its forces from Europe (i.e., whether they would welcome or regret this news). Through the early 1980s, a solid majority of West Germans replied that they would regret such a step. Following Gorbachev's ascent to power in the mid-1980s, however, West Germans were divided on this issue as well, and by the spring of 1990 some 49 percent replied that they would welcome the announcement of an American troop withdrawal (see Table 3-4). Moreover, a breakdown according to age and party affiliation clearly showed that support for an American troop presence is weakest among the younger

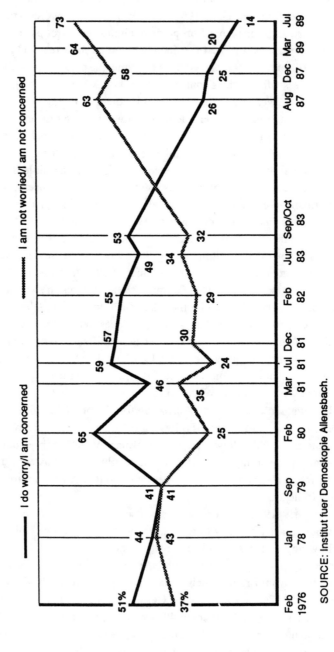

I do worry/I am concerned

I am not worried/I am not concerned

| Feb 1976 | Jan 78 | Sep 79 | Feb 80 | Mar 81 | Jul 81 | Dec 81 | Feb 82 | Jun 83 | Sep/Oct 83 | Aug 87 | Dec 87 | Mar 89 | Jul 89 |

51% 44 41 65 46 59 57 55 49 53 63 58 64 73

37% 43 41 25 35 24 30 29 34 32 26 25 20 14

SOURCE: Institut fuer Demoskopie Allensbach.

Figure 3-2 Question: Are you or are you not concerned about a threat from the East?

	Guaranteed %	No longer guaranteed %	Impossible to say %
May 1970	20	50	30
May/June 1973	24	47	29
June/July 1987	33	35	32
July 1988	37	37	26
December 1988	34	34	32
July 1989	43	32	25
March 1990	54	21	25

SOURCE: Institut fuer Demoskopie Allensbach

Table 3-3

Question: Assuming that there would no longer be any American forces in the Federal Republic, could our military security be guaranteed or no longer guaranteed?

	Welcome %	Regret %	Undecided %
June 1962	12	59	29
April 1969	17	56	27
May 1970	22	51	27
May/June 1973	23	45	32
June 1976	15	54	31
August/September 1979	11	60	29
September/October 1981	17	59	24
October 1982	21	55	24
March/April 1987	34	32	34
September 1987	32	38	30
July 1988	36	34	30
December 1988	33	33	34
July 1989	38	30	32
March 1990	49	22	29

SOURCE: Institut fuer Demoskopie Allensbach

Table 3-4

Question: If tomorrow you were to read in the newspaper that the Americans were withdrawing their forces from Europe, would you welcome or regret this news?

age groups. Similarly, whereas the parties of the Bonn coalition are roughly split on this question, a solid majority emerged on the Left and among the electorate of the SPD and the Greens in favor of an American troop withdrawal (see Table 3-5).

The trends just outlined could be exacerbated by the unification process if the addition of some 17 million former East Germans to the security debate added a new variable to the equation governing overall German attitudes toward the American role in Germany. Yet existing evidence on East German attitudes toward the United States is still fragmentary. Systematic polling started only recently, and attitudes in the GDR are obviously in a state of flux; after having been bombarded with 40 years of propaganda presenting the United States and NATO as the leading cause of tension and as a possible catalyst for war in Europe, East Germans might initially harbor overly critical attitudes toward the United States and American policy.

An initial United States Information Service (USAI) poll conducted in the GDR in June 1990 prior to the final agreements on a future security arrangement for Germany nonetheless found significant differences between West and East German attitudes toward German membership in NATO. A mere 26 percent of East Germans wanted a unified Germany to be in NATO, with 56 percent favoring neutrality; a similar poll conducted the same month in the FRG produced a 58 percent majority favoring NATO membership, with some 31 percent preferring neutrality (see Table 3-6). Similarly, some 70 percent of all East Germans favored the withdrawal of all American military forces from Western Europe (see Table 3-7).[88]

It is hardly surprising that the dramatic events of the last year have produced major shifts in public opinion, above all in a country where security has been defined and discussed in very narrow terms and in which the threat has been defined only in the context of the need to deter a direct and immediate Soviet threat. Moreover, such polls must be seen as a barometer of the public mood, not necessarily as a prescription for future political decisions, because politicians react to as well as shape public opinion.

At the same time, such polls underline the credibility gap that must be closed if German public support for NATO is to remain cohesive. They also demonstrate how rapidly diminishing threat perceptions have led to a significant erosion in public support for an American presence on German soil, thereby making it necessary that the Alliance develop a new rationale and legitimization for an ongoing U.S. troop presence. Arguments that have been used in favor of an American troop presence in years past (i.e., that they have acted as a stabilizing force for German democracy) are likely to be largely irrelevant for a younger generation of Germans. It will be increasingly difficult and perhaps impossible

	July 1989			March 1990		
	Welcome %	Regret %	Undecided %	Welcome %	Regret %	Undecided %
Population as a whole	38	30	32	49	22	29
Men	39	31	30	52	23	25
Women	37	29	34	47	21	32
AGE GROUPS						
16-29 years	48	20	32	56	16	28
30-44 years	40	28	32	50	23	27
45-59 years	30	35	35	49	25	26
60 and over	31	39	30	41	25	34
PARTY AFFILIATION						
CDU/CSU	24	49	27	33	34	33
FDP	29	45	26	38	37	25
SPD	46	18	36	62	13	25
Greens	63	9	28	75	5	20
Republikaner	56	21	23	53	16	31

SOURCE: Institut fuer Demoskopie Allensbach

Table 3-5

Question: If tomorrow you were to read in the newspaper that the Americans are withdrawing their forces from Europe, would you welcome or regret this news?

Question: As you may know, the FRG is currently a member of NATO
(that is, the North Atlantic Treaty Organization of Western
Europe, the United States and Canada). In your opinion,
should a united Germany belong to NATO, or should a
united Germany be a neutral country and not a member of
NATO?

Country:	GDR	FRG
Date:	06/90	06/90
Sample size:	(774)	(504)
United Germany should belong to NATO	26%	58%
United Germany should be neutral, not a member of NATO	56%	31%
Don't know	18%	11%
Total:	100%	100%

Note: The data from the Federal Republic of Germany were obtained
from a June USIA survey conducted by telephone, whereas the
GDR data were obtained by means of a personal interview
survey. Differences in samples may be sufficient to make direct
comparisons of results from face-to-face and telephone polls only
suggestive of the general direction and magnitude of differences in
public opinion in the two Germanys.

SOURCE: USIA

Table 3-6
East and West German attitudes toward NATO

to justify either a strong Bundeswehr or a residual allied troop presence solely in
terms of a residual Soviet threat, above all at a time when Germany is pursuing a
policy of rapprochement and assistance toward the USSR. Not only is it politically inopportune to stress such risks at a time when the German government is
eagerly constructing a new relationship with the Soviet Union, but the presence
of Soviet troops on German soil for the next four years will continue to give
Bonn an interest in not offending Moscow.

Recognition of this problem has led Bonn to take a lead role in advocating a
fundamental change in the policies and structure of the Alliance as well as a

---

East Germans want Soviet troops withdrawn

Question: Some people have advocated the withdrawal of all Soviet
military forces from Eastern Europe. Others say it is
important to keep some Soviet military forces in Europe to
maintain stability. Which view is closer to your own?

Date:	06/90
Sample size:	(774)

Withdraw all Soviet forces	75%
Keep some Soviet forces to maintain stability	19%
Don't know	6%
Total:	100%

East Germans also want American troops withdrawn

Question: Some people have advocated the withdrawal of all
American military forces from Western Europe. Others say
it is important to keep some American military forces in
Europe to maintain stability. Which view is closer to your
own?

Date:	06/90
Sample size:	(774)

Withdraw all American forces	70%
Keep some American forces to maintain stability	22%
Don't know	8%
Total:	100%

SOURCE: USIA

Table 3-7

broader definition of German security interests, including new and expanded roles for German, American, and other NATO troops. Atlanticists in Germany also urge the forging of a new strategic partnership between a unified Germany and the United States—a partnership that would obviously continue to be rooted in geopolitical factors. The bottom line of the German–American relationship remains rooted in a security partnership based on geopolitics—namely the need for the United States to balance the USSR as a continental superpower, above all in the nuclear realm. Without a clearly recognized sense of geopolitical interests, the presence of American troops will be increasingly difficult to justify.

At the same time, geopolitics is not enough. The future of the American presence in Germany will not hinge entirely on perceptions of a residual Soviet threat. Instead, it will be seen in a broader context (one that takes into account the need to develop coordinated strategies in the realm of transatlantic commercial and economic issues as well as a joint policy toward the USSR and Eastern Europe). German officials point to the need to expand on Secretary of State Baker's speech in December 1989, in which he called for a new relationship between the United States and the EC. Not only is such a relationship in American economic interests, but it would also create a broader political and economic base for an American role in Europe as well as an institutionalized mechanism with which to ensure that tensions over trade and commercial issues do not cause undue harm to the transatlantic strategic relationship.

German officials also underscore the need for a joint Western *Ostpolitik* that includes the United States. In theory, German and American interests in the East will continue to run in parallel even in the face of a disintegrating USSR. Both countries will be interested in preserving an American presence and engagement to help fill a potential major power vacuum in Europe, and both will be strongly interested in retaining a good relationship with a rump Soviet state that will presumably continue to control a significant quantity of nuclear weapons. Moreover, both will be interested in preserving as much stability as possible in Eastern Europe and in the western portions of the USSR and will thus be inclined to negotiate agreements with the remaining Soviet or Russian state on these terms. Finally, while it is recognized that Germany has a key and perhaps decisive role to play in the region, no one—including the Germans themselves—wants to see the role of managing orderly change in the region to become exclusively Germany's.

These are the potential elements of a new strategic bargain between Germany and the United States. In the final analysis, major adjustments will be required in the way the United States sees its role in Germany and in Europe. Specifically, American influence in European affairs will be more limited and diffuse. Moreover, Germany will be a more equal, assertive, and independent-minded partner that will want the United States to remain involved, but increasingly on terms defined by the Germans themselves. Future German attitudes toward the United States will hinge on American attitudes in areas deemed essential to German interests. Should German–American differences emerge on how to deal with the USSR, Eastern Europe, CSCE, or trade issues—all areas in which German political and diplomatic energies are likely to flow in the next couple of years—the American role could be marginalized in the Germans' perceptions.

GERMANY'S TRIPLE TRANSITION

The unification of Germany has launched the country on a triple transition. The first such transition resulted from the merging of the two German states, the augmentation of German resources and influence, and the consequences for the existing balance in Europe and beyond. Both the domestic and foreign aspects of unification have been accomplished under conditions that would have been considered wildly optimistic only a few years ago. Yet unification was not the result of diplomatic machinations but rather was a product of self-determination and of a popular, peaceful, democratic, and pro-Western revolt by the East German populace. Moreover, the key components of a final security arrangement for a unified Germany include NATO membership, a continuing American nuclear guarantee, and modest constraints on the Bundeswehr—in short, conditions that so obviously correspond to Western interests that few experts would have dared to sketch out such a result in past scenario writing.

German unification, however, must not be seen in isolation. Fundamentally, it is the result of a basic shift in the balance of forces in Europe whose ramifications extend well beyond Germany or Central Europe and that resulted both from the collapse of communism in East-Central Europe and from the pending withdrawal of massive Soviet military force from Central and Eastern Europe. Its result, however, is a fundamental change in the European security environment—one that will touch on the interests of all European actors. Its impact on Germany has nonetheless been direct and has certainly been more far-reaching than on other Western European or NATO countries. Not only has Germany been unified, but the FRG has been transformed from a divided front-line state exposed to massive Soviet power to one of the strongest actors on the European stage surrounded by friendly, democratic, and weaker countries.

The second transition lies in the internal political transformation that will accompany the unification process. It would certainly be premature to predict how the reintegration of two halves of a nation divided for 40 years by ideology will affect the future political culture and fabric of a unified Germany. Yet there is every reason to assume that the well-tested democratic institutions of the FRG are ideally suited to guarantee a quick transition to democratic rule in the former GDR as well as to lay the basis for successful democratic rule in an all-German framework. Nonetheless, one should not forget that at least a generation elapsed before West German democracy matured to the point at which Germans as well as their neighbors developed full confidence in that system.

While the learning curve in the GDR will be steep, the political education and adaptation of some 16 million Germans with little practical experience in the ways of democracy will inevitably take time. Roughly 20 percent of a future all-German parliament will consist of delegates from the former GDR—delegates whose political and intellectual baggage is quite different from that of their West German counterparts. Many will have to be convinced of the merits of much of what has long become established consensus in West Germany.

This will also be a process that will differ from the West German experience in at least one important way. In the 1950s, a generation of West Germans turned to the West, above all to the United States, for inspiration and ideas for buiding a new democracy. In the 1990s, East Germans will turn to a successful West German model for inspiration rather than seeking inspiration from an American model, whose attraction has faded in light of America's own internal problems. If one believes that the FRG's experience with the United States as a society, as well as with key Western European countries such as France, was critical to the internal evolution of an open, liberal German democracy, then the Europeanization and Atlanticization of the Germans in the GDR will be a key task for Bonn and its Western allies.

Unification also coincides with a crucial generational transition in both former parts of Germany. German unity has been accomplished by a generation of German leaders who knew a single, unified Germany in their youth and who rejoice in seeing a development that many had long assumed they would never witness in their lifetimes. This was also a generation, however, that grew up bearing the heavy burden of the crimes of National Socialism and the holocaust, and for whom nationalism and the cultivation of national pride were thus suspect if not taboo.

This was, in addition, a generation that sought to give Germans a new identity in the context of Europe and the Atlantic Community and for whom America was not only a strategic ally but a conduit for Western and democratic ideas. All these factors combined to make German leaders in many ways the least national in terms of style and substance. At the same time, there was also a correlation on a societal level. Public opinion polls over the years have documented the ongoing ambivalence of postwar West Germans on questions of national identity and national pride, leading Elizabeth Noelle-Neumann of the Allensbach Institute to comment that Germany was a "wounded nation."[89]

The building of a new Germany will be performed by a new generation of Germans that is emerging on the political scene. A generation that is solidly pro-democratic but one that is also far more self-confident. It has been raised without many of the doubts concerning the stability of German democracy that characterized its forefathers and has instead come to know Germany's postwar accomplishments with pride. It is also a generation that is growing weary of having Germany's democratic credentials and commitment to the West repeatedly challenged, and one whose sense of dependence on Bonn's allies, above all the United States, is far less pronounced. It is, moreover, a generation for whom patriotism and national pride are increasingly seen as normal. The weight of German history will undoubtedly continue to cast a shadow, but this shadow will grow shorter with the passage of time.

Unification will reinforce German national pride for several reasons. First, the German elite's handling of the unification process has already given German self-confidence and national pride a tremendous boost. Second, unification offers Germany the opportunity to rid itself of the identity crisis that plagued the FRG throughout the postwar period. The anomaly of the FRG and the GDR as two states of a common nation has been overcome—and with it many of the aspects of the "wounded nation" of the postwar period have been overcome as well. Germany will become more national if for no other reason than that those factors that once made it so difficult for Germans to cultivate a sense of national pride are slowly dissipating.

The result is likely to be a Germany that is democratic, liberal, and capitalist but also one that is more Protestant, more strongly oriented toward the East, and more consciously German. Whether this means that the country or individual parties are going to swing to the Left or the Right is not yet clear, as this will hinge on the ability of the parties to respond to new issues that emerge in German politics. But the comfortable and predictable patterns of postwar West German politics as most Western analysts have come to know them are likely to change in new, interesting, and often unpredictable ways.

Furthermore, a new unified Germany is likely to be increasingly engaged and preoccupied with the East. This has nothing to do with any ostensible *Drang nach Osten* but instead reflects the need to come to terms with potentially serious political and economic ferment that could arise on Germany's eastern flank. No country has a greater interest in the rapid consolidation of stable democratic rule and economic progress in the former communist countries of Central and Eastern Europe than Germany. Should the countries on Germany's eastern border fail in their attempts to move quickly to a new political and economic order, forces could easily be unleashed ranging from mass migration to growing nationalism, which would place a tremendous burden on Germany's social system and patience and could fuel a national backlash.[90] Maintaining political and economic stability on Germany's eastern flank is likely to become Germany's primary security concern.

The third transition concerns German attitudes toward power, the use of power and influence as a tool of diplomacy, and the goals to which newly acquired German influence will be applied. This is, first and foremost, a question of the psychological transformation of a formerly divided, medium-sized power into the dominant political and economic actor on the continent. Throughout much of the postwar period, the FRG assumed a low foreign policy profile. Burdened with the weight of German history, the role of a front-line state, and an identity crisis rooted in partition, the FRG's leaders deliberately chose to maintain a low profile and became masters at pursuing their goals through multilateral institutions, thereby avoiding any direct leadership role or direct responsibility of leadership.

Such factors have also profoundly affected the West German domestic debate about foreign and security policy. For much of the early postwar period, any discussion of separate German "national interests" was taboo. Similarly, geopolitics as a school of thought or as a rationale for strategy was largely discredited in the public eye owing to its misuse under Hitler, and it thus survived only among elite circles of security policy analysts. The result was a style of foreign policy that was well tailored to the FRG's needs as a divided, medium-sized country located at the East-West divide.

There have long been signs that such a role was anachronistic and perceived as such by both Germans and their allies. Twenty years ago, Willy Brandt pointed to the mismatch between German capabilities and its political responsibility when he termed the FRG an economic giant but a political dwarf. And in the early 1980s, Helmut Schmidt pushed his country to assume a greater leadership role in East-West affairs as the question of German dependence on Washington became a major domestic issue throughout the INF debate. As Germany unites against a rapidly changing political landscape, the country will inevitably have to question whether its old agenda and, above all, its old style and instruments of foreign policy are fully adequate to meet the new challenges.

How will Germans accommodate themselves psychologically to their newly acquired power and influence? Will they maintain the mentality of a medium-sized country, or will they again start to think and behave like a great power? In the mid-1980s, at the height of the peace debate centered on INF deployment, West German historian Hans-Peter Schwarz wrote a book entitled *The Tamed Germans* in which he lamented that his countrymen had come full circle from their previous preoccupation with power politics to a total disregard for geopolitical thinking and a tendency to view such thinking as highly immoral.[91] Will such thinking prove to be an enduring part of the postwar German psyche, or will a healthy sense of democratically based geopolitical thinking emerge?

The prospect of Germany coming to terms with itself and the basic question of national identity should be a positive one for all neighbors in both East and West. In the final analysis, it offers the hope of a Germany that is more predictable both as a society and as a foreign policy actor. The prospect of Germany developing a normal and healthy sense of patriotism based on its postwar accomplishments is a development that should be greeted, not feared.

Quo vadis Germany? The course of German political behavior in the last year offers ample testimony to how strong the German commitment remains to preserving the structures that have served the FRG so well in the postwar period. At key junctures in the unification process, Bonn proved itself willing to assume considerable costs to ensure that unity was achieved along the lines of Article 23 of the Basic Law. Similarly, Bonn was willing to make considerable financial concessions to the USSR to ensure that a future Germany would be allowed to retain the foreign policy structures that have served West German interests so well in the postwar period.

If such structures will remain the same, a unified Germany will still differ from either of the two German states as we have come to know them in the postwar period. The Germany that emerges from the unification process will not simply be an enlarged FRG. Such changes will not only be a function of the influence of Germany's eastern part on German political culture; equally important will be the results of generational change and the maturation of Germany as a country that comes to terms with the past and again assumes a dominant role in European affairs.

Similarly, German foreign policy will evolve for the simple reason that the country's strategic and foreign policy environment has been altered—and because the challenges now confronting a unified German state are so radically different from those that the FRG was compelled to deal with for four decades. The key challenge for Germany is to balance the requirements of Western integration with the need to confront the extremely difficult task of the political and economic reconstruction of the East. In the wake of the collapse of communism in Eastern Europe, Germany will be more likely than any other country in the Western alliance to see the promotion of political and economic stability in the East as a foreign policy imperative of the first order.

With regard to foreign policy instruments, Germany's clear preference will be to seek to accomplish its goals through existing multilateral institutions. Germany is likely to continue to see NATO, the EC, and the CSCE as important institutions through which it can pursue its multiple agendas of preserving geopolitical balance, pursuing European unity, and building a new Europe from the Atlantic to the Urals. At the same time, a unified Germany will continue to seek to use its new influence to shape these institutions according to its wishes and preferred approaches.

Perhaps the most important question, however, is whether and when Germany is prepared to reassume the role of a major actor both in Europe and beyond. Are the Germans ready for such a role, and is the rest of Europe and the world ready for it as well? The Germans are only starting to realize that their position in Europe, their resources, and the potential power vacuum that could emerge in Eastern Europe could quickly thrust an enormous responsibility upon them; not surprisingly, many of them are hesitant to play such a role. Yet Europe needs German resources, skill, and leadership if it is to master the challenges it faces.

The United States has been the key country throughout the postwar period that has facilitated the political rehabilitation of the FRG from its status as a defeated country and the maturation of Germany as a responsible European power. This also helps explain the early and decisive support of the current administration for German unity, in contrast to the initial reticence of several other Western allies. This American attitude has in part been the luxury of a superpower that enjoys greater distance. Yet it has also reflected a desire to move toward a more equal and balanced partnership.

This process has certainly had its high and low points as the relationship between the two countries has evolved, as Germany has recovered from the wounds of the Second World War, and as sporadic fits of rebellion against the influence of their erstwhile mentors have sent occasional waves through the German body politic and German–American relations. Similarly, it would be misleading to suggest that Americans have not shared others' concerns regarding certain trends in German politics. Yet the United States has repeatedly nurtured the process of rehabilitation of Germany.

German unification has undoubtedly altered the context of German–American relations, and many in both countries already question the future significance of the German–American relationship. Yet the United States still has a crucial role to play in Germany and in Europe—not as a controller or a mentor but rather as a key partner in Western leadership. It is a senior partner, first and foremost, in its role as interlocutor with the USSR on security issues. It is also in everyone's interests that Germany outgrow its previously narrow security mindset and that it not become preoccupied with itself and the sole Western power heavily engaged in the East. The best guarantee against such a scenario is to ensure that the problems of the East are dealt with jointly by the key countries of Western Europe in a multilateral guise that includes the United States.

Finally, the United States can and should encourage Germany to become involved in broader issues touching on common Western security interests. This does not mean that Germany should resort to the types of aggressive policies on the world stage that spelled disaster so often in the past or that it should pursue an expanded international role on its own. Yet unification must also mark the end of geopolitical and international abstinence.

It is only in this way that the German–American relationship will remain healthy and thrive. A division of labor in which the Germans deal solely with the East and in which the United States concentrates on crises in the Persian Gulf or elsewhere could simply accelerate a process of erosion and marginalization on both sides of the Atlantic. It would be a tremendous irony of history if the United States, after playing such a decisive role in building German democracy, promoting Germany's rehabilitation, and facilitating the achievement of German unity, should now become a marginal force in German and European politics.

NOTES

1. For background on German demographic trends, see the article by Josef Schmid, professor of demography at the University of Bamberg, entitled "Der Druck nimmt zu," in *Rheinischer Merkur*, October 12, 1990.

2. On the integration of refugees from the East, see Klaus Leciejewski, "Zur wirtschaftlichen Eingliederung der Aussiedler," *Aus Politik und Zeitgeschichte*, January 12, 1990.

3. See the interview with Rudolf Kuznetsov, chief of the Visa Department in the USSR Ministry of Internal Affairs, in *Pravda*, September 26, 1990.

4. Bonn's Basic Law foresaw two possibilities based on Articles 23 and 146 respectively. The latter called for a new constitution to be drawn up by a future all-German parliament. It was initially favored, above all on the West German Left, by critics of West German democracy, who saw unification and a chance to modify West German laws or provisions in the constitution. Such sentiments reflected early hopes of the West German Left that they would benefit from unification and could therefore push for constitutional revisions that would reflect an expanded commitment to social and economic quality. It also had support among those in the East German Left who saw Article 146 as an issue of pride and equality and as giving them a chance to have a greater say in determining the "new" German state rather than simply being absorbed on West German terms.

5. As one worker exclaimed to great applause on the streets of Leipzig in mid-December in reponse to calls for an indigenous East German experiment in democratic socialism, "I have worked hard for 40 years, paid my rent on time, am still with my wife, I haven't seen the world, and my city is decaying. I won't allow myself to become a guinea pig again." As quoted in *Frankfurter Allgemeine Zeitung*, December 13, 1989.

6. See *Sueddeutsche Zeitung*, August 29, 1989.

7. Kohl, for example, was widely criticized in West Germany for raising the issue of a divided Germany and unification in his talks in Moscow in July 1983 with Yuri Andropov.

8. For further details, see Ronald D. Asmus, *The Politics of Modernizing Short Range Nuclear Forces in West Germany*, The RAND Corporation, R-3846-AF, 1989.

9. Kohl's desire to stake out his position on German unity was reflected in the fact that Genscher was not even consulted prior to Kohl's unveiling of his ten-point plan for German unity in November 1989. For Genscher's view, see his interview in *Der Spiegel*, October 1, 1990.

10. See Ruehe's interview in *Rheinischer Merkur*, No. 6, February 9, 1990.

11. Ibid.

12. See the article by Elisabeth Noelle-Naumann in *Frankfurter Allgemeine Zeitung*, March 23, 1990.

13. See Ruehe's interview in *Der Spiegel*, No. 25, June 18, 1990.

14. For LaFontaine's views on the future of the SPD, see "Der Sozialismus und die neuen sozialen Bewegungen," *Die neue Gesellschaft*, Sonderheft, January 1990; and Oskar LaFontaine, *Deutsche Wahrheiten: Die nationale und soziale Frage* (Hoffmann and Campe, Hamburg, 1990).

15. See, for example, the interview in which Willy Brandt acknowledges that he and others prematurely expected a renaissance of social democracy in the former communist regimes of East-Central Europe, including the GDR, in *Horizont*, No. 29, 1990, pp. 6–9.

16. See for example, the speech by Wolfgang Thierse, deputy SPD chairman and former chairman of the SPD in the GDR, at the SPD party congress held in Berlin on September 27, 1990 (author's private copy).

17. See *Frankfurter Allgemeine Zeitung*, October 29, 1990. See also the statement by the PDS treasurer Wolfgang Pohl admitting his role in, and his motivations for, the transfer of funds—as broadcast by ADN International Service, 1630 GMT, October 26, 1990.

18. See Guenther Gaus, *Wo Deutschland liegt* (Hoffmann and Campe, Hamburg, 1983).

19. See Heym's remarks to the November 4 rally in East Berlin in *die tageszeitung*, November 9, 1989. As quoted in Daniel Hamilton, "After the Revolution: The New Political Landscape in East Germany," *German Issues*, No. 7 (American Institute for Contemporary German Studies, Washington, DC, 1990).

20. See the interview with Manfred Stolpe in *Der Spiegel*, No. 27, July 2, 1990, pp. 42–43.

21. See Karl-Rudolf Korte, "Die Folgen der Einheit: Zur politischen-kulturellen Lage der Nation," *Aus Politik und Zeitgeschichte*, B27, June 29, 1990, p. 38.

22. Kohl's speech honoring Alfred Dregger in *Bulletin* (published by the Press and Information Office of the German government), No. 92, July 17, 1990.

23. See Hans-Peter Schwarz, "Das Ende der Identitaetsneurose," *Rheinischer Merkur*, September 7, 1990.

24. See Kohl's interview in *Rheinischer Merkur*, September 28, 1990.

25. See Genscher's speech at the United Nations in *Bulletin*, No. 115, September 27, 1990; and in Wuppertal in mid-October in *Bulletin*, No. 122, October 14, 1990.

26. For further details, see the paper by Horst Siebert, president of the Kiel Institute of World Economy, presented at the United States-German Economic Policy Group Meeting in Bad Honnef, June 7–9, 1990.

27. See *Germany: OECD Economic Surveys 1990* (OECD Publication Service, Paris, 1990).

28. See the estimate compiled by the German Institute for Economic Research in 1987 entitled "Vergleichende Darstellung der wirtschaftlichen und sozialen Entwicklung der Bundesrepublik Deutschland und der DDR seit 1970," published in the *Materialen zum*

Bericht zur Lage der Nation im geteilten Deutschland (Bundesministerium fuer innerdeutsche Beziehungen, Bonn, 1987, pp. 241–796).

29. See Siebert, op. cit.; and Deutsche Bank, *Special: East Germany* (Deutsche Bank, Frankfurt, 1990, pp. 7–11).

30. See Pohl's interview in *Die Zeit*, No. 25, June 15, 1990.

31. See Juergen Becker, "Das Ringen um die Wirtschaftsreform in der DDR," *Deutschland Archiv*, May 1990, p. 687.

32. The obsolete level of telecommunications technology in the GDR was directly linked to investment, or rather to the lack thereof. Whereas the West German Bundespost spends nearly 17 billion DM per annum for investment in telecommunications, the GDR postal service under the old SED regime received the modest sum of 600 million East German marks per annum (figures supplied by Deutsche Bank).

33. For an excellent overview of the evolution of German thinking on the economic aspects of unification see W. R. Smyser, "A New Economic Miracle?" *Washington Quarterly*, autumn 1990, pp. 159–176.

34. The fund's total volume will amount to some 115 billion DM; some 20 billion DM will come from budgetary savings of the central government, and the rest will be raised outside normal budgetary channels. The fund will shift a sizable amount of funding for unity outside normal budgetary channels, thereby taking pressure off federal and state finances. It was designed to remove any need to raise taxes during the politically sensitive election year. Interest and principal payments will be born half by the central and half by the state governments. It is modeled after off-budget credit-raising mechanisms used in West Germany after the war to aid economic recovery. It is scheduled to be paid out in the following allotments: 1990, 22 billion DM; 1991, 35 billion DM; 1992, 28 billion DM; 1993, 20 billion DM; and 1994, 10 billion DM.

35. West German Economics Minister Helmut Haussmann openly admitted that Bonn underestimated the administrative obstacles Bonn encountered in implementing many of the changes decided upon. See Haussmann's interview in *Der Spiegel*, No. 27, July 2, 1990. Similarly, West German Finance Minister Theo Waigel conceded that one of Bonn's key problems lay in the fact that their East German counterparts were simply overtaxed by the enormity of the task facing them and unable to react quickly enough to defuse emerging problems. See Waigel's interview in *Die Welt*, August 6, 1990.

36. The working compromise established in the state treaty stated that property will be returned except in cases where such a step would entail significant social hardship, in which case the former owners will be compensated. As for industrial property, the state treaty clearly states that firms will be allowed to buy private property and that "adequate amounts" of property will be made available and that GDR companies will be able to include their land in their balance sheets as property so that they can borrow and attract investors. See the text of the treaty in *Bulletin*, No. 63, May 18, 1990.

37. According to West German press reports, current plans call for the EC to invest some 4 billion DM in the GDR, of which 2 billion DM will be for infrastructure improvement, 1.6 billion for agricultural supports, and some 300 million for the environment. In return, the GDR will contribute some 3 billion DM through customs duties and the VAT. See *Sueddeutsche Zeitung*, August 22, 1990.

38. See Dieter Loesch and Peter Ploetz, *Soziale Marktwirtschaft-jetzt* (HWWA/Institut fuer Wirtschaftsforschung, Hamburg, 1990, p. 42).

39. In June 1990, West German Economics Minister Haussmann stated in public that unemployment will not be allowed to exceed 10 percent in a unified Germany. See *Sueddeutsche Zeitung*, June 10, 1990.

40. Private sources, Deutsche Bank.

41. See "Gesamtwirtschaftliche Auswirkungen der deutschen Waehrungs-, Wirtschafts-, und Sozialunion auf die Bundesrepublik Deutschland," *DIW Wochenbericht*, No. 20, May 17, 1990.

42. *Frankfurter Allgemeine Zeitung*, October 22, 1990.

43. *Financial Times*, October 23, 1990.

44. See *Frankfurter Allgemeine Zeitung*, October 1, 1990.

45. "DDR Wirtschafts-und Waehrungsunion" (Deutsche Bank, Frankfurt, June 1990).

46. The first signs of a "GDR effect" in German trade patterns are already visible. A study completed in the summer of 1990 by the Federal Ministry of Economics in Bonn concluded that there had already been a modest "GDR effect" in the first five months of 1990 as the growth in West German exports to EC countries had slowed along with a considerable jump in exports to the GDR. The study also estimated that German exports to Eastern Europe would grow from 3.5 to 8 to 10 percent as a result of unification *(Sueddeutsche Zeitung*, August 21, 1990).

47. See Balcerowicz's comments in *Die Welt*, June 25, 1990.

48. See Haussmann's interview in *Die Welt*, July 5, 1990.

49. See the analysis by David D. Hale, chief economist of Kemper Financial Services, published in the *Washington Post*, July 1, 1990.

50. See Kohl's speech in *Bulletin*, No. 58, May 28, 1990.

51. See *Bundesbank Monthly Report*, "FRG Exchanges with Planned Economies," July 1989.

52. See Kohl's speech "Opening to the East: Opportunities for All," delivered at the 125th anniversary of the founding of BASF in *Bulletin*, No. 44, April 11, 1990.

53. See, for example, Michael Stuermer, *Das ruhelose Reich* (Severin and Siedler, Berlin, 1983); and Michael Stuermer, *Die Reichsgruendung: Deutscher Nationalstaat und europaeisches Gleichgewicht im Zeitalter Bismarcks* (Deutscher Taschenbuchverlag, Munich, 1984).

54. See Kohl's speech delivered in the final plenary session of the Disarmament Conference of the Interparliamentary Union, published in *Bulletin*, No. 68, May 29, 1990.

55. In his first policy address as chancellor, Kohl termed the Alliance part of the *raison d'etat* of the FRG state, a position he has retained in the face of criticim from the German Left.

56. Ibid.

57. See Kohl's speech "Ein geeignetes Deutschland als Gewinn fuer Stabilitaet und Sicherheit in Europa," *Bulletin*, No. 68, May 29, 1990.

58. See Stoltenberg's speech delivered at the Hungarian Military Academy in Budapest in July 1990 and reprinted in *Bulletin*, No. 92, July 17, 1990.

59. The most forceful advocate of this line of thinking has been Alfred Dregger, who has for decades advocated the vision of a Europe stretching from Poland to Portugal emerging as a third superpower between the United States and the USSR. See Alfred Dregger, *Der Vernunft eine Gasse. Politik fuer Deutschland. Reden und Aufsaetze* (Universitas Verlag, Munich, 1987). See also Dregger's speech at the 36th CDU Party Congress, recorded in *CDU Dokumentation*, No. 19, 1988.

60. "If we don't help our neighbors—in the first instance Czechoslovakia and Poland —get their economic homes in order, then we will experience great refugee migrations into the more prosperous areas of the West. We have to do everything we can to ensure that these people receive a means of subsistence at home. Precisely on the day of German unity I think of our East European neighbors who played such an important part in the toppling of the Wall and the opening of the borders. We always say that we are thankful. But they can't buy anything with such declarations. They want to become members of the European Community. I see a great deal of hesitation on the part of the prosperous EC countries to accept our poorer relatives in the East. In my opinion, the Federal Republic has an obligation to be a broker for the interests of these countries in the EC. One has to invite these countries to join and not to wait for their applications. They have become democratic and market-oriented. They have furthered the cause of freedom and peace in Europe and they therefore belong to the European family that has organized itself in the EC. Germany should take the lead in making an initiative along these lines." See Graf Otto Lambsdorff's interview in *Der Morgen*, October 2, 1990.

61. See Kohl's article in the *Financial Times*, October 29, 1990.

62. See Teltschik's article on Germany's future role in Europe in *Die Welt*, September 22, 1990.

63. See Genscher's speech at the annual meeting of the German Foreign Policy Society, printed in *Europa Archiv*, No. 15, 1990, pp. 473–478.

64. See Genscher's interview in *Der Spiegel*, October 1, 1990.

65. See Genscher's interview in *Sueddeutsche Zeitung*, August 29, 1990.

66. According to Genscher, "Certainly, the economic development in Central and Eastern Europe is not something that we can manage alone, nor do we Germans have this ambition. I hope our Western partners will realize that we all have to make our contribution to creating a single Europe through participation in the economic development of Central and Eastern Europe. We do not want a new division in Europe. I see a great responsibility in this. A year ago it was important to prevent the building of a wall of missiles by stationing short-range nuclear weapons. Now it is necessary to prevent the building of an economic wall." See Genscher's interview in *Sueddeutsche Zeitung*, August 29, 1990.

67. See Brandt's article in *Die Zeit*, No. 47, November 17, 1989. Perhaps the best example of a prominent leftist German intellectual bitterly opposing unification was the writer and SPD member Guenter Grass. See Grass's speech at the SPD party congress in December 1989, reprinted in Guenter Grass, *Deutscher Lastenausgleich: Wider das dumpfe Einheitsgebot* (Luchterhand, Frankfurt, 1990), pp. 7–12.

68. See the SPD position paper issued in late April and published in *Stichworte zur Sicherheitspolitik*, No. 5, May 1990, pp. 24–27.

69. See Gerhard Heimann, "Die Aufloesung der Bloecke und die Europaeisierung Deutschlands," *Europa Archiv*, No. 5, 1990, pp. 168–269. See also Egon Bahr, "Sicherheit durch Annaeherung," *Die Zeit*, June 29, 1990.

70. See LaFontaine's speech at the SPD congress in Berlin on September 28, 1990, and his concept of a "Europa der zwei Geschwindigkeiten" (author's private copy).

71. See Karsten Voigt, "German Unity and a Pan-European Structure for Peace and Security," March 28, 1990 (author's private copy).

72. See Peter Glotz, "Renaissance des Vorkriegsnationalismus? Deutsche Umbrueche —Oder ein sozialdemokratisches Programm fuer Europa," *Die neue Gesellschaft*, No. 1, 1990, pp. 40–41.

73. Differences remain on conditions under which German armed forces can be committed to such actions. The CDU position is that German forces should be allowed to participate in any multilateral Western action. As mentioned above, Genscher has limited his support to UN-sponsored missions as has the SPD.

74. See the opening remarks of Volker Ruehe at the Bundeswehr Forum at the CDU's Konrad Adenauer Haus on March 29, 1990, in *CDU Pressemitteilung*, March 29, 1990.

75. See Stoltenberg's speech delivered at the Kommandeurtagung of the Bundeswehr on June 13, 1990, and reprinted in *Bulletin*, No. 76, June 14, 1990.

76. According to Dieter Wellershoff, "Forward defense is the most natural task of any state. A state will defend itself there where it is attacked, namely at the border. But forward defense had a special historical meaning in the defense strategy of the alliance as the allies pledged themselves to defend at the borders of their partners. *This should not be changed in an integrated alliance. At the same time, the previous concept of arranging forces in a layer cake, i.e., side-by-side in battle areas needs to be altered after unification and the removal of Soviet troops from Central Europe*" (emphasis added). See Wellershoff's article in *Welt am Sonntag*, August 16, 1990.

77. German officials have stated publicly that they expect some 150,000 allied troops to remain in a unified Germany. See Stoltenberg's interview in *Welt am Sonntag*, August 12, 1990.

78. See NATO's London Declaration in the *Guardian Weekly*, July 15, 1990.

79. In March 1990, Volker Ruehe stated that the optimal size of a future German army would be 400,000. The opposition Social Democrats had proposed a reduction to 240,000, and Soviet officials had floated proposals also pinning a future Bundeswehr to some 250,000. The final result negotiated by Kohl was closer to the initial position suggested by the Ministry of Defense in Bonn.

80. See Ulrich Weisser, *Toward a New Security Structure in and for Europe: A German Perspective*, The RAND Corporation, P-7667, August 1990 .

81. See Willy Wimmer, "Sicherheitspolitische Lagebeurteilung in Europa—Bundeswhehrplanung," *Wehrtechnik*, No. 6, 1990, pp. 12– 15 .

82. See Simon Webb, *NATO and 1992: Defense Acquisitions and Free Markets*, The RAND Corporation, R-3758-FF, July 1989.

83. See Teltschik's article in *Die Welt*, September 22, 1990.

84. While his views should not necessarily be taken as representative of the French government or President Mitterrand, the views of Defense Minister Jean-Pierre Chevenement in this regard are noteworthy. In a speech delivered in late May 1990 on the future of French defense policy and France's role in the world, Chevenement underscored two "irreversible" factors as crucial for French and European security. The first was the decline of Soviet power and an increase in German power and the possibility of a new Rapallo: "As we have been able to observe in the past, changes in the balance between these two countries—both of which tend to be expansionist—can lead to an accord for the subsequent period. There is an old connivance between these two peoples which has taken many forms from Catherine II to Bismarck. Our century has witnessed examples of this as well. Everybody remembers Rapallo and the Hitler–Stalin Pact. Let us not forget that it was the FRG that gave the starting signal for detente." The second factor singled out by Chevenement was the future of German public opinion, which he also saw as being influenced by developments in the USSR and likely to result in "some race for influence in Central Europe" between Germany and the USSR. According to Chevenement, "Whatever happens, it is predictable that German public opinion—without going

so far as to wish for a return of Weltpolitik—will probably impose an active foreign policy consistent with that great power's traditions and potential." See Chevenement's speech, published in *Defense Nationale,* July 16, 1990, pp. 9–28.

85. See Genscher's speech thanking former Hungarian Foreign Minister Gyula Horn in *Bulletin,* No. 68, May 29, 1990.

86. See USIA Research Memorandum, "West Europeans Reject Total Withdrawal of American Troops but Fewer Deem NATO and U.S. Military Presence Essential," April 11, 1990.

87. See USIA Research Memorandum, "Support for NATO Unshaken by Collapse of Communism, but West Europeans Prefer EC for Future Security Decisionmaking," July 9, 1990.

88. See USIA Research Memorandum, "East Germans Don't Want a United Germany in NATO," July 9, 1990.

89. See Elisabeth Noelle-Neumann and Renate Koecher, *Die verletzte Nation: Ueber den Versuch der Deutschen ihren Charakter zu aendern* (Deutsche-Verlags Anstalt, Stuttgart, 1987).

90. The plight of thousands of Poles trying to enter Germany to work illegally or simply to engage in black market transactions, together with the subsequent decision of the German authorities to reinstitute visa requirements after growing tensions in the border area, has already led commentators to refer to the Oder-Neisse river on the German-Polish border as the new Rio Grande in Europe.

91. See Hans-Peter Schwarz, *Die gezaehmten Deutschen: Von Machtbesessenheit zur Machtvergessenheit* (Deutsche Verlags-Anstalt, Stuttgart, 1985).

Chapter 4

France

Gregory Flynn

Current and future French policy cannot be understood without understanding the basic assumptions that underpinned de Gaulle's policies. Charles de Gaulle, in turn, cannot be understood without understanding how France perceived the new order it confronted in postwar Europe.

The security framework that emerged in the Cold War was not one that corresponded to French preferences. Nonetheless, France somewhat grudgingly accepted the realities of the Cold War and sought to adjust. The main adjustment was to the emergence of the Soviet Union as the primary threat to French security.[1]

During the late 1940s and early 1950s, the primary challenge for French security policy was to find a way to deal with the Soviet threat while ensuring that Germany could never become a threat again. The dilemmas became acute after the outbreak of the Korean War, when it became clear that West Germany would have to be rearmed in order to strengthen Western defenses. France's solution was to bind the German Federal Republic as tightly to the West as possible within a set of institutions that would contain the growth of West German power. After failing to ratify the treaty creating the European Defense Community in 1954, France accepted West Germany's integration into NATO as a tolerable means of harnessing new German military capabilities. In addition, building on the initial success of the European Coal and Steel Community, the institutions of the European Economic Community (EEC) would help channel German economic energies and provide the republic with a Western vocation. The Franco–German Treaty of 1963, providing for regular bilateral consultations, was to symbolize how inextricable the destinies of the two states had become.

Whereas the Western Alliance provided the basic framework for meeting France's security needs, France was never entirely comfortable with the power relationships that prevailed in the world of the Cold War. The reduction of France's status in the international system to that of a medium power and the constraints of strict solidarity with allies produced a sharp ambivalence toward the arrangements that provided French security. The result was the search for ways to express an independent identity. The most concrete manifestation was the development of France's own nuclear arsenal. While continuing to resist the Soviet challenge through NATO, the *force de frappe* provided the symbol for the profile France sought, as well as the additional increments of security that dependence on others could never yield.

When de Gaulle returned to power in 1958, the basic dilemmas associated with providing France with security had been resolved. The key decisions of alliance and on developing the *force de frappe* had already been taken. But France was still at war with itself, and the realities of being dependent had been made painfully clear during the Suez crisis in 1956. For both domestic and foreign policy reasons, de Gaulle felt it necessary to assert French independence more forcefully, a course that would earn him both scorn and admiration.

De Gaulle's policies were based on the assumption that the structures that had been erected at the height of the Cold War provided essential French security needs. The guarantee of basic security provided the flexibility to pursue other policy objectives, as long as it did not undermine the security framework. This is what produced the dualistic approach to East–West relations that characterized the Gaullist period and in many ways remains valid today: firmness toward the Soviet Union and solidarity with the United States in times of acute East–West crises (e.g., Berlin and Cuba) and dialogue with the Soviet Union and enlargement of France's diplomatic margin of maneuver with the United States through a policy of calculated differentiation in periods of relaxed tensions.[2]

Despite de Gaulle's rhetoric, a functioning Atlantic Alliance was a *sine qua non* for the policies he pursued, and he apparently believed that the Alliance did not require special attention to remain robust for the immediate future. But because he also believed in the transitory nature of regimes and international structures, he concluded that the Alliance would not indefinitely remain viable or necessary. Only states endure, not regimes or institutions. He was convinced that the basic East–West division of Europe could ultimately be overcome and that French policy could contribute to this. A more appropriate role for France could be created in a future European system.[3]

These beliefs were based on specific assumptions about the three critical actors that have determined France's perception of its basic security needs throughout the postwar period: the Soviet Union, the United States, and West Germany. For de Gaulle, by the mid-1960s the Soviet Union was no longer the same kind of direct military threat that it had become after the end of World War II and was at the height of the Cold War. Moreover, there was a belief that France and the Soviet Union, the two great European continental powers, shared a strategic interest in preventing any resurgence of German power in the center of Europe. The United States, all rhetoric about its newly acquired vulnerability notwithstanding, was assumed to be sufficiently engaged in Western Europe and its nuclear umbrella still viable, if slightly weakened. West Germany was considered firmly anchored in the West, and existing Western institutional arrangements were believed adequate to satisfy German security needs (NATO) and to provide a surrogate fatherland.[4] NATO would provide the necessary counterweight to Soviet power and the political framework for German ambition in all foreseeable circumstances.

The importance of the assumptions about the United States should not be underestimated, precisely because of the accompanying rhetoric. The development of French nuclear weapons clearly did embody, as part of its long-term rationale, a belief that nuclear weapons could be used only in defense of one's own national territory, and that American engagement in Europe would inevitably weaken with time. But this was all at a high level of theory and abstraction. In the short term, not only was French policy not a response to a perceived weakening of American commitment to Europe, French strategy was viable only in a context of continued American commitment to Europe. The credibility of the *force de frappe* was enhanced by the existence of a link to the American deterrent; the doctrine of proportional deterrence really makes sense only in a world where it is an add-on.

In the 1960s the assumptions made by de Gaulle about each of the three actors brought him to the conclusion that French security requirements no longer needed integration in the NATO military structure and that he was free to pursue what might be called a policy of security plus. It was a rare period in which France could have its cake and eat it too. France lost nothing in security (at least in the short term) by the path he chose, and it was able to gain: above all in terms of restored national pride and prestige, and in being able to lift security issues out of domestic politics in the name of independence.

The period of high Gaullism was one where image and reality were never close. The systems did not exist to match the claims. But it did not matter, and indeed the image created by the rhetoric of independence and the *force de frappe* together made a national reality, and eventually a reality that reached beyond as well. Ironically, however, just as image and reality of French capabilities began to converge, the context began to shift.

SHIFTING CONTEXT AND CHANGING ASSUMPTIONS

Geopolitical Trends

During the 1970s and early 1980s, the strategic environment in Europe began to change in important ways, prompting a reconsideration of Gaullist assumptions about all three of the key actors that determine how France views its security requirements.[5]

Thinking about Germany was the first to be affected. The most important factor conditioning new perceptions was brought about by the new German Ostpolitik in the early 1970s and the FRG's conclusion of the Moscow Treaty with the Soviet Union. With Germany accepting the territorial status quo in Eastern Europe, Bonn acquired a new quality of relationship with Moscow. The Federal Republic now possessed its own channel to the East for dealing with the consequences of the postwar settlement, which created the potential for West Germany being less firmly anchored to its Western moorings. For France, this is precisely the specter that grew in the late 1970s and early 1980s as the Federal Republic wrestled with its declining confidence in NATO's force posture and the American guarantee, combined with domestic political convulsions surrounding the INF modernization decision.[6]

There was also reassessment of the Soviet Union as a politico-military threat to French interests. Here there was an internal and an external dimension to the evolution. The internal is generally referred to as the Gulag effect: a reconsideration among the intellectuals, triggered by the publication of *The Gulag Archipelago,* that began to focus on true nature of Soviet society. The result was a much less tolerant domestic filter for Soviet behavior. Moreover, when France elected Francois Mitterrand in 1981, it gained a president who had deep-seated anticommunist convictions (as well as an incentive to demonstrate these in his foreign policy).

The external dimension was conditioned by two factors. First, the new Soviet–German relationship that emerged from the Ostpolitik gave Moscow a new ability to influence the tone and direction of German policies. As a result, France became a less important partner for the Soviet Union. Moscow could pursue European strategic objectives more easily by dealing directly with West Germany, which diminished the importance of the overarching strategic interest shared by France and the Soviet Union. By the late 1970s, these new Eurostrategic conditions converged with a growth of Soviet military power and the shifting East–West balance of forces, the emergence of new generations of Soviet nuclear weapons and NATO's difficulty in responding, and the more aggressive use of Soviet military power, especially in Afghanistan.

During the early and mid-1980s, U.S. policy provoked French concern about American commitment in Europe. Although the harder line Reagan policies toward the Soviet Union coincided with France's own predisposition, the Strategic Defense Initiative was seen as indicative of growing insularity. Moreover, serious pursuit of strategic defense by both superpowers could undermine the credibility of French nuclear forces, as well as destroy public support for nuclear deterrence. Further, the United States reiterated the need to enhance NATO's conventional capabilities to raise the nuclear threshold, which it was feared could erode what credibility remained of extended deterrence and thus open Europe up to conventional war. The Reykjavik summit sent a shiver down the spine of French (and most European) cities because the United States negotiated without consultation over the heads of Europeans on matters of vital interest to Europe, and the French simply did not believe in the value of major nuclear reductions in Europe. Finally, there were the U.S. budget deficit and growing pressures in Congress to reduce overseas commitments and enhance burden sharing. For the French, the United States had become in reality, not just in theory, a less reliable and predictable factor in the European security equation.

Thus France began to see a potential unraveling of postwar geostrategic stability in Europe. The Soviets were becoming more menacing, German confidence in American protection was declining, German temptations toward pacifism and neutralism in exchange for amelioration of Germany's division were seen as growing, and NATO's ability to keep nuclear deterrence robust was sharply reduced, despite its ultimate success in deploying the Pershing II and Cruise Missiles.

Policy Adjustments

The first major reforms to move French policy away from purist Gaullism were undertaken by Giscard. At the level of assumptions, Giscard represented those who had always had a different perspective on building Europe and the role Europe would have to play in both defining and protecting French national interests over time. Along with Helmut Schmidt, he brought into being the European Monetary System. In military policy, Giscard, through the idea of the enlarged sanctuary, attempted to broaden the definition of French security interests, one that included France's immediate neighbors.[7]

The most important of Giscard's military reforms was his reorganization of the French army. The army's internal structure inherited from de Gaulle and Pompidou made any European or allied role problematic at best. In 1975, large divisions were transformed into smaller maneuver divisions to make them capable of fighting alongside France's allies. Correspondingly greater attention was given to the conventional equipment portion of the defense budget, which reached a high point in the late 1970s.[8] Arrangements were made between the French and American governments "to assure that war reinforcements and supplies arriving from the United States could have access to French seaports, airports, pipelines, railways, and highways, rather than be confined to more vulnerable lines of communication in West Germany."[9]

Both the enhanced collaboration with the allies and the greater European orientation were carried forward under Mitterrand. His concern with the shifting context was never more dramatically demonstrated than in his unprecedented intervention before the Bundestag in January 1983, when he urged German deployment of the Pershing II and Cruise Missiles. Under his presidency, the French government has undertaken several force posture adjustments to further improve the interface between French and NATO forces, or to symbolize closer solidarity with France's allies.

First, in 1981, there was a further reorganization of French army divisions. It had been determined that the divisions created in 1975 were in fact too light for maximum compatibility with the allied divisions they were to be capable of fighting alongside. As a result, French divisions were strengthened from just under 8,000 men to roughly 9,000 men. Then, over the next few years,

> French and NATO planners worked out arrangements whereby if Paris judged war to be near, French ground forces would take up positions in central Germany and fall directly under NATO commanders there. Operational coordination of tactical air forces and NATO air forces in Central Europe became considerably tighter. Selected French airfields were earmarked and surveyed to serve as potential dispersion bases for NATO's airborne early warning system."[10]

Second, France had long faced a doctrinal conundrum that involved the range of the Pluton missiles and the way these were integrated into the operation of the French First Army.[11] The fact that the Pluton would be deployed into the combat zone as the First Army was moved forward meant that it would have to fulfill its principally political mission of *ultime avertissement*[12] from a position that was incompatible with the central control by the French president. This cast considerable doubt on whether the army would indeed be available to fulfill its role as a NATO reserve. With the decision to move forward with the increased range Hades ground-launched missile (Mitterrand now refers to a range of just under 500 km), however, the French chose a weapon that could remain well away from the battlefield and whose command structure could be separated from that of the First Army, rendering the role of both more credible. The extended range also would enable the French tactical nuclear warning shot to reach beyond West Germany.

Third, high level consultations between the chief of staff of the French Armed Forces and SACEUR on nuclear war plans were intensified and became more specific. Although stopping short of formally committing French forces to NATO, target lists have been exchanged and French plans have apparently been adapted to take into account NATO's priority on restraint and limiting collateral damage in the early phases of nuclear use.[13]

The fourth and highly visible manifestation of French commitment to security in the forward areas was the creation of the *Force d'action rapide (FAR)*. This five division force, particularly its air mobile and light armored divisions, was expressly designed for rapid force projection into forward battle areas.[14] The force has been criticized for its lack of infrastructure and the incompatibility of its communications links with those of NATO, which clearly render it less effective than it could be. But it is potentially capable of credible military action in a major conflict between NATO and the Warsaw Pact.[15]

The most recent innovation in force posture involves the constitution of a Franco-German brigade. While it reached full strength in 1990, it will have to overcome numerous obstacles if it is to be operationally important. Substantial problems stem from differing French and German operational concepts, and from equipment incompatibility that currently requires parallel infrastructures. The unit falls outside NATO's integrated military command, and there are questions about how French nuclear weapons can protect the French troops without implicitly extending protection to their German colleagues.[16] Even more than the FAR, therefore, the Franco–German brigade is primarily a symbol of French commitment to German and allied security rather than a major change in French contribution to Western military strength.

At the level of policy process, there have been many indications of greater French concern with West European security and a desire to cooperate more intimately in the consultation process among allies. Throughout the 1980s, concrete steps have been taken to facilitate the development of a European consensus on defense and security issues. Bilaterally, in 1982 the French and Germans created a joint Committee for Security and Defense, which was upgraded in early 1988 to the status of a Joint Defense Council. Since 1985, foreign and defense ministers have met at the thrice-annually Franco–German summits under the provisions of the 1963 Elysée Treaty. There have also been unilateral official French statements, such as that by Chirac in his December 1987 speech to the Institut des Hautes Études de Défense Nationale, when he asserted that no one should doubt that in case of an attack on Germany, the engagement of France would be immediate and without reserve.

At the multilateral level, the French have become more active in the North Atlantic Council and its dependent committees. While they do participate in more

NATO activities, also they are simply more present.[17] Probably most important, they have played an instrumental role in reviving the Western European Union (WEU) as a forum for consultation among the European allies on security issues. It is the only forum in which foreign and defense ministers of the members meet simultaneously, an innovation that many consider important. There are also consultations at the level of political directors of foreign ministries, with related staffs, to discuss and coordinate issues related to European security. The French government was instrumental in getting the WEU to adopt a security charter that embodies the basic principles of nuclear deterrence, defense of member national borders, and the need for U.S. military presence in Europe.

The range of military and political initiatives moving France away from purist Gaullism and toward greater collaboration with its allies has thus been impressive during the 1980s. Moreover, there is no longer the same anti-NATO flavor of efforts to create a greater European profile in defense. But a net assessment must still conclude that much of the movement has remained at the level of symbols.

Despite the successive reorganizations of the French army to enhance compatibility with NATO forces and the greater attention to the forward battle, there is no indication of any substantial shift in French military doctrine to emphasize conventional operations or a shift in the portion of the defense budget devoted to conventional forces and their equipment. Indeed, the contrary is the case, given the progressive cuts in the size of the army over the past decade and stretching out of conventional arms modernization programs. Nuclear deterrence remains the heart of French defense policy and nuclear forces the core of France's military posture.

This is not to underestimate the value of either the concrete adjustments in the conventional posture or the symbols in a period of strategic change in Europe. It is an open question, however, whether and how the symbols will be translated into further concrete steps that link France's destiny more directly with those of its European allies. By the late 1980s, France was still straddling the dilemma of how to reconcile its basic strategic doctrine with the desire to bind Germany more tightly to the West and to keep the United States engaged in the defense of Europe.

EMERGING POLICY CONTEXT

Future French security policy will be determined by the interaction of three basic contextual factors: the effect of Mikhail Gorbachev and reform in the Soviet Union on the geopolitical trend lines in Europe; the emergence of fiscal constraints on French defense options; and how both affect the viability of domestic political consensus on defense.

The Gorbachev Effect

The effect of Mikhail Gorbachev on French thinking about European security has been complex, even contradictory. Initially, French assumptions about Gorbachev and his reforms were more cautious than elsewhere in Europe. The French saw no basic change in Soviet strategic objectives in Europe, despite "new thinking." In general, Gorbachev was seen as needing a tranquil European and international environment in order to give himself the best chance for success at home. He also needed the financial support he hoped would come with reduced East-West tensions. His policies could well ultimately reduce the Soviet military threat to the West, but the proof of the pudding would have to be in the eating.

The French, along with everyone else, were caught off guard by the revolutionary events of 1989. Although the future of the Soviet Union still remains in question, it is now clear that the nature of the Soviet threat has been profoundly changed. The new situation is quite different from what provoked the shifts in European French policy away from purist Gaullism. Indeed, French assumptions about the direct Soviet military threat have begun to move closer to those of de Gaulle than to the assumptions of recent years. The perception of a declining Soviet military threat, however, has not had the same effect on French security thinking in the 1990s as it did in the 1960s. The rest of the world is not the same as it was under de Gaulle. Germany is a less constrained actor on the European stage and the United States feels less capable of sustaining its levels of global engagement.

The most important Gorbachev effect for France has been his influence on the basic trend lines of German and American policy, both of which are of substantial concern to the French. By opening up the possibility of German unity and more normal interaction in the center of Europe, Gorbachev reinforced French concern about a Germany eager to extend its influence into East-Central Europe at the expense of its Western integration. And by moving toward reducing the level of military confrontation in the center of Europe, he reinforced French concern about the future of U.S. engagement in Europe.

If Gorbachev fails and the Soviet Union reverts to a more hostile form of coexistence, this could, of course, move French assumptions back toward a more predictable, comfortable world, with a more menacing Soviet adversary also reducing German drift and American disengagement. In the more likely case, at least in the next few years, of continued Soviet experimentation and promise of change, the French will have to contemplate a world in which Europe remains in a phase of some geostrategic flux.

This is a world, however, that already poses challenges for France much more dramatic than those that promoted the evolution of French policy from the mid-1970s to the mid-1980s. The postwar order in Europe has collapsed and a new order must be built. The task is no longer simply how to maintain Western institutions while overcoming the legacy of Yalta, but how to build the institutional framework for the new Europe and how to remold French consensus to these new conditions.

The dilemma is how to adapt without undermining the foundations that for the foreseeable future will remain indispensable to security. It is a world in which neither the Gaullist nor the NATO-integrationist solutions provide an answer. The search now is for a new framework that will continue to incorporate elements of both independence and alignment but will address the far more challenging environment of a new Europe that is beginning to emerge.

Fiscal Constraints

The alternatives available to France in pursuing its security interests over the coming period are going to be considerably more constrained than they have been in the past because of a growing defense resource problem. In large part this is the result of three factors: a prolonged period of low economic growth rates and sluggish world economy, which together have produced austerity conditions in all government spending; the fact that the cost of sophisticated high technology weapons is rising even faster than the rate of inflation; and the structure and missions of the French armed forces. It has become increasingly difficult to maintain a credible nuclear posture, a credible conventional commitment to European defense, and adequate interventionary forces to project power into areas of French influence in the Third World.

In the mid-1980s, France was spending roughly 3.9 percent of Gross Domestic Product on defense, considerably up from its low point of 2.95 percent when Giscard became president in 1974. Giscard was committed to increasing spending to 4 percent, a point never reached. Although spending declined somewhat in the late 1980s, the real problem is that static spending would not have been enough to maintain projected programs and force levels.

The initial signs of the current problem had become visible in the 1983 Military Program law.[18] Spending was constrained, but virtually all major modernization programs were maintained, most of which were inherited from procurement decisions taken by Giscard, but whose funding had been delayed. Funding for new weapons was front-loaded, assuring that many costly systems would be maturing at precisely the same moment in the early and mid-1990s. The operational budget of the armed forces took the direct hit, with manpower being cut by 20,000 men over the five-year life of the law.

After the 1986 elections and the arrival of Chirac at the Matignon, a new military program law was developed. All modernization programs were to be continued and enough money was to be allocated to implement these, although it has been argued that the figures cited in the law would not have been nearly sufficient to meet spending requirements in the out years of 1991–1992.[19] No further personnel cuts were mandated. The law was voted by an overwhelming majority of the *Assemblée Nationale*, including the Socialists.

Following the elections in May and June 1988, a limited review of the law was conducted by the Socialist government as it prepared the 1989 budget for presentation in the fall. In that budget, Defense Minister Jean-Pierre Chevénement foreshadowed some of the difficulties that still lay ahead: additional, if limited, cuts were made in the armed forces, bringing the total reduction since 1981 to roughly 26,000 (315,000 to 289,000); the S4 missile was put on hold to offset development cost overruns on the new generation of ballistic missile submarines; the number of new generation tanks to be procured was cut by as much as 50 percent because of massive cost overruns; the number of new generation attack helicopters (jointly developed with the Germans) was reduced by roughly 50 percent, also because of massive cost overruns; and several other programs were stretched.[20] The trade-offs (except for the cuts in personnel) were kept within the same categories of systems, but it was already clear that more significant cuts would be necessary in the next budgetary cycle if more money did not become available, which no one considered likely. It was impossible to sustain existing French program commitments across the board on the same budget.

The problem came to a head during the spring of 1989, when the government conducted a full review of the Military Program Law (a midterm review had been planned from the outset, with the idea that spending projections would be adjusted according to need). There was considerable tension between Prime Minister Michel Rocard and Defense Minister Chevénement over the final amounts to be allocated to the procurement budgets for the years 1990–1993, to the point that Mitterrand finally had to arbitrate. When the revised projections were finally presented in early June 1989, the budgetary restrictions were justified in terms of an international climate that had become more permissive and the fact that "defense policy can only be durably credible if it respects economic equilibria."[21] Nonetheless, the impact was considerable.

Rocard had been partisan of making fundamental choices and cancelling specific modernization programs; he was obliged to allocate more than he wished to procurement. Chevenement was asked to maintain all major modernization programs, but he was not given the money he considered necessary to meet that objective. In the end, the nuclear arsenal escaped almost unharmed (a slight delay in the first of the new generation submarines and a reduction from 33 to 28 the annual number of Mirage 2000 to be purchased during the life of this law, although the S-4 missile remained on hold), but other programs judged to be less important are to be stretched and in some cases the numbers to be procured reduced considerably.[22] Although cancellation of the new generation Rafale fighter aircraft alone could relieve much of the pressure on the procurement budget, the plane will suffer only a slight delay; it has become a symbol of both the government's commitment to maintain French technological capacity and its need to take into account the "industrial, economic, and social stakes, giving French defense industry the means to maintain its competitiveness."[23] The nuclear-powered aircraft carrier has been delayed by two years until 1996, but that is the one substantial system that remains the object of speculation about possible outright cancellation in the future.

The 1989 review does not resolve the basic defense resource problem confronting French policy makers and thus the issue will be revisited over the next few years. For the moment, France refuses to abandon any of the three basic missions assigned its armed forces: the strategic nuclear; the European conventional; and the intervention forces. Moreover, it continues to pursue these capabilities largely through national armaments programs. On the other hand, a convergence of armaments programs in the mid-1990s that will require more resources than are currently being projected if the programs are to be maintained.

This need not pose a problem any greater than in the past; programs can be stretched once again in order to avoid cancellation. Indeed, people have forgotten how many times the programs currently being debated have already been stretched. However, delays and cuts in equipment will eventually impinge upon the capacity of the French armed forces to perform their missions. Some already voice concern that the army has basically been stretched to its limits if it is to fulfill the European mission it has been given (assuming that mission is to act as a reserve force for the central region until American reinforcements can arrive). The numbers of troops are a concern, but it is above all materiel and sustainability that are the cause for deepest concern: specifically, training, readiness, and stockpiles. Only a few places could bear cuts and not risk undermining future capacity to perform current missions (reserves, the nuclear carriers, possibly some aircraft).[24]

The changes underway in Europe, however, may help the French to square this circle. The French conventional mission on the continent could well be defined in the emerging context in a way that would reduce the need for resource commitments and make stretching further or cancelling some systems more acceptable. This would also reduce the potential of financial constraints to become a significant factor in domestic political debate over French defense policy. At the same time, the larger issues raised by the transformation of the European order may well pose the greatest test yet for the future of political consensus on French security policy.

The Domestic Political Environment

In the protest environment in Europe of the late 1970s and early 1980s, France was often regarded as a model of political consensus in the areas of foreign and defense policy. More recently, however, there have been some indications that the famed French consensus may not be as solid as was thought. Indeed differences have appeared among contending political groupings over the appropriate configuration of the French nuclear deterrent and over the financial constraints discussed above. The question, of course, is whether these are important enough to make the basics of French defense policy once again descend upon the realm of domestic politics.

Consensus around the *force de frappe* and independence were not automatic in France. During his tenure, de Gaulle's policies were politically controversial. But he enjoyed an electoral system that guaranteed him a parliamentary majority and a constitution that gave him sweeping powers. Nonetheless, the primary symbols of Gaullist foreign and defense policy became the benchmarks for all parties to establish the legitimacy of their claims to govern. When Mitterrand reorganized the Socialists and the party began its long climb to power, one of his early moves was to forge his nuclear credentials by reversing much of socialist doctrine on defense. The Communist party, too, eventually rallied to nuclear deterrence (although they have since virtually deserted it once again). Defense policy was thus extracted from daily domestic political strife, but the new doctrinal norms became highly political in the sense that any deviation from purism would be a sanctionable offense. At least that was the fiction that everyone upheld.

When Giscard introduced his reforms in the mid-1970s, he created substantial controversy, precisely because it was seen as a deviation from Gaullist principles. There were really two lessons of the period for understanding the evolution of political consensus on defense in France. First, Giscard's reforms confronted some of the paradoxes of Gaullist doctrine head-on. He created a debate on principles, not interests. There was not yet a sufficient perception of a changing international context to permit deviation from purism. At the same time, and this is the second lesson, all the controversy really had no effect on the important dimensions of the reforms, given the power of the executive in this domain.

By the early 1980s there existed across the main political parties a more general acceptance of changing international conditions and the need to adapt policy. At the same time, Mitterrand has been smart enough to avoid presenting his various initiatives in terms of a need for modifying doctrine. He has simply taken action and called it necessary. The most important changes in both conventional and nuclear policy were also closely guarded; much of what transpired was suspected, but it only became public in 1989.

The most important political evolution has taken place within the Gaullist party, the changing international context coinciding with the declining power of the Gaullist barons. In the past, conservative governments have often attempted to cultivate good relations with the Soviet Union not only as a consequence of basic Gaullist belief in the special relationship between Paris and Moscow, but also in the hope that Moscow would use its influence on the Communist party to prevent the Left from coming to power. Since the arrival of the Socialists in government in 1981, the parties of the Right have concentrated heavily on the persistence of the Soviet threat and have taken a much harder stance than in earlier periods. The Gaullists particularly have continued this line, even after Gaulist Prime Minister Chirac's forced *cohabitation* with Mitterrand, in an attempt to use defense as an issue to challenge the president and his party.

The Gaullists also have evolved in their approach to the ingredients of national security policy. In particular, the *Rassamblement pour la Republique* (RPR) under Chirac has ceased to be the guardian of the nuclear holy scriptures. Indeed, during the period of cohabitation (1986–1988), it was the Gaullists who began to change the language used when talking about tactical nuclear weapons, expressing the French need for a capacity to avoid the all or nothing choice. It was also Chirac who became most forthcoming about the French commitment to forward defense, previously Gaullist anathema, and about the desirability of coordinating French and American strategies.

The Socialists, too, have evolved. When Mitterrand came to power in 1981, it was the first time that the Gaullist republic had a chief executive with a markedly anti-Gaullist past. Moreover, as leader of a government that included communists, he was placed in a delicate situation with regard to policy toward the Soviet Union. Many expected this coalition would attempt to position France as an intermediary between East and West, but the reality was actually quite different. Having brought the communists into his government, Mitterrand was all the more inclined in his first years in office to take a hard line toward the Soviet Union to show French voters and his Western allies that he was not a prisoner of the Communist party. Mitterrand's return to a more flexible approach to relations with the Soviet Union began about the same time that the socialist-communist coalition was approaching its end. Although it would be hard to draw a solid link between the two events, the latter condition made the former politically easier.

The more differentiated policy since the mid-1980s permitted some of the contending strains of thought within the Socialist party to reemerge. Some party members continue to support a rather hard-nosed approach to the Soviets and the ambitious plans to modernize the French defense posture. But there has also been a current of thinking that places much greater emphasis on "existential" deterrence[25] and on disarmament, even at a time when official French policy is openly suspicious of European arms control. Mitterrand himself has become more of a purist on nuclear issues, for example, renaming the *arme tactique nucléaire* to be the *arme préstratégique* to emphasize the unbreakable link between all nuclear weapons. Indeed, the Socialist party has found it uncomfortable trying to reconcile its skepticism about the Soviet Union, the exigencies of being a governing party, and its desire not to become isolated among the socialist parties of Western Europe.

These differences are real, but their potential to promote a breakdown in basic French consensus should not be overestimated. The debates over the French defense budget illustrate less the emergence of profound political cleavages than they do how difficult it is to use this as an issue in political debate. Chirac has attempted to advance the right through attacks on Mitterrand for being weak on defense. But in reality his case has lacked political plausibility. Mitterrand has kept French defense priorities on nuclear forces, he has taken France into the new negotiations on Conventional Forces in Europe, he has set stiff conditions for French participation in any future nuclear talks, and he has attempted to keep France's positions from becoming too distinct from those of its European partners. Given that he has not shifted French doctrine or the basic rhetoric of independence, it is very difficult to make a strong case that he has sacrificed French position or interests. And it is difficult to mobilize support for more defense spending in the current European environment, even in France. There is no real nascent Left/Right split in France on defense, largely because the terrain is not fertile.[26]

The structure of political institutions in the Fifth Republic prevents the kinds of differences that are voiced publicly from being amplified or having a major impact on policy. Decision making is highly centralized, and even the contending views that surfaced in the current government on the appropriate French approach to controversial Alliance issues such as short-range nuclear forces are largely irrelevant. In France, the power of the presidency in the domain of national defense is so great that he may essentially determine policy.

Moreover, there has been a general reduction of the polarization in French political life, a narrowing of the gap between Left and Right. There is no longer an obvious deep internal social division of the kind that dominated France from between the wars through the early postwar decades. An internal loosening up has accompanied, and permitted, the loosening of France's external posture.

As the result of this evolution of political opinion, the basic domestic political constraints on French defense policy are really only at the level of the commitment to nuclear deterrence, the *force de frappe*, and nonintegration in NATO military commands. Below this level, adjustments in the name of changing conditions and maintaining the viability of the French posture may create political noise but will create little political fallout.

At the same time, it is going to be increasingly difficult even for an astute politician like Mitterrand to adapt French policy to emerging conditions in Europe without calling into question the basic tenets of independence. There are already signs that Chirac and the Gaullists may attempt to make a political issue out of the sacrifice of French sovereignty entailed in moving the European Community toward economic and monetary union, and then on toward political union. There have not yet been any moves by Mitterrand in the area of defense policy itself that can be construed to violate these basic constraints, but many observers feel it will be necessary for France to move closer to its allies once again in the military field in order to avoid Germany seeking to emulate France's special military status in NATO. To do this without being liable to the charge of reintegration in NATO will require a major feat of statesmanship by Mitterrand. French political consensus may well be subjected to acute strains in the period ahead.

FUTURE POLICY DIRECTIONS

In response to the evolving geostrategic conditions in Europe, French policy will have as a primary objective to prevent undesirable shifts in the basic power relationships among the key actors in the European security equation. In particular, France will want to make sure that major movement in the East-West relationship does not alter the relative balance of power between France and the Federal Republic, or more correctly, remove the conditions currently making that balance irrelevant. It must be borne in mind that the Soviet Union was able to become the primary threat to French security only because Germany was divided after the war and each half integrated into the Alliance of one of the superpowers. Even if the form would be different today than in the past, France does not want to exchange the Soviet threat for the reappearance of Germany at the center of its geostrategic preoccupations. Above all, it wants to avoid a situation in which Germany once again becomes a strategic rival in Europe, but in which the Soviet challenge remains, and perhaps is even strengthened.

Mitterrand and those close to him look at the current European situation in terms of three interactive dynamics: change in the Soviet Union and Eastern

individually instead of in battery) and kept in service to provide additional flexibility to the land-based prestrategic nuclear arsenal.

These systems will be complemented by a modernized airborne component of the *force de frappe*, although the role of the airborne forces is being diminished in favor of the land-based systems. The current five-squadron, 75-plane force of Mirage IIIEs and Jaguars is scheduled to be replaced by three squadrons of Mirage 2000N and two squadrons of Mirage 2000N'. The aircraft are identical and all will be fitted with an air-to-surface missile (ASMP), although the 2000N' will be dual capable. Each is also scheduled to receive a new longer range ASMP (reportedly 300 km) in order to allow it to fire from a safe distance and to attack deeper targets of supporting echelons. These systems have not yet been developed and cannot be ready before the year 2000. The navy will only retrofit one of their carriers, the *Foch*, to handle the Super-Étandard, which will carry the same ASMP. The carrier *Clemenceau* will continue to handle only the Super-Étandard carrying gravity bombs (AN-52).[31]

None of these nuclear programs except the S-4 has been substantially affected in the budgetary decisions made in 1989. Basically, Mitterrand, like his predecessors, is committed to guaranteeing that France has a modern panoply of nuclear arms.

Ambiguities in French doctrine—particularly when France would actually use its nuclear arsenal—will remain, despite the greater coordination with NATO in recent years. There is no incentive for France to describe more precisely under what conditions it could cross the nuclear threshold or to be more explicit on the role of tactical nuclear weapons. It is believed that to do so would weaken their deterrent value, and it is one of the few remaining areas that could provoke a breakdown in domestic consensus. It is clear, however, that the new tactical nuclear arsenal will be considerably more diversified, flexible, survivable, and capable of a larger range of military missions, thus presenting the French president with greater choice in executing his *ultime avertissement*. When combined with French presence in the forward battle, these new systems are assumed to heighten Soviet uncertainty.

Conventional and Nuclear Arms Control

France has an interest in seeing progress on the European arms control front, stemming from a belief that reducing military confrontation on the continent will not only increase security but, more importantly, will consolidate the evolution in the relationship among the European states and the breakdown of blocs on the continent. The positions France defended in the preparation for the Negotiations on Conventional Armed Forces in Europe (CFE) in Vienna, the first time France has participated in an East–West arms control forum, symbolized French commitment to promoting the goal of breaking up the blocs. Hence the insistence on a nonbloc-to-bloc format and counting rules that are global rather than East versus West. Hence also the proposals (regional quotas and quotas of nonnational forces in a country) attacking the key factor guaranteeing a continuation of blocs: Soviet conventional preponderance in Eastern Europe. These proposals have a security content, but were primarily political in their motivation.

In a narrower sense, the French enumerated two specific goals for the talks, which began in March 1989: to eliminate the ability of the Soviet Union to launch a surprise attack, and to ensure that troop cuts could be verified. In the development of the Western opening proposal, the French sought to limit any offer of Western reductions. When the Germans attempted to introduce the idea of cutting deeper than 95 percent, the French blocked it categorically. Among the reasons seem to be a French desire to avoid both reductions of their own on French territory. The French were certainly not thrilled with President Bush's initiative at the May 1989 NATO summit because they are convinced that the inclusion of aircraft in CFE will open the way for the Soviets ultimately to gain control over France's nuclear-capable aircraft. Indeed, the French have long suspected that one of the prime Soviet objectives in CFE is to find a way finally to draw French and British nuclear forces into an arms control regime.

Among the most interesting of Mitterrand's statements on CFE was in his speech before the United Nations in September 1988. He said he believed the talks only had two years to achieve a substantial breakthrough and to forestall the introduction of more advanced weapons into the European theater.[32] Most observers link this to reports that the French might be willing to forego deployment of the Hades, and the delay coincided with a final go-ahead for their deployment.[33] Mitterrand has consistently denied any linkage between conventional and nuclear considerations by time and again emphasizing the unbreakable link between tactical and strategic nuclear weapons, but he has nonetheless sought to soften the rhetoric of the French approach to nuclear arms control.

Mitterrand's three conditions for French participation in nuclear arms negotiations are well known: the reduction of superpower arsenals to a level comparable to those of the French forces; the cessation of all competition in strategic defense, antisatellite warfare, and anti-submarine warfare; and the correction of conventional force disequilibria.[34] But in the fall of 1988, Mitterrand went further, both by asserting that he wanted France "to be associated intellectually, psychologically, and morally with efforts at disarmament," and by juxtaposing the fact that French forces would be guided by a concept of "strict sufficiency," to the overarmament of the superpowers.[35] This was his strongest signal that France may not forever be absent from the nuclear negotiating table.

But the conditions will have to be met. The new tone is meant to convey that the French are not just setting unreasonable conditions, but want to encourage the emergence of a new geostrategic context. It is in this light that one should read the Elysee statements about the Hades and enhanced radiation weapons (ERW): "It would be paradoxical to proceed with building a neutron bomb in a context of disarmament."[36] The purpose of not yet moving forward with the manufacture of the ERW is explicitly to encourage Soviet moderation. The idea of reconsidering such nuclear programs as the Hades if the Soviet threat shrinks dramatically—that is, if fundamentally new conditions emerge—is totally consistent with Mitterrand's overall philosophy about French participation in nuclear disarmament. What is new is the explicit reference to tactical nuclear systems and the implicit delinking of their consideration from overall strategic nuclear balance questions.

The idea of unilaterally renouncing the Hades or other nuclear systems under the right conditions is also consistent with the position Mitterrand took beginning in February 1988 on NATO's tactical nuclear modernization. He publicly argued that there was no urgency for the short-range nuclear force (SNF) modernization, a position that seems to run contrary to his proclaimed concern about denuclearization in Europe and his opposition to consideration of a third zero or inclusion of nuclear systems in the Vienna talks. Bonn apparently convinced Mitterrand that forcing the modernization issue would bring down the Kohl government, a government he clearly wants to continue in power during the current diplomatic phase. The basic notion of NATO testing the Soviet Union—with the threat of SNF modernization being held in reserve if movement on CFE is not forthcoming—was not, however, consistent with the approach Mitterrand was taking with his own Hades. But in this case, as in all others, Mitterrand holds his cards closely, and precise French policies with regard to non-French nuclear weapons cannot be known.

For France itself, Hades continues on track, with full funding. The French want to avoid any notion of a bargaining chip and are capable of doing so. Even under emerging conditions, the French definition of a substantial reduction in the Soviet threat is likely to be so dramatic that almost no START or CFE agreement would satisfy their conditions for participating in nuclear arms control negotiations, at least not for the foreseeable future. If France engages in reductions of its nuclear arsenal, this will in all probability be unilateral, with the Hades still being the most likely candidate. It is increasingly difficult to reconcile French desires to use a Franco-German axis to accelerate European integration with the maintenance of the Hades. At the same time, the French have positioned themselves to be able to justify proceeding with the Hades deployment. It should not be overlooked that the Hades acquires a certain political value in the world of geostrategic flux described earlier.

Relations with NATO

France's formal military relationship with NATO is governed by a series of technical agreements negotiated after the French withdrawal from the military command in 1967. There is no automaticity to the substance of the agreements, but the levels of interaction between the French armed forces and NATO commands are clearly extensive. French has observer status in the Military Committee and has liaison officers with SHAPE, SACLANT, AFCENT, and CENTAG.

France's special status in NATO once again came under criticism with the acceleration of movement toward German unity in early 1990. The worry was that Germany might seek a similar status at some point for domestic political reasons, or in order to respond to Soviet concerns. If France were to remove this special status, many feel it would have strengthened the West's position on NATO membership for a united Germany.

In part for reasons of its own domestic politics described earlier and in part for reasons of conviction about the emerging European order, there is no chance that France will decide simply to reintegrate within existing NATO military structures. There is a generally positive French predisposition to becoming more active in a NATO modified to emerging conditions, but the modifications will have to be significant. The French understand that their position does create undesirable options for a reunited Germany, but Mitterrand's answer has been to push for a greater assertion of a European security identity within the framework of the EC. This is not incompatible with NATO, but would imply a NATO with much more prominent European face within it. This is the type of adaptation, however, that would probably allow the French to collaborate more closely in the Alliance.

Barring this evolution, it is in the nature of the technical agreements between France and NATO that the real key to French-NATO collaboration in wartime can be reduced primarily to the capacity of French forces to fight alongside their NATO allies. The primary objective of the 1975 and 1981 restructuring of the French army was to enhance this interface. Since the late 1970s, several technical agreements have also been concluded that further enhance the interface. Nonetheless, substantial potential barriers to joint operations remain between France and its NATO allies.

Enhanced interoperability and harmonization of operational concepts would clearly be desirable from the NATO perspective, and many of these could yet be resolved through technical agreements or future modifications of French doctrine. It can be argued, however, that the most important dimension of the future French relationship with NATO from the NATO perspective concerns less whether additional agreements can be negotiated on these technical issues and more whether or not the French army is kept strong and modern. Most important will be whether the trend toward cutting into the army and reducing its sustainability are continued into the future, as the fiscal crunch on the French defense budget worsens, rather than as the result of a reduction of the Soviet threat. Sufficiency is clearly a concept that the French plan to apply to their conventional forces as well. Some observers worry that recent moves could foreshadow a major drawdown of French conventional forces, and the only question is whether this will occur within the context of CFE or outside it.

The army is considering a major revision of its barracking arrangements, reportedly to find a more rational disposition of forces to correct for its current wide dispersal throughout the country. The new plan supposedly will create concentrations that will ultimately be more efficient and, in the long term, less costly.[37] Minister of Defense Chevénement has also announced a major restructuring of the army, Plan Armées 2000. Under this plan, the precise dimensions of which are still unfolding, the First Army will be reduced from three to two corps. Most units will be divided between the two corps to make them "more complete and more capable of acting in either of the two main strategic directions, east or northeast, in case of a European crisis."[38] This will reportedly involve a reduction of 7,000 troops but is being done primarily to bring into greater harmony the size and missions of the corps.

It is still too early to tell what the precise impact of these decisions will be either on military capability, or on compatibility with NATO's forces. The French clearly are rationalizing a force structure that had grown hollow because of reductions in manpower over the past decade. The question is whether there is some bottom line that coincides with a definition of conventional force sufficiency, or whether this could provide a context for recommencing the process of thinning out all over again. In any case, the plans were drawn up prior to the revolutions of 1989 and without the expectation of such radical changes in the East-West environment.

The French have made the case in the context of CFE that they do not want to envisage more dramatic reduction scenarios involving French forces because these would already be reaching minimum levels for foreseeable requirements if an agreement were reached along the lines of the NATO proposal in Vienna. But the effect of the emerging East-West climate combined with a continuing fiscal crunch is likely to be significant. Army morale has already been affected by the 8 percent reductions made during the 1980s, but it is clear that conventional forces do not have Mitterrand's highest priority.

Franco–German Cooperation

Franco–German cooperation has been a subject of great interest and speculation as the numbers of meetings and exchanges between the two countries has proliferated during the 1980s. The French objective has clearly been to reinforce the image that German and French security are intimately linked, thereby binding Germany more closely to its Western European destiny. These bilateral efforts, although symbolically important, should not be misconstrued in the larger picture of French policy. The new Europe is the primary tool for controlling German drift. And the primary military relationship between France and Germany still runs through NATO. Thus, although bilateral military consultations and maneuvers will continue to develop over the next few years, they will be more important politically than militarily.

One of the basic obstacles to increased Franco–German military cooperation during the coming period will be the fact that France is concentrating on its nuclear posture while Germany is increasingly interested in reducing the role of nuclear weapons in Europe. The ratification of the protocol creating the Joint Defense Council was in fact held up due to problems over finding an acceptable reference to the necessity of nuclear deterrence. The Germans barely disguise their displeasure about the French modernization plans for the Hades, and despite the extended range and its separation from the French First Army, this is likely to remain a bone of contention. The fact that the Hades will in all likelihood carry a neutron warhead will heighten its negative effect on German opinion. German concern was not reduced by the French offer in 1986 to consult with them on the use of French nuclear weapons, within the limits imposed by the rapidity with which these decisions are reached, and considering that nuclear authority cannot be shared.[39] Nor was it by French emphasis that these systems cannot be used to conduct limited nuclear war.

The primary area where progress in Franco–German cooperation may well still increase is in collaborative procurement, although the prospects will be heavily dependent on the evolving East–West environment and whether the efforts to accelerate West European integration are successful. The record has thus far not been spectacular, with the dramatic failures of the tank and fighter aircraft projects. But the joint helicopter has been a real success, as have several smaller projects.[40]

Mitterrand seems to place collaborative European arms production at the center of the possibilities for a new European defense effort, but he also seems to have a multilateral vision. He refers to Franco–German successes, but in general talks disparagingly about progress in arms collaboration. He seems to believe that little of importance can be accomplished before 1992–1993, which he apparently hopes will help break down barriers that currently have prevented progress.[41] And even then, attitudes toward future Western European defense collaboration will be contingent on the evolution of relations between the two halves of Europe that occurs in the interim.

Franco–German bilateral cooperation will continue in the defense area. But expectations about its importance should not be exaggerated. The most important collaboration between the two countries over the next few years will be in the elaboration and execution of the European idea, which is first and foremost political, and in its translation into a pan-European concept that provides a framework for dealing with change in the East.

CONCLUSIONS

The movements currently taking shape throughout Europe are bringing about the most fundamental change in the European order since the late 1940s. Gorbachev's programs and proposals and the effects they have been allowed to precipitate in Eastern Europe have dramatically altered the character of relations between the two halves of Europe. The basic European context is clearly evolving and with it the assumptions France must make about its strategic requirements.

Gaullism was based on solid security structures and a belief that French policy would help break down the stalemated East–West relationship. When the structures began to weaken and the stalemate appeared to harden, French policy moved back toward reinforcing Western institutions and relationships. Today, the prospect of overcoming the stalemate has become a reality, but this can no longer be viewed against the comfort of stable Western security relationships. It is to this new combination of conditions that French policy is now responding, with all of the contradictory impulses born of ambivalence.

More than any other West European country, France is fundamentally ambivalent about change in the European order. On the one hand, there is a desire to encourage movement that ameliorates the basic relationship between the two halves of Europe. On the other, there is a strong desire to consolidate Western and especially European institutions in order to control unwanted shifts in power relationships among key actors. France's security policy and its relationship with its allies will be an attempt to reconcile these objectives.

NOTES

1. For greater detail on French security thinking during the early period, see Alfred Grosser, *The Western Alliance* (New York: Vintage Books, 1982).

2. See Dominique Moisi and Gregory Flynn, "Between Adjustment and Ambition: Franco-Soviet Relations and French Foreign Policy," in Gregory Flynn (ed.), *The West and the Soviet Union: Politics and Policy* (New York: Martin's Press, 1990).

3. For an excellent discussion of de Gaulle's world view, see Phillip Cerny, *The Politics of Grandeur* (Cambridge: Cambridge University Press, 1980).

4. The notion was that the process of Western European integration would provide the Federal Republic with a constructive outlet for energies that might otherwise be more actively directed at overcoming the division of Germany.

5. Compare Robert Grant, "French Defense Policy and European Security," *Political Science Quarterly,* 100, 3 (Fall 1985), 411–426.

6. A primary political/military impulse for the double-track decision came from the German government's concern with the combined implications of parity and the impending SALT II treaty (which was to exclude the SS-20 and Backfire Bomber from restrictions) for the viability of flexible response and extended deterrence. The same government, however, confronted growing domestic support for using arms control as a tool to reinvigorate detente, as well as increased allergy to nuclear weapons. The French were quick to conclude that the politics of defense in Germany would never be the same.

7. For an elaboration of the concept of the enlarged sanctuary, see Guy Mery, "Une Armée pour quoi faire et comment?" *Défense Nationale* (June 1976), pp. 11–33.

8. See David Yost, "France's Deterrent Posture and Security in Europe; Part I: Capabilities and Doctrine, *Adelphi Paper,* No. 194, International Institute of Strategic Studies, London, 1984–85.

9. Richard H. Ullman, "The Covert French Connection," *Foreign Policy,* No. 75 (Summer 1989), p. 23.

10. Ibid.

11. Grant, "French Defense," pp. 415, 418.

12. Translated as "Final Warning."

13. Ullman, "Covert," pp. 24–25.

14. The FAR was designed and configured not only for force projection in Europe, but to strengthen France's intervention capabilities in the Third World, especially Africa, as well.

15. See John L. Clarke, "New Directions in Franco-German Military Cooperation," *Parameters* (September 1988), pp. 82–84.

16. For a more complete discussion, see ibid., pp. 38–40.

17. See Peter Berger, "Cooperative Ventures: The French Connection," *Armed Forces Journal International* (November 1988), pp. 38–40.

18. See Jolyon Howorth, "Resources and Strategic Choices: French Defense Policy at the Crossroads," *The World Today* (May 1986), pp. 77–80.

19. Conversations in the French Ministry of Defense.

20. See "L'armee de terre devra reduire ses commandes de chars et d'helicopteres," *Le Monde,* 1 November 1988.

21. See "Les grandes lignes," *Le Monde, 9* June 1989.

22. For details, see Jacques Isnard, "La programmation militaire," *Le Monde,* 25 May 1989.

23. "Les grandes lignes," *Le Monde, 9* June 1989.

24. It is legitimate to look at the situation as a glass half full. Over the past several decades, the French army would have always had difficulty fulfilling its NATO missions, and current modernization programs, even if reduced or further stretched, can only help but continue to improve the situation.

25. The common French way to denote the belief that deterrence in the nuclear age flows from the existence of the nuclear arsenal more than from specific configuration of the arsenal.

26. For a more skeptical assessment, see Pierre Hassner, "Un chef-doeuvre en peril: le consensus francais sur la défense," *Esprit* (March 1988), pp. 71–82.

27. See Pierre Hassner, "Vers l'Est du nouveau?" *Esprit* (March–April 1989), pp. 108–116.

28. See Henri de Bresson and Luc Rosenzweig, "La France est la RFA souhaitent une concertation europééne sur les rapports avec l'Est," *Le Monde*, 5 November 1988.

29. See Jean Guisnel, "Budget Defense Chevenement rogne, l'armée grogne," *Libération*, September 16, 1988.

30. See Jacques Isnard, "La France prépare une modernisation de ses armes nucléaires prestratégiques," *Le Monde, 5* November 1988.

31. Ibid.

32. Joseph Fitchett, "At UN Mitterrand Ties France to Initiatives on Arms Control and Debt," *International Herald Tribune*, 30 September 1988.

33. Joseph Fitchett, "France Studying Delay in Missile," *International Herald Tribune*, 23 September 1988, and "French Officials Deny Shift on Hades Missile," *International Herald Tribune*, 24 September 1988.

34. Speech before the Institut des Hautes Etudes de Défense Nationale on 11 October 1988, *Le Monde*, 23 October 1988.

35. Ibid.

36. Ibid.

37. See Jacques Isnard, "L'armée de terre dans les turbulences," *Le Monde*, 29 September 1988.

38. "A Metz, l'état-major du ler corps d'armée sera dissous," *Le Monde*, 22 June 1989.

39. See text of Mitterrand declaration of 28 February 1988, published in *Le Monde*, 2–3 March 1988.

40. See Peter Berger, "French Defense Initiatives: Emergence of Second Pillar in NATO?" *Armed Forces Journal International* (August 1988), pp. 50–54.

41. Allocation Prononcée par Monsieur Francois Mitterrand, Président de la République Francaise sur la Défense de la France, Paris, 1988.

Chapter 5

The United Kingdom

Phil Williams

British security policy from the late 1940s to the late 1980s exhibited a consistency of purpose and a continuity of design that was challenged but not undermined by the perennial need to adjust to straightened economic circumstance and that did not change in essentials despite the rise and fall of East–West tensions. Although Britain was clearly not oblivious to changes in the climate of East-West relations, especially at the superpower level, these changes had a limited impact on the evolution of British defense and security policy. With the revolution in Eastern Europe in the last months of 1989, however, the context changed dramatically and posed fundamental questions for British policy makers and planners with the responsibility of adapting defense policy to post-Cold War Europe. Indeed, it may prove much harder for the United Kingdom to adapt to the changed security environment than for other European states. The constancy of purpose and the resistance to change in British policy are not entirely surprising as Britain, more than any other West European country, was the major architect of the postwar security system in Europe. The Labour government of the late 1940s concluded that there was a threat from the Soviet Union that could be met only by the commitment of the United States to the defense and security of Western Europe. It was Ernest Bevin rather than his predecessor, George Canning, who really called in the New World to redress the balance of the old. By encouraging Western Europe to engage in self-help and engaging in skillful bilateral diplomacy, the United Kingdom played a major role in entangling the United States in the security affairs of Western Europe. Having been pivotal in the creation of the Atlantic Alliance, Britain has also been extremely solicitous of its welfare. The belief that NATO provides the most appropriate security architecture in Europe remains uppermost in British policy. Although there have been suggestions in France and Germany that the Conference on

Security and Cooperation in Europe might provide the most appropriate security framework for post-Cold War Europe, the Thatcher government has remained committed to NATO as the security organization of first resort. Yet there has also been an acknowledgment in Britain that NATO itself has to change. There is not great enthusiasm for change—it is simply that reform is accepted as the only alternative to either increasing irrelevance or disintegration.

The transition from Cold War Europe to post-Cold War Europe poses major problems of adjustment for Britain. This is not simply a matter of British conservatism, but a reflection of the importance that the Atlantic Alliance has had in British security policy since 1949. Perhaps the most important single impulse driving this policy has been the desire to uphold the transatlantic security framework and ensure that the U.S. commitment to Western Europe is maintained. This was evident in the 1950s when the failure of the European allies to establish a European Defense Community provoked American threats to reappraise its commitment. It was Britain that took the lead in promoting the Western European Union as the framework for West German rearmament and ensuring that there was no U.S. disengagement. Similarly, Britain has always attempted to play the role of conciliator or intermediary within the Alliance and has been wary of developments that might prove divisive in Atlantic relations. Consequently, Britain has traditionally had a somewhat cautious, not to say skeptical, attitude toward West European defense cooperation, especially where this was presented as an alternative to the American security guarantee.

Yet British policy has always had a more muted theme, which complemented reliance on the United States with a simultaneous desire to maintain ultimate responsibility for British national security. In the final analysis, Britain, no less than France, has been unwilling to rely exclusively upon another state for the provision of security. The British nuclear deterrent, although partly an embodiment of concerns over status, has also manifested a continuing desire for independence and a reluctance to rely completely on the United States. Britain has never been as explicit as France about the dangers of excessive reliance on the United States for security, yet its nuclear policies have been based on Gaullist logic if not Gaullist rhetoric. The rationale for British nuclear policy has been very similar to the logic underlying the French independent deterrent. This has been obscured by the fact that the acquisition of British nuclear weapons has been done in cooperation with the United States. If Anglo–American nuclear link has been a reflection of the desire for strategic and political independence, it has also been a reflection of continuing dependence on the United States.

In one sense, this can be seen as the logical result of the limited resources available to Britain. At another level, the willingness to rely on the United States and the desire for independence seem to be contradictory or inconsistent. Yet the tension between them may be more apparent than real, and not simply because of Anglo–American nuclear collaboration. British policy has implicitly rested upon a two-tier concept of security that involves both structure and strategy. By structure is meant the existing security arrangements in Europe based on the division into two blocs and the U.S. willingness to underwrite the security of Western Europe. At the level of structure, the U.S. connection has been regarded by Britain as particularly important if potentially fragile; at the level of strategy, however, Britain has attempted to play a more European and more nationalistic role. Not only have successive British governments preferred Alliance strategies that emphasize deterrence through threats of escalation rather than through conventional defense or denial—a preference that reflects the realities of Western European geopolitics—but they have been anxious to maintain an independent nuclear deterrent as both a weapon of last resort and a contribution to deterrence in Europe. In one sense the nuclear component of British strategy fortifies and sustains the security structure; in another it acts as a hedge against the collapse of the structure.

This dual approach has run into problems because of limited resources. As a result, the structural dependence on the United States has been accentuated by a technological and strategic dependence. Nevertheless, the British desire for independence has rested upon concerns, which as recent research has pointed out was evident in the chiefs of staff committee during the late 1940s and early 1950s—that there might be circumstances such as international crisis in which British and American interests would diverge.[1] This has been particularly evident at the level of strategic doctrine, where British governments since the 1960s have been reluctant to accept American strategic preferences. More recently British concerns over SDI and President Reagan's aspirations to move toward a world free of nuclear missiles highlighted once again that even in the relationship of close allies, differences of perspective and interest are unavoidable.

If British security has depended partly upon structure and partly upon the possession of certain military capabilities, security has not been seen simply in terms of deterrence and defense. There has been a third component in British security policy—the search for accommodation and ultimately, it is hoped, agreement on arms limitation with the adversary. Whereas the United Kingdom readily accepted the division of Europe into two blocs, not least as a solution to the German problem, it was anxious to ensure that the military stalemate did not develop into direct confrontation and conflict. This was evident in the early 1950s when Winston Churchill, in a series of major speeches, called for an "easement of tensions" between East and West.[2] Indeed, one student of British policy during this period has suggested that although "the British government was not alone in pressing for a Detente . . . no other Western state matched the

British commitment to a normalization of East-West relations during the first half of the 1950s."[3] Furthermore, this strand in British policy was deepened under Macmillan. Writing in the early 1980s, therefore, Fred Northedge could claim that "British policy towards the Soviet Union since 1945 has followed a consistent course of armed vigilance against aggression, coupled with a search for detente and all manner of agreements to ease international tension, as and when opportunities for making these presented themselves."[4]

In short, British defense planning throughout most of the postwar period has been carried out within consistent and enduring policy framework, that is, a set of judgments, assumptions, and expectations about the threat to security and what has to be done to meet it. As a result, it was possible for Britain to maintain a balanced security policy in which the three components of security—the framework of political arrangements in Europe and across the Atlantic, the nuclear strategy, and the dialogue—were mutually reinforcing. Even before the last quarter of 1989 crucial elements in the international environment had begun to change in ways that posed a challenge to this three-pronged policy. The revolution of 1989 posed an even more fundamental challenge: as result of the changes in Eastern Europe, the new attitudes in the Soviet Union, the drawdown of Soviet forces in Eastern Europe, and the reunification of Germany, most of the traditional tenets of British security policy appear increasingly outmoded or irrelevant.

This is all the more pertinent because of changes in the domestic political context within which security policy is formulated. During most of the postwar period, foreign and defense policies were formulated by a small policy making elite operating within bipartisan consensus and not subject to political challenge. This too has altered. The Labour party during the 1980s advocated radical shifts in British security policy. Having realized belatedly that its support for unilateral nuclear disarmament was a major electoral liability, however, it abandoned unilateralism and reembraced multilateral disarmament. Even so, it is arguable that the Labour party is more attuned than the government to the shifting security environment and more inclined to see the changes that have taken place as an opportunity rather than a problem.

Yet even for a Labour government adjusting to the new Europe would not be easy. One of the main purposes of this chapter is to explain why Britain will find it harder to adapt to post-Cold War Europe than most other countries. In order to do this, it is necessary to identify more fully the underlying assumptions of British defense policy. The chapter then examines the changes that have taken place at the domestic level and in the international arena. Particular attention is given to those developments that will not only shape the security environment of the 1990s but that very clearly challenge the traditional tenets of British policy.

ous assault ships, thirty submarines, and forty mine countermeasures vessels. In the 1989 Defence White Paper, the government reaffirmed its commitment to maintain a 50-frigate and destroyer navy. Although it has occasionally engaged in out-of-area activities, in recent years the navy's main role has centered on Europe. In hostilities, the navy would contribute to forward defense in the Norwegian Sea, and by intercepting Soviet submarines contribute to reinforcement and resupply across the Atlantic. In addition to these major roles, the United Kingdom also provides a brigade of marines to the UK/Netherlands amphibious force, which would reinforce NATO's northern flank in a crisis. It also contributes a national contingent of 2,300 men to the Allied Command Europe Mobile Force and one Harrier and two Tornado squadrons, as well as Canberras equipped for electronic warfare, to SACEUR's Strategic Reserve (Air). This underlines once again just how comprehensive the British contribution to the Alliance order of battle actually is.

As well as making a contribution to deterrence and defense in Europe, the United Kingdom has acknowledged that, whereas the bloc structure and a strategy based on a comprehensive range of capabilities are necessary conditions for West European security, they are not sufficient conditions. This is not to imply that British governments have had an uncritical approach to East–West detente or have seen detente and arms control as a substitute for deterrence. On the contrary, the approach has been pragmatic and the appraisal hard-headed. Nevertheless, there has long been a recognition that the unilateral measures on which security primarily depended need to be buttressed by arms control or confidence-building measures. East–West competition was not regarded by Britain as a zero-sum situation in which the losses of one side translated automatically into the gains of the other. In addition, it was accepted that it was possible to introduce measures that enhance the security of both blocs in Europe. This has sometimes put the British government more in line with its European allies than with the United States, which, at times, has approached security much more in zero-sum terms. At other times, the United States appeared to place its common interests with the Soviet Union above its obligations to allies, and this became a source of concern for West European governments, including Britain.

The British approach to arms control, therefore, was generally cautious but positive. Arms control was seen as an important supplement to—but not a substitute for—national and alliance defense efforts. Indeed, the United Kingdom adopted what might be described as a managerial concept of arms control, which saw it primarily as a means of stabilizing the strategic environment and not a step on the road to total disarmament.[9] This led the United Kingdom to participate in arms control negotiations—sporadic and desultory as they sometimes appeared—and, on occasion, to take important initiatives in them. Britain clearly shared the objective, held by its NATO allies, of encouraging greater military transparency in the Soviet Union, thereby helping to reduce fears over a possible surprise attack by Warsaw Pact forces. In the latter half of the 1980s Britain also laid great stress on conventional force negotiations, emphasizing the urgency of asymmetrical reductions that would lead to stability at lower levels. Gorbachev's announcement at the United Nations in December 1988 that he was initiating substantial unilateral cuts in Soviet forces deployed forward in Eastern Europe eased Britain and allied concerns. Even so, the Soviet willingness to implement further reductions and move away from a force configuration geared up for offensive operations was still regarded as a litmus test of real change in Soviet strategic objectives. Britain also insisted that a conventional arms control agreement was a precondition that had to be met before negotiations on reductions in short-range nuclear forces could begin.

Indeed, the 1987 accord eliminating NATO's (and Soviet) intermediate nuclear forces was unsettling for the Thatcher government even though Britain formally endorsed the INF agreement. Yet this is only one of the trends that, in recent years, has challenged the three-pronged approach to security traditionally pursued by British governments of both major political parties.

CHALLENGES TO THE POLICY FRAMEWORK

The traditional policy framework has been subjected to a series of challenges that have not only made it more difficult to sustain but threaten to undermine the equilibrium among the three components. Although the policy framework has survived the challenges of the 1980s, it is not clear that it will prove equally robust during the 1990s.

The Domestic Challenge

One of the challenges has come from domestic factors. In the late 1970s defense policy, which had hitherto been the prerogative of a narrow elite, was challenged by a populist revolt. The left wing of the Labour party became the institutional home of the peace movement; the Conservative government continued with policies that differed little from those of its predecessors. The impact of these internal changes should not be exaggerated, however. The Labour party, having fought and lost two elections on a unilateralist plank, moved back to the center on defense issues. It was widely, although certainly not universally, acknowledged in the party that the commitment to unilateralism cost Labour as much as 3 to 4 percent of the votes in the last two general elections, and the party modified its stance by dropping unilateralism and embracing multilateral disarmament. This move was made in the face of determined opposition from the left wing of the party and from trade union leaders such as Ron Todd. But although it encountered considerable difficulties at the 1988 party conference, at the 1989 conference there was a much clearer endorsement of the leadership's position.

The Labour party's move back to a more pragmatic stance on nuclear weapons was facilitated by the decline of East–West tension. This trend, along with progress in arms control, gave defense a lower salience than in the early 1980s. Even if this had not taken place, however, the impact of dissent on government policy should not be exaggerated. So long as the government has a substantial majority in the House of Commons, the lack of consensus need not be inhibiting. The British government has considerable discretion in determining the main features of its security policy.

The making of Britain's nuclear policy, in particular, has been characterized by small group decision making, high levels of secrecy, the influence of specialist advice from the scientific and technological experts involved in defense policy making, and limited parliamentary and public scrutiny. Although the level of parliamentary oversight improved as a result of the work of the House of Commons Defence Committee, it is still rather startling to recall that the full Commons debate on nuclear weapons held on January 24, 1980, was the first of its kind for 15 years.[10] And even though the revival of partisanship on defense issues in the early 1980s led to increased activity in Parliament, debates on defense remained infrequent and desultory. All things considered, therefore, it is hard to disagree with McInnes that, although parliament is able to embarrass governments, its effect on the decision-making process is minimal.[11]

Other areas of defense policy making are less exclusive than the nuclear dimension. Even so, the decision-making process is effectively a closed one. To some extent this is a feature of British political life in general. Defense policy makers and planners may object to this by pointing out that, almost alone among government departments in Britain, the Ministry of Defense provides an annual statement for parliamentary and public scrutiny and debate. Yet the annual White Paper on defense is partly an attempt by government to set the parameters within which debate is to occur and, although revealing of the judgments and assumptions underlying the British defense policy, is sometimes designed to hide "at least as much as it reveals."[12] As one observer has noted, it is a "summary of all the news of the defence community's discourse that is fit to print; though it is the government that defines what is 'fit'."[13] Even so, the publication of the annual statement on defense does provide an opportunity for parliamentary and public debate. The fact that this debate is rarely very satisfying is not simply the responsibility of the government and the Ministry of Defence. The level of interest and expertise in the British House of Commons on defense is limited. A Gallup survey carried out in June 1988 covering 171 Members of Parliament and representing 28 percent of the total number of Conservative and Labour MPs in the House of Commons revealed that there is a dearth of knowledge and understanding of defense issues among MPs. Nearly one-quarter of MPs questioned had no idea of the proportion of GNP allocated to defense and 42 percent of those surveyed exaggerated the figure. Similarly, only 30 percent realized the British nuclear force accounts for only a small proportion of the defense budget. As striking as the errors was the high percentage of "don't knows." It is hardly surprising, therefore, that one analyst commented that "the most unfortunate finding of the survey . . . is that there are so many widespread misconceptions particularly in such vital and controversial areas."[14]

The lack of detailed knowledge about defense issues is widespread at the public level, too. Indeed, there is very limited public interest in defense—a point that is sometimes obscured by the intensity with which political activists express their opinions on the subject. The activities of the peace groups in the first half of the 1980s, however, led to an increased awareness of defense issues among the electorate. It also reflected and accentuated a polarization of the public debate.

This polarization has deep roots in British traditions of thinking about foreign policy and security issues. There is a long history of dissent from British foreign policy, which can be traced back to Cobden and Bright in the nineteenth century, through the Union of Democratic Control in the early twentieth century, and which has found expression in the postwar period in the Campaign for Nuclear Disarmament. The dissenters not only refuse to accept establishment thinking but offer alternatives of their own.

For much of the postwar period, dissent was largely suppressed by a bipartisan consensus about foreign policy and defense. The first challenge to this consensus in the late 1950s was relatively short-lived. The second challenge occurred in the late 1970s and early 1980s partly in response to the increase in Soviet American tensions. The decline of detente and the reversion to Cold War policies by the United States seemed to challenge one of the three pillars of British security policy—the need for accommodation and dialogue with the Soviet Union. It was not surprising, therefore, that although the Thatcher government was sympathetic to the hard line approach of the Reagan administration, the other political parties were much more critical. Furthermore, the belligerent rhetoric of the first Reagan administration fueled fears in Britain and other European nations that Western Europe might be dragged into a superpower confrontation that started elsewhere. It encouraged what one observer has described as the "institutionalization of British anxiety about a Third World

War."[15] Once cruise missiles were actually deployed in the UK, however, the peace movement began to lose much of its momentum. This was further diminished by changes in the climate of Soviet American relations and by the INF Agreement, which gave the protesters what they had long demanded. As the superpowers moved toward a new detente, so the urgency of protest diminished.

One legacy of the protest movement though is a divided public opinion that is considerably more sympathetic to the Soviet Union than might have been expected. Throughout the 1980s opinion poll results clearly reflected what is sometimes described as the growth of "equilateralism" in British thinking about the superpowers. One question that has consistently been asked by Gallup is "How much confidence do you have in the ability of the United States to deal wisely with present world problems?" In 1977 48 percent of those who responded answered "very great" or "considerable"; while 36 percent had "little" or "very little" confidence. The percentage of positive answers fell below 30 percent in 1982 and did not go above it again until late 1987. During the same period the negative answers rose considerably and from 1982 onward rarely fell below 50 percent.[16] A Gallup poll conducted June 9–13, 1988, in the aftermath of the Moscow Summit resulted in 39 percent providing positive answers and 46 percent claiming to have little or very little confidence in the United States. In this last poll, the same question was asked about the Soviet Union—with 47 percent providing positive answers and 38 percent expressing little or very little confidence. The Gorbachev effect was even more apparent in an additional question about whether confidence in the superpowers had gone up or down. Only 16 percent answered that their confidence in the United States had gone up, whereas the corresponding figure for the Soviet Union was 53 percent. The same poll recorded a 32 percent approval rating for the acquisition of Trident as against 57 percent disapproval, although when asked whether Britain should "give up relying on nuclear weapons whatever other countries decide," 53 percent thought this was a bad idea and only 38 percent thought it was a good idea.

In April 1989 on the eve of Gorbachev's visit to London, a MORI survey conducted for the *Times* and the Council for Defence Information confirmed most of these findings. When asked which of the two superpowers wished "to extend its power over other countries," 35 percent chose the Soviet Union and 33 percent the United States. This was a remarkable shift from 1981 when 70 percent chose the Soviet Union and 31 percent chose the United States, or even from 1983 when the figures were 59 and 26 percent, respectively. The much less negative image of the Soviet Union in British public opinion was also reflected in the fact that only 17 percent thought Soviet policies were harmful to Britain, a figure that had declined from 42 percent in 1981. Rather strangely, only 14 percent believed that

Gorbachev's judgment is sound—although even this reflected a marked increase from 1983 when only 3 percent thought Andropov's judgment was sound.

If there was a feeling that Gorbachev had improved East-West relations, however, there was also considerable caution and not a little conservatism in British public opinion on defense issues. Even if the superpowers agree to cut strategic forces, for example, only 21 percent believed that Britain should get rid of its deterrent. Although 36 percent thought that in these circumstances Britain should also reduce its strategic nuclear forces; 33 percent believed there should be no change in British capabilities. There was also a strong feeling—expressed by nearly half those interviewed—that it would be in British interests if the existing level of U.S. troops remained in Europe. At the same time, the vision of a nuclear-free world had some appeal; 37 percent of those asked thought Britain would be safer and 39 percent thought that it would be as safe as it is at the moment if all nuclear weapons were abolished by the year 2000.

Several conclusions can be drawn about these polls. The first is that on British nuclear weapons, they are relatively permissive, although the past two elections provide telling evidence that there is only limited popular support for unilateralism. The second is that there has been a long-term decline in British public confidence in the United States. To a large extent this was a response to the Reagan presidency, although the trend downward really began in the last half of the Carter era. The third observation is that Gorbachev has very clearly had a considerable impact on British popular attitudes and has created a far more favorable image of the Soviet Union than ever before.

The implications of all this are uncertain. It does suggest, however, that the traditional assessment of the Soviet Union as a threat to British security will not go unchallenged in the future. This view is reinforced by a study of media coverage of the Soviet Union. Although in traditional coverage of Soviet relations with Britain, the "USSR generally appears as a protagonist, a threat or an enemy" this appears to be diminishing, partly as a result of Gorbachev's personal image, partly as a result of the domestic reforms he has initiated, and partly as a result of a much more conscious and effective effort at news management by the Soviet Union.[17]

If Gorbachev seems to have had considerable public impact, at the level of Parliament and the parties his main impact seems to have been to confirm images rather than to change them. Although the poll of MPs referred to above revealed great support for the INF Treaty from members of the two main political parties, it also highlighted an important difference among the parties. Compared to Labour MPs, "conservatives are more likely to regard the Soviet Union as a threat, and nuclear deterrence as an appropriate response. They are more worried about the conventional balance in Europe and more skeptical about Gorbachev's disarmament proposals."[18]

Whereas 93 percent of Labour MPs support Gorbachev's proposal to abolish nuclear weapons, over half the Conservatives are skeptical. As well as a divergence about the nature of the threat, there is also considerable difference over how best to meet it. This was especially the case in relation to nuclear weapons, with 114 out of 116 Conservatives supporting Trident and only 9 out of 54 Labour MPs.

There is a sense in which much of this is irrelevant. The party differences are hardly surprising, and they reinforce the basic point that the government has considerable discretion so long as it has a clear majority in the House of Commons. There does, however, seem to be a long-term trend away from the traditional perception of the Soviet Union as a threat. This could make it more difficult for the government to justify increases in defense spending, especially in a period when it is attempting both to restrict public spending and to meet demands for increased resources on domestic programs such as health and education. Indeed, insofar as public opinion has any impact on British security policy, its effect is likely to be felt mainly in an indirect way, with the government response most evident at the level of resource allocation.

The implication of all this is that in the absence of a Labour government, the internal political dimension of British security policy is unlikely to be decisive in bringing about change. Nevertheless, the lack of consensus and the resource constraints complicate matters and add to the uncertainties about whether or not British policy can adapt to the external changes that are already apparent and seem likely to become much more salient during the 1990s. These changes are now examined more fully.

The International Challenge

The detente of the late 1980s began by default, with the superpowers drifting into it without any kind of conceptual underpinning. Even so it promises to be far more enduring and substantial than the detente of the 1970s. Consequently, although it offers considerable opportunity, it also poses serious problems for the traditional British approach to security, challenging several of the assumptions on which this approach has been based.

The first assumption that has been challenged by the new detente is the traditional conception of the Soviet Union as a direct threat to British security. Although Thatcher developed a good working relationship with the Soviet leader, prior to the events of late 1989 the government and the Ministry of Defence were not convinced that there had been a fundamental shift in the threat. There was less emphasis than in the past on the ideological dimension of the Soviet challenge and rather more on the way the threat has been institutionalized in Soviet and Warsaw Pact military capabilities. The British defense establishment accepted the significance of new thinking in Gorbachev's approach to foreign policy and security, especially his emphasis on reciprocity and reasonable sufficiency, but there was considerable uncertainty about the implementation of the new ideas. The difficulties that Gorbachev faces from his domestic critics and opponents as well as the possibility that, at some stage, he could be ousted from power, were presented as reasons for caution. Furthermore, there was at least some skepticism about whether or not there had been a real shift in Soviet objectives. Gorbachev was seen by more critical members of the policy making elite as a leader who was simply pursuing traditional Soviet goals through more subtle and skillful tactics than those pursued by his predecessors.

This is not to suggest that policy makers have been oblivious either to the changes taking place in Soviet domestic and foreign policies or to the need to react positively to them. Recognition of change was most apparent in the Foreign Office where the prime concern was not the military threat but the political opportunities and challenges posed by the Soviet Union. There was considerable sensitivity to the potential for political movement in Europe but also a fear that Gorbachev could exploit this to his advantage. In the Ministry of Defence, there was also a sense of the opportunities especially at the level of conventional arms control, but this was accompanied by a belief that a significant diminution in the Soviet threat had yet to materialize.

As a basis for military planning, the shift in Soviet declaratory policy was not accepted as a good indicator of a reduced threat until accompanied by concrete measures that reduce Soviet capabilities for sudden and decisive military action against Western Europe. Throughout most of 1988, it was claimed that such measures were still lacking and "when you look at the evidence, whether it be the economy, research and development, forward equipment programmes, military infrastructure, logistics or deployment," there has been no significant change.[19] Those who hold to the orthodox view of the Soviet threat "point to the continuing 2.5 to 1 imbalance in favor of the Warsaw Pact in terms of tanks; to the 30 divisions they can mobilize within 48 hours . . . to the 90 days of Warsaw Pact stocks compared to NATO's 30."[20] In view of the lack of change in these basic indicators, it was not surprising that the intelligence community and the defense policy making elite were "still to be convinced that aggressive designs have been placed in the Kremlin's own dustbin of history."[21]

In the event, Gorbachev's December 1988 announcement went some way to meeting what had clearly become another litmus test for the Soviet leader. In his speech at the Wehrkunde Conference in January 1989, Sir Geoffrey Howe acknowledged that new thinking seemed to apply to military issues as well and that there were grounds for optimism. Yet there was also considerable caution in the speech and the foreign secretary reiterated that although Gorbachev had recognized a long-standing Western concern about forward-deployed Soviet armor, the huge Eastern preponderance in tanks and artillery remained. Furthermore, "Soviet military procurement continues at an unjustifiably high level," giving the Soviet Union "a well-stocked hat full of well-armed rabbits and the Soviet Union will be able to go on surprising us by drawing rabbits from that hat for many years to come, but a lot less will have to be spent on guns before the Soviet consumer stops queuing for butter."[22] Another problem was that Soviet procurement belied Soviet theoretical analyses, which highlight the desirability of moving to a nonnuclear world by the year 2000.

This caution was also evident in the 1989 White Paper on defense. Although the statement acknowledged that recent Soviet foreign policy had displayed "new flexibility, pragmatism and sensitivity to the security concerns of others," there was a continuing concern over the imbalance of military capabilities in Europe and a reluctance to rely completely on Soviet pronouncements.[23] In the official view, it was necessary to be sure that the changes in the Soviet Union were fundamental and irreversible. Moreover, even if this test is met, there is still the problem that the Soviet Union remains the preponderant power on the European continent. In a sense, this is where geopolitical considerations and ideological considerations diverge. A reformed, more pluralistic Soviet Union would remove the ideological component of the British threat assessment but not the concern over the balance of power. This is perhaps a uniquely British preoccupation, which predates the Cold War and will not necessarily be abandoned simply because the Cold War is over. This explains much of the caution in British policy statements of the late 1980s, which emphasized that although the relationship between the Soviet Union and the West had improved as a result of Western policies of strength and determination on the one side and new Soviet flexibility on the other, the threat had not disappeared. Even after the events of 1989 there was still a reluctance to conclude that the Soviet threat was no more.

If the threat to British security could no longer be taken for granted, neither could the nuclear component of the strategy to meet it. There have been several challenges to the traditional emphasis that Britain has placed on the role of nuclear weapons in European security. As the Reagan administration pursued what appeared to be a visionary arms reduction policy, the Thatcher government found itself increasingly uncomfortable. In the aftermath of Reykjavik, in particular, the government was particularly vigorous in criticizing the idea of eliminating ICBMs in the second phase of an agreement dealing with offensive systems. It accepted that reductions of up to 50 percent in strategic offensive forces would not fundamentally alter the strategic landscape, but was perturbed at anything that threatened to go beyond this. Such an attitude is hardly surprising. Not only did the government hold to the belief that American ICBMs are crucial to the integrity of extended deterrence, it also recognized that if the superpowers make large-scale reductions in their strategic forces, then the strategic nuclear deterrent forces of Britain and France begin to loom much larger in the East-West balance. Part of the concern was over a dilution of extended deterrence, which was regarded as one of the pillars of the security structure in Europe, and part of it was over the possibility of constraints on national nuclear forces, which provides the insurance against a crumbling of this pillar. At best the British strategic nuclear forces could be seen as hindering further progress on arms control; at worst there would be considerable pressure to include these forces in a START 2 agreement—something that is a major problem given the minimal nature of the force. From this perspective, part of the response to Reykjavik was a preemptive attempt to preserve Britain's independent nuclear capability.

At the time of Reykjavik, the challenge to nuclear deterrence seemed to be coming from the United States. In the period following the INF Agreement, however, it was to come from a different direction as the British government found itself at odds with the Federal Republic of Germany and, to a lesser extent, Belgium over the issue of short-range nuclear force modernization. Although the Thatcher formally welcomed the double zero option enshrined in the INF Agreement, there was also a recognition that the direction of future arms control negotiations might pose problems for the Western Alliance. Concerns over "cascading denuclearization" made the prime minister reluctant to consider a third zero in short-range nuclear forces and anxious to ensure that modernization of NATO's short-range nuclear forces through the deployment of a Lance follow-on system went ahead.

It was felt that removal of the remaining U.S. land-based nuclear forces from Europe would sever the linkage between the two parts of the Alliance and that this would have serious repercussions for NATO's ability to maintain deterrence and defense in Europe. On this particular issue the United States and Britain were aligned against the Federal Republic of Germany, which believed it had been "singularized" and was therefore reluctant to accept modernization of short-range nuclear systems. The prevailing sentiment in Bonn was "the shorter the range, the deader the German"; in London it was concern over ensuring that coupling is maintained. Accordingly, the prime minister exerted considerable pressure on Bonn for a commitment to modernize NATO's short-range nuclear arsenal through the deployment of the follow-on to Lance.

Although it appeared in April 1989 that a compromise had been reached, the Federal Republic's desire to respond to Soviet overtures to begin negotiations on short-range nuclear forces gave the issue a new twist and an added urgency. Part of the concern in Britain was that Bonn's position would alienate U.S.

opinion and precipitate an upsurge of support for the proposition "no nukes, no troops." In the event, President Bush was able to fashion a compromise at the NATO Summit of May 1989. This, too, though was overtaken by the events in Eastern Europe, and in 1990 Britain and the United States accepted that the issue of short-range nuclear force modernization was dead. The liberalization of Eastern Europe and the effective disintegration of the Warsaw Pact had undermined any rationale for the deployment of a new short-range missile system.

The events of 1989 not only challenged the traditional assumptions about the Soviet threat and the role of nuclear weapons in meeting it, but it also raised questions about the future of NATO's strategy. The fact that the period of warning time that would precede any Soviet aggression against Western Europe had increased very substantially meant that the necessity of large standing allied forces deployed in West Germany was no longer self-evident. At the same time, the process of German reunification raised interesting and complex issues about the future of forward defense. It was not clear where the defense of the West began now that the East-West divide in Europe had effectively disappeared.

In short, the revolution of 1989 and its aftermath posed a serious challenge to British judgments and assumptions about strategy and force posture. The challenge to the existing security structure in Europe was even more fundamental. The Atlantic framework had not only contained the Soviet Union but had also been important in containing the German problem. The American commitment to Western Europe was crucial to this framework. It maintained the balance of power between East and West in Europe while also helping to promote cooperation and harmony in Western Europe itself. Consequently, the United Kingdom, along with the other European allies, was able to rely on the United States for the provision of security.

Even before the revolution of 1989, there were several developments indicating that the period in which Western Europe was a net security consumer was coming to an end and that increasingly Western Europe would have to become a more vigorous security producer. There was growing dissatisfaction in the United States with the level of resources devoted to the security commitment to Western Europe, especially in view of what was widely seen as a lack of European reciprocity in terms of burden sharing. Moreover, the growing concern in the United States that it was a superpower in decline accentuated demands for retrenchment. This was not surprising. The original commitment was based on notions of U.S. primacy and West European weakness. These notions no longer seemed relevant as Western Europe moved toward the creation of a single European market. Indeed, it appeared possible that increased economic cooperation would undermine U.S. willingness to underwrite West European security to the same extent as in the past. At the same time as the U.S. inclination to reduce forces in Europe was increasing, so were the opportunities—stemming from the growing superpower detente and the opening of negotiations on conventional arms reductions in March 1989. The possibility of U.S. troop cuts was placed firmly on the agenda by President Bush at the NATO Summit when he proposed an equal ceiling of 275,000 troops in Europe for the United States and the Soviet Union. This proposal was very shrewed in domestic political terms. Not only did it help forestall congressional pressure for unilateral troop cuts, but it also made it clear to the allies that the United States was determined to obtain its share of the burden relief that might be possible as a result of conventional arms control.

The events of 1989 added another dimension to the debate over the U.S. commitment to Western Europe. With the lessening of the Soviet threat and the movement toward German reunification, it appeared that the American presence in Western Europe was less crucial and more problematic than ever before. In his State of the Union address in January 1990, Bush proposed that U.S. and Soviet forces in Central Europe be cut to 195,000 (with another 30,000 U.S. personnel elsewhere in Europe). Many commentators have argued that this will be only the first phase of a more drastic reduction in the American military presence in Western Europe. In other words, by the mid- or late 1990s, there will be far fewer American troops in Europe, an eventuality that successive British governments have attempted to avert.

Nor is it only the American commitment to Western Europe that has been questioned. With the changes that have taken place in Europe, the future of NATO itself has become far less certain. As the profound nature of the changes in Eastern Europe in 1989 have been assimilated, there has been increasing discussion about the need for a new security architecture in Europe that transcends the old division between East and West. France in particular has argued that in the new Europe it is necessary to replace integrated military blocs by a pan-European security structure.

The implication of all this is that the traditional judgments and assumptions underlying British security policy in the postwar period are crumbling. Moreover, the problem is partly one of structure and partly one of strategy. Indeed, it is this dual nature of the challenge to British security policy that makes it so difficult to contain. One response to concerns over the weakening American commitment to the existing security structure, for example, would be to place more emphasis on the national strategy. Yet the same kind of developments that are challenging structure are also challenging both NATO and British strategy. Conversely the challenge to strategy would be less disturbing were it not being accompanied by challenges to the security structure. What, then, of the British response to these challenges?

ADJUSTING TO CHANGE

Adapting to the new security environment of the 1990s will be extremely difficult for Britain because the demands of structure, of strategy, and of accommodation are diverging to a far greater extent than ever before. A policy based on clear convictions about the Soviet threat, the continuing U.S. security guarantee, the primacy of the "special relationship," the role of nuclear weapons, and the contribution of detente and arms control becomes much more uncertain when each of these elements is changing. In 1989 the changes were momentous. Yet, British policy at the end of the 1980s was still based on familiar responses and traditional patterns. The difficulty is that although a stable policy framework is appropriate when change in the international environment is marginal, it is less suitable when the pace of change increases.

The British government's response to the end of the Cold War in Europe has had several key elements. The first—and most predictable—has been to emphasize that the forces of continuity should not be obscured by the forces of change. The 1990 White Paper on Defence emphasized the uncertainties attendant upon the reform process in Eastern Europe and the Soviet Union. As it noted, "change on this scale and at this pace is rarely a tidy and consistent process. We cannot foresee its development and we certainly cannot assume that it will stay smoothly on its original heading. . . . the very suddenness of recent upheavals, welcome as their initial impulse has been, carries its own warning. The range of possible outcomes remains wide and not all the possibilities are comfortable."[24] Moreover, even if the more dangerous outcomes are avoided, the statement identified what might be termed the existential nature of the Soviet threat: "despite all the changes, and despite the promises which President Gorbachev has made in evident good faith, the Soviet Union remains an enormous military power, with massive nuclear armoury."[25]

In other words, there is still a need to maintain the existing and familiar security framework in Europe. As the White Paper noted, "Defence arrangements . . . cannot sensibly be made the leading agent of political change."[26] Not surprisingly, therefore, the Thatcher government has been anxious to reassert the relevance of the familiar Atlantic framework against the claims of France and some elements in Germany that a new structure or security architecture is essential. Britain, along with the United States, has seen the Conference on Security and Cooperation in Europe as a possible supplement to, but certainly not a substitute for NATO. The preference for the Atlantic framework is partly a matter of pragmatism, the Alliance has worked in the past and still remains the most effective means of ensuring continued American involvement in European security affairs while also reflecting a conservative distrust for new and relatively untried institutions.

The British government has also continued to see nuclear weapons as retaining a crucial role in the security order in post-Cold War Europe. The 1990 White Paper reiterated that a superpower arms control agreement would not reduce the requirements for British strategic nuclear forces. "Even after a START Treaty had been implemented, our Trident force would still represent a smaller proportion of Soviet strategic nuclear warheads than did Polaris when it entered service. Reductions in US and Soviet strategic nuclear arsenals would have to go much further before we could even consider including the British deterrent in any future negotiations on strategic nuclear weapons."[27] Yet Britain remains crucially dependent on the United States for technological support in maintaining the efficacy of its strategic forces, and at some point the United States could see a possible conflict between continued support for Britain and progress toward deeper cuts in superpower strategic forces. Although the issue has been sidestepped in START as the superpowers move to START II, British and French strategic forces will loom much larger in the equation, and their pressures for their inclusion will become more insistent.

Indeed, one result of the changes in the strategic environment is that although France and Britain have very different positions on future European architectures, there are also pressures impelling them into a closer bilateral relationship. Both have residual concerns over the reemergence of a powerful united Germany in the center of Europe; both the Conservative government and the French government retain their faith in their independent nuclear deterrent forces. Anglo-French cooperation, therefore, could appear an attractive option. Indeed, in the early part of 1990 it appeared that the two governments were moving to enhance cooperation in several ways. Britain was considering acquiring the French stand-off air-to-surface missile, the ASLP, as a means of ensuring that its airborne nuclear weapons retained their efficacy. By exploring the possibility of Anglo-French nuclear cooperation, the government is hedging and trying to ensure that even if the familiar structure of European security collapses, the national strategy will remain intact. The difficulty is partly that British preferences about structure are very different to those of France and partly that Anglo-French cooperation has to overcome a residue of historical distrust between the two nations, a distrust accentuated by the continued British preference for cooperation with the United States.

In another words, the response of the Thatcher government to the changes in the security environment in Europe has been predictable and unimaginative. The process of responding to the changes, however, has only just begun. Consequently, there are many future choices that have to be made. These choices will be determined to a very significant degree by the party in office. As suggested above, a Conservative government will almost certainly be reluctant to move too fast down the arms control road, especially where this is seen as undermining the structural and strategic elements of British security. A Labour government, in contrast, would be more enthusiastic about arms control at all levels and would be much more ready to include Trident in strategic arms control negotiations. The Labour party has long argued that defense is only one component of security, which is best achieved through cooperation rather than confrontation with the Soviet Union. As such it could be more in tune with the detente policies of the European allies and the United States.

The nature of the government could also influence the British response to moves toward greater West European defense cooperation. The Thatcher government has always been hostile to a West European defense identity on the grounds that it could prove divisive in NATO. The argument has been that if the European allies are too self-reliant, this might convince the United States that it is no longer needed in Europe; at the very least it could provide a pretext for American troop withdrawals that the United States, for budgetary and political reasons, is anxious to take. Not surprisingly, therefore, Thatcher has been suspicious of moves in this direction and in the mid-1980s warned the French and Germans that their efforts to achieve a greater degree of cooperation were in danger of creating divisive substructures within the Atlantic Alliance.

How salient this issue will be, of course, remains uncertain. If the creation of the single European market provides an impetus to greater cooperation in defense and if the U.S. commitment to West European security is seriously in question, then greater European self-reliance in defense could appear a matter of urgency. In contrast, if the process of East–West accommodation continues without any major setbacks stemming, for example, from upheaval in the Soviet Union, the incentives for greater West European defense cooperation could decrease in spite of these other developments. In the event that moves are made to provide an alternative structure for maintaining West European security, however, a Labour government would be better placed than the Thatcher government to adopt policies that respond positively not only to new opportunities in East-West relations but also to the cooperative process among West European states. The postwar Labour government played a crucial role in the creation of the postwar security structure, and a post-Cold War Labour government in the 1990s would be very well placed to create new security structures that are based on close cooperation with Britain's West European allies and with the erstwhile adversary.

Whatever government is in power, though, the 1990s will almost certainly prove a difficult one for ministries of defense and the armed forces. Justifying level funding, let alone increased defense spending, is difficult in an environment when it appears that the Cold War has been won, that peace has broken out in Europe, and that arms control offers an opportunity to dispense with existing force structures. Indeed, budgetary constraints are already in evidence. As David Greenwood has pointed out, when expressed in constant prices, British defense spending for 1989–1990 is 8.5 percent less than actual expenditures in 1984–1985.[28] Furthermore, although the Thatcher government—which remains more sympathetic to military spending than any alternative government—has pledged to provide 5 percent more cash for defense for the early 1990s, this could prove insufficient to cover the increase in costs resulting from inflation. To compound the problem, the British armed forces confront demographic problems that are not entirely different from those facing West Germany. The declining birth rate of the 1960s and 1970s means that in the first half of the 1990s there will be much smaller pool of the 16- to 19-year-olds who provide three-quarters of all new recruits. This in turn means that in order to maintain force levels, the services have to attract a larger portion of this group. If they are to deal with the problem of manning and recruitment through the lean years of the 1990s, however, they will have to make military service more attractive. The more money that is spent on personnel, the less there will be for procurement in a period when major reequipment programs are in train.

The implications of all this is that during the 1990s the United Kingdom will find it more difficult than ever before to play the role of "good ally," at least in terms of its contribution to the Alliance. Yet this is not so urgent as in the past as in May 1990 the Alliance agreed formally to abandon the commitment to the 3 percent per annum real increase in defense spending. This reflected widespread public and parliamentary expectations that, in the aftermath of 1989, savings can safely be made in the defense budgets. Whereas the problems could be alleviated somewhat by higher rates of economic growth, defense spending in the first half of the 1990s is likely to be characterized by declining or at best static budgets and rising costs. In such circumstances, it will be very difficult for the United Kingdom to continue doing all that it has been doing in defense.

This became evident in the summer of 1990 when the Conservative government announced details of its Options for Change study, which in effect was a defense review by another name. The preliminary results of this review were outlined in the House of Commons by Secretary of State for Defence Tom King on July 25. Although King made it clear that the national review process will continue in tandem with the studies on NATO force structure and strategy that are underway at the Alliance level, even the preliminary results reflected a willingness on the part of the government to make hard decisions about priorities. It was revealed that the army will be cut by 40,000, from 160,000 to 120,000; the air force will be cut by 14,000, and the navy by 3,000. In addition, there will be a cut of 21,000 in civilian personnel. The forces in Germany will be cut from the current level of 55,000 to between 20,000 and 25,000 by 1995, while the number of air bases will be cut from 4 to 2 and the number of squadrons in RAF Germany from 15 to 9.

Although the cut in ground forces in Germany is the most drastic change in the British order of battle, the other services have not escaped. The surface navy will go from the current level of 48 frigates and destroyers to 40, largely through retirement of older vessels. The three carriers and the amphibious capability will remain, but the submarine fleet will be reduced from 27 to 16, although 12 of those remaining 16 will be nuclear powered. The navy, however, will still have the responsibility for the strategic deterrent force, and it was confirmed by King that the UK will be acquiring a fourth Trident boat rather than leaving the number at three.

There are several points about this announcement that are particularly worth noting. The first is that in some aspects it reflects a reversal of the priorities since the last attempt at establishing a clear hierarchy of roles and missions took place under John Nott in the early 1980s. At that time the navy was the prime candidate for reductions. Now it is the army which has to accept the largest share of the cutbacks. Although the surface navy is also being reduced, the decision to retain the three carriers and to create a special strategic reserve with a headquarters in Britain and a capacity to respond to out-of-area contingencies, reflects the shift of focus beyond Europe. Trends such as the spread of ballistic missile technology and chemical warfare capabilities mean that insecurity and instability in the Third World in the 1990s are likely to increase rather than diminish. This danger was dramatically underlined by the Persian Gulf crisis, which has reaffirmed the belief that the main threats to European security in the 1990s will originate outside Europe.

Although the review reflects the fact that many of the judgments and assumptions underlying British defense policy have been called into question, in certain respects it is rather cautious. More radical options were considered and rejected, and the implementation of the relatively modest measures that were announced was made conditional upon a CFE agreement. Even so, it is clear that the review represents the beginning of an effort to reappraise outmoded assumptions and adjust priorities in a way that is both rational and orderly. Yet this process has to go much further as Britain attempts to catch up to its NATO allies in responding to the changes that have taken place in the European security system. The task is not an easy one. The "bonfire of the certainties" has proved very uncomfortable for defense policy makers and planners. Moreover, the difficulties are exacerbated by the complex interplay between the choices that are made at the military level regarding the interservice balance and the choices that are made at the political level about whether security is best achieved through a national West

European, pan-European, or Atlantic framework. Formidable as these problems may be, however, they have to be confronted. In a world where the pace of political change has transformed the security environment and the security agenda, there are no easy options and no escape from painful dilemmas. British defense policy makers and planners have to recognize that the decisions of the 1990s will be more momentous than any of the choices that have been made since the 1940s.

NOTES

1. I am grateful to Nicholas Wheeler, The University of Hull, for this point.
2. This is discussed more fully in B. White, "Britain and the Rise of Detente," in S. Smith and R. Crockatt, eds., *The Cold War: Past and Present* (London: Allen and Unwin, 1987) pp. 91–109.
3. Ibid., p. 99.
4. Quoted in Ibid., p. 109.
5. *Statement on the Defence Estimates 1986,* Vol. 1 Cmnd.9763-1 (London: HMSO, 1986), p. 2.
6. Ibid., p. 6.
7. See J. Stromseth, *The Origins of Flexible Response* (London: Macmillan, 1988), especially Chapter 8.
8. *British Defence Policy 1988–89* (London: Ministry of Defence, 1988), p. 21.
9. The term "managerial arms control" is used in Lawrence Freedman, *Arms Control: Management or Reform?* Chatham House Paper 31 (London: Routledge, 1986).
10. This paragraph rests heavily on C. McInnes *Trident, The Only Option?* (London: Brassey's, 1980), p. 17.
11. Ibid., P. 31
12. M. Dollon, "Britain" in M. Dilon (ed.), *Defence Policymaking: A Comparative Analysis* (Leicester: Leicester University Press, 1988), p. 15.
13. Ibid, p. 15.
14. P. Towle, *MPs and Defence: A Survey of Parlimentary Knowledge and Opinion,* Occasional Paper 36 (London: Institute for Defence and Strategic Studies, August 1988), p. 18.
15. P. Sabin, *The Third World War Scare in Britain* (London: Macmillan, 1986), p. 47.
16. I have drawn heavily here on a paper by M. Clarke, "British Perspectives on the Soviet Union," which contains an excellent analysis of British opinion about the Soviet Union.
17. See B. McNair, *Images of the Enemy* (London: Routledge, 1988), pp. 47, 196–198.
18. Towle, *MPs and Defence,* pp. 17–18.
19. P. Hennessy, "Little Cause Found for Optimism over the Cold War Heartlands," *The Independent,* May 23, 1988.
20. Ibid.
21. Ibid.

22. Text of speech by Sir Geoffrey Howe at the Wehrkunde Conference in Munich, January 28, 1989, reprinted as Appendix 12 of the House of Commons Foreign Affairs Committee *First Report on Eastern Europe and the Soviet Union*, Session 1988–89 (London: HMSO, March 1989).

23. See *Statement on the Defence Estimates 1989*, Vol. 1 Cmnd.675-I (London: HMSO, 1989), p. 1.

24. *Statement on the Defence Estimates 1990*, Vol. 1 CM1022-I (London: HMSO, April 1990), p. 16.

25. Ibid.

26. Ibid.

27. Ibid, p. 14.

28. Paper presented at conference organized by Department of War Studies, King's College, London, July 19–20, 1989. The analysis of economic and demographic constraints draws heavily on David Greenwood's work in this area.

Chapter 6

Italy

Ian Lesser

Consideration of Italy's place in the Atlantic Alliance suggests a number of
stock images: the loyal ally with limited resources; the democratic and increasingly prosperous ally that, nonetheless, seems to be in a perpetual state of political and economic crisis; the peripheral or neglected ally with aspirations toward
a wider role in European, Atlantic, and Mediterranean affairs. There is a good
deal of truth in all these images, yet taken at face value they do not adequately
reflect the character of Italy's role and future within the Alliance. After almost
40 years in which Italian attitudes toward NATO could reasonably be understood on the basis of such images, the security debate in Italy has become more
active and complex. To a large extent, this has been a consequence of developments that have affected the Alliance as a whole, including controversies over
German reunification, INF (intermediate-range nuclear force) modernization
and elimination and, not least, Mikhail Gorbachev's extraordinary diplomatic
and reform initiatives, and the political revolution in Eastern Europe.

The growing assertiveness of Italian foreign and defense policy reflects a natural desire for an international role commensurate with the country's level of
economic development; it also reflects the four-decade transition from a defeated and politically constrained power to one with the status of a central, if not
entirely influential, member of the Atlantic Alliance and the European Economic Community (EC). One consequence of the new attention to security questions is that certain tensions that have always existed in some form are becoming more visible and are the subject of more explicit discussion, with important
implications for policy toward the two postwar pillars of Italian external relations, NATO and the EC. The first of these tensions concerns the balance
between Atlantic and European relations; the second embraces the competition
between Italy's role in NATO's central region and the rediscovery of traditional

interests, and the perception of new threats in the Mediterranean. The nature of these tensions is such that they are unlikely to be "resolved," and their continued existence will play essential role in defining Italian relations within the Alliance.

Overall, future Italian policy toward NATO is unlikely to represent a radical departure from past behavior—Italy will almost certainly remain a loyal and cooperative ally, but the tensions outlined above and increasing Italian assertiveness on security questions will make the course of Italian policy more difficult to predict in detail and Italian support for U.S. and NATO initiatives less automatic.

The purpose of this chapter is to assess the prospects for Italy in the Atlantic Alliance through the mid-1990s based on certain assumptions about the external and internal environments—that is, the context in which Italian attitudes and policies will be formed. Proceeding from these assumptions, the most likely direction of Italian policy with regard to a range of important Alliance issues is explored. Finally, some possible variations on the likely case—"wild cards" and their implications—are suggested.

KEY ASSUMPTIONS

The following assumptions are offered as a departure point and a guide to the principle external and internal factors likely to drive Italian policy toward NATO in the period under discussion.

Soviet Policy

In the very near term, it is likely that Soviet policy will continue to be directed toward a relaxation of political and military tension in Europe, encouraging a reduced perception of threat, and holding out the prospect of new trade and security relationships between East and West. The prospects for the continuation or acceleration of this trend over the next five to 10 years are far less certain. The primary question is whether Gorbachev will remain in power or whether he will be replaced by a reactionary leadership. Beyond this and assuming that Gorbachev manages to maintain his position, there is the question of the extent to which his economic and political initiatives will be successful and what the consequences of this will be. In the extreme case, a period of profound and suc-cessful restructuring of the Soviet economy might occur (accompanied by a tac-tical detente), after which the Soviet Union would emerge as a more capable and aggressive power ready to resume political and strategic competition with the West on more favorable terms. A more likely alternative would be a continuing struggle toward economic reform, accompanied by structural changes of a more or less permanent nature in the character of the Soviet system and its external relations. Any reversal of the Soviet withdrawal from Eastern Europe could be accomplished only at great political and economic cost and would surely bring with it a renewed perception of threat in Western Europe.

Soviet policy toward the Mediterranean is unlikely to be marked by real activism as long as both domestic and Central and Eastern European developments remain the focus of concern. Efforts to improve the Soviet Union's political and security relationships in the region might be made, including access to better naval facilities, should suitable opportunities present themselves. The size and activities of the Soviet fleet in the Mediterranean have essentially leveled off at their 1979 peaks, and barring a major regional crisis, it is unlikely that this presence will be increased.[1]

U.S. Policy

The presence of moderate Atlanticists in key foreign and defense policy positions is unlikely to signal any substantial reduction in the U.S. political commitment to Europe or the determination to remain a European power, although almost certainly at lower levels of military presence. It is likely that the United States will press ahead with strategic and conventional force reduction efforts, as well as with short-range nuclear modernization initiatives. The latter will face very strong opposition from many quarters, and indefinite postponement of any decision on this question—if not outright abandonment— is the most probable outcome. Overall, the approach to developments in the Soviet Union is likely to be characterized by caution and may continue to be rather reactive.

At the same time, there will be growing pressure from Congress on the issues of defense spending and burden sharing in Europe and elsewhere. This will be driven not only by the deficit problem and detente in Europe, but by uncertainties surrounding the future U.S.–European trade relations before and after 1992. To the extent that negotiating with the EC bureaucracy for access to European markets may be difficult and unappealing, bilateral "portals" will become much more attractive and Italy could prove to be a good candidate for such an approach.

U.S. defense budgets will almost certainly decrease substantially in real terms, and this will probably have a pronounced effect on force structure, including naval forces. the U.S. naval presence in the Mediterranean is unlikely to be strongly affected, however, as the perception of risks emanating from the Persian Gulf, the Middle East, and North Africa continue to demand a substantial presence in the region. The Soviet pressure to include naval forces in conventional force reduction talks will continue to be resisted—probably, but not inevitably, with success.

Unlikely, but not altogether impossible, variations on the above scenario would include very substantial troop withdrawals from Europe (beyond the conventional force cuts already proposed), serious bilateral or Alliance-wide political crises resulting from an out-of-area dispute, a "trade war" with EC, or a major recession followed by a substantial strategic retrenchment.

Policies of Other NATO Member States

The Italian security relationship with the United States has historically provided the crucial bilateral context for Italian relations within NATO, but the behavior of other Alliance members in Europe will play an increasingly central role in determining Italian policies and attitudes. The influence of the European environment will be particularly pronounced in two areas: European defense cooperation and the movement toward a single European market.

Joint European defense initiatives—and particularly Franco-German cooperation—will most likely continue to be pursued with varying degrees of vigor depending upon the nature of German reunification, the perceived health of the U.S. security commitment to Europe, and the status of conventional and nuclear arms control negotiations. Whether Franco–German arrangements will proceed along lines that will lend themselves to broader Italian participation is also unclear. This will undoubtedly be an area of concern for the Italian leadership, which is supportive of European initiatives but uncomfortable with the notion of Franco–German collaboration alone. In this sense, a broad-based security role for the European Community, and bilateral relations with the United States represent the principle counters to German or French domination of the European security environment. Another less prominent but potentially important "hedge" would be expanded cooperation among the southern region allies, along the lines already being pursued by Italy, France, and Spain in the area of maritime surveillance.[2] Additional Mediterranean initiatives of this sort can be expected over the next five to 10 years; they will probably be designed to promote defense-industrial development as much as improved defense capability.

Without attempting to predict the precise extent to which Europe will represent a single market after 1992, it is likely that substantial progress will eventually be made toward this goal. The very high degree of Italian economic interdependence, together with very marked differences in its financial and commercial structures, suggests that the post-1992 environment will pose serious challenge for Italian policy, not least because Italian attitudes toward European integration are intimately bound up with broader political and security concerns.[3]

In the absence of another shock on the order of Czechoslovakia or Afghanistan, Europe—with the possible exception of Britain—is likely to be much less cautious than the United States in responding to developments in the Soviet

attempt to make a virtue of necessity). In this sort of budgetary environment, there will be some question of the Italian ability to proceed with expensive modernization programs, despite assurances to the contrary. Indeed, there have been reports that the 10-year, $22-billion modernization plan maybe cut by at least half. The government has stated, however, that it will make efforts to insulate key programs that "cannot be compromised," including those that have required special legislation (for example, naval aviation) or that are multinational in character (EFA, Patriot, the NATO Standard Frigate, and satellite communications and surveillance programs).[19] The most likely scenario with regard to Italian conventional defense improvement will be a firm verbal commitment in principle, coupled with very selective modernization in areas with clear defense industrial benefits and/or with cooperative aspects. Economic constraints and the widespread belief that detente in Europe and conventional force reduction talks will render any general expansion of conventional capability unnecessary will be the key factors in this regard.

The debate over conventional strategy in Italy—to the extent that one exists —will continue to focus on the tension between defense or collective security to the northeast and defense in the Mediterranean. To a significant extent, this is as much a political dilemma as a strategic one, a perception reinforced by the apparent evaporation of the Warsaw Pact threat across Italy's borders. The issue is not so much one of making a "choice" between central region security and Mediterranean defense—Italy will continue to have evident interests in both areas—but of managing the very different coalition aspects of security in each region. Thus a focus on the central region brings with it a greater degree of involvement in the core concerns of the Alliance and, potentially, European defense cooperation. In contrast, a southern focus could suggest an even closer strategic relationship with the United States, with all that such a relationship implies. In the remote case of a general war with the Soviet Union, the defense of Italian interests in the central Mediterranean would clearly depend on operations elsewhere (for example, at the Dardenelles and in the Suez Canal), for which Italy must rely on allied, and particularly U.S., forces.[20] In non-NATO contingencies, the actions of Italy's principal ally can just as easily be the cause of political friction, as was the case with the U.S. airlift to Israel in 1973 or with the Sigonella incident in 1986.

Italy has already made clear that, as a matter of general principle, it will not permit the use of U.S. bases on Italian land for non-NATO purposes (emergency cooperation is not strictly excluded). On the basis of past Italian refusals in 1973 and again in the operations against Libya it would be unrealistic to assume that this position will change. Indeed, the reiteration of this policy has been a centerpiece of the new Italian "assertiveness" on security questions, the only serious opposition to which is found in strong Atlanticist circles within the Republican and Liberal parties. In contrast, access to Italian facilities in any NATO-related contingency, including operations in the Mediterranean to counter Soviet operations elsewhere, can be regarded as certain.

Nuclear Forces and Deterrence

Apart from the broadly based tradition of support of arms control and disarmament referred to earlier, the Italian approach to the role of nuclear weapons and nuclear deterrence in NATO strategy is not driven by particularly deep political and philosophical forces. In this, as in many other Alliance matters, the Italian attitude has been characterized by a high degree of strategic pragmatism. Two pints bear mentioning in this context. First, the trend toward the "conventionalization" of NATO strategy was greeted with reservation by members of the Italian defense and foreign policy elite because they perceived the nuclear dimension of flexible response as having a unifying effect within the Alliance, binding together the security fate of Central Europe and the flanks. From the Italian perspective, it has been essential not only to assure the strategic coupling of the United States to Europe, but also to maintain the coupling between deterrences in the central and southern regions. Nuclear weapons in Europe do this very well; conventional forces alone do not provide the same confidence. Second, strengthening conventional forces to the point where they might begin to assume the deterrent role provided by the nuclear weapons would be extremely expensive and, as practical matter, beyond Italian means. Moreover, nuclear and conventional forces are in no sense equivalent in their ability to encourage a perception of shared risk within the Alliance. The current environment of uncertainly in Europe has bolstered the Italian interest in preserving the nuclear dimension of deterrence with its strong transatlantic associations.

Nuclear issues have been excellent vehicle for the Italian desire to be helpful within NATO without taking on expensive new commitments. Such a policy probably does have its limits, however, and they are likely to be defined by the Italian desire to stay within the mainstream of Alliance opinion on nuclear questions. Thus Italy can be expected to support the continued presence of nuclear systems in Europe in some form (perhaps at a reduced level, perhaps only air-based—but not complete elimination, for preference). Yet Italy probably would not be forthcoming as in 1979 on the issue of nuclear modernization, including any follow-on to Lance, unless the decision was really in the balance within NATO, and this is not likely to be the case.[21] The prospect of substantial and asymmetrical cuts in conventional forces would, of course, encourage support for early negotiations on a third "zero" embracing short-range missiles.

Although there has not been a great deal of interest in ATBM (antitactical ballistic missile) programs among Italian political parties or defense figures, this situation may change over the next few years with growing evidence that several states around the Mediterranean, including Libya, are acquiring ballistic missiles of a range that would threaten Italian territory. They accompanying threat of chemical and nuclear proliferation will serve to increase this concern. Participation in SDI (Strategic Defense Initiative) research has been more divisive issue, but even here, only the PCI and Radicals have been seriously opposed. To the extent that ATBM can be divorced from SDI and treated as an air defense effort, a more active role will become possible.

Economic and Defense-Industrial Relations

Italy has traditionally been a firm supporter of European economic and political integration, having seen greater European coordination on international questions as a means of promoting its own role in many areas. In this sense, the EEC, not unlike NATO, serves as an important political "club" membership that confers a sense of influence and prestige along with more practical advantages. Italy has made a consistent point of objecting to the discussion of key economic and political issues in restricted forums, such as the Guadeloupe summit in 1979, that do not provide for Italian participation. This remains a point of particular sensitivity and one that has emerged again in connection with the 2+4 discussion on German reunification. Italy will continue to be wary of European political and economic initiatives that are not firmly anchored in the EEC structure, and Italian politicians have also spoken out strongly against the notion of a German hegemony, or Franco–German or Franco–German–British directorate within the EC.[22] Italian attitudes in this area, even (perhaps especially) after 1992, will continue to be characterized by the formulation "for Europe, against European coalitions." Not surprisingly, Italian policy makers have expressed concern over the potential consequences of German reunification for the future of European integration (possibly slowed, at worst dominated by German economic and political power). With regard to the Community's relations with Eastern Europe, Italy will inevitably prefer deepening to broadening.

One probable consequence of 1992—the accelerated movement toward greater European economic integration—is that the distractions between the political, economic, and security dimensions of Italy's relations within Europe will become increasingly blurred. This, in turn, is likely to complicate the Italian preference for an evolutionary development of European institutions that does not threaten the Alliance relationship with the United States. The specter of European protectionism, real or imagined, that has already begun to affect perceptions about Europe and the Atlantic Alliance in the United States will be an issue of particular importance through the mid-1990s and beyond. Italy currently runs a substantial trade surplus with the United States, and the Italian position on future EC trade policy, though nonprotectionist with regard to the movement of goods within the EC, may well be quite protectionist overall. The principal Italian—indeed, West European—concern in this regard will probably be Japan, but measures in this area would also have clear implications for trade with the United States.[23]

One alternative might be a scenario in which the United States, if frustrated in its attempts to negotiate unencumbered access to the European market in Brussels, might seek out bilateral "portals" in Europe. Thus even if the broader trade climate worsens, there may still be scope for greater cooperation between U.S. enterprises and the Italian private sector, much of which is very well equipped to compete in this new European environment and will regard 1992 as a great opportunity. (The real problems of adjustment after 1992 will be in the extremely cumbersome Italian public sector.)[24] Overall, however, Italy is unlikely to oppose any European movement toward protectionist policies vis-à-vis the United States, a movement that could be expected to have serious consequences for Alliance cohesion as well as for the climate of U.S.-Italian relations.

The Italian defense industry is easily the most highly developed in NATO's southern region and is competitive in many areas with its counterparts in Britain, France, Germany, and the United States. The Italian government has been broadly supportive of NATO armaments cooperation and standardization efforts; one can expect this cooperation to continue, particularly as Italian arms sales in the Third World face new constraints. Italy, once the fourth largest arms exporter, has slipped to twelfth over the past few years, largely as a result of domestic political pressure and government restrictions. The decline in traditional exports to the Third World is likely to lead to an even greater emphasis on joint projects, along the pattern of EFA and the Brazilian–Italian AMX fighter-bomber.

European Defense Cooperation

The Italian attitude toward European defense cooperation—the development of a European pillar within the Alliance— is in some respects analogous to the Italian position on European economic and political integration: European initiatives are widely favored; coalitions or blocs within Europe are not. More specifically, Italian concerns regarding future European defense are likely to focus first on the degree to which such efforts represent an alternative to the bilateral security relationship with the United States (that is, Europe versus the Atlantic),

Chapter 7

The Low Countries

Richard A. Bitzinger

Belgium and the Netherlands, largely by virtue of their small size and populations, have never been major actors within the Atlantic Alliance. Yet their proximity to the central front in Germany and, in particular, their ports, airfields, and other critical lines of communications mean that, should war ever break out in Europe, they would play important roles in the successful defense of the West. Both Belgium and the Netherlands commit nearly all of their armed forces to the defense of Germany. Their ground forces comprise almost half of the Northern Army Group (NORTHAG), and two of its corps sectors; their air forces make up nearly 40 percent of NATO's 2nd Allied Tactical Air Force (2ATAF). For two countries whose combined populations total less than 25 million, this is not an inconsiderable contribution.

In addition, the Low Countries have long been some of the more dependable partners of the United States and NATO. Today, however, the security policy of Belgium and the Netherlands is in the process of undergoing significant change, much to the detriment of this traditional relationship. The seeds for this change extend back a decade or more. At the same time, the seismic developments currently unfolding in Europe are having the effect of accelerating and exacerbating this process.

DOMESTIC DEVELOPMENTS AND THE SECURITY CONSENSUS

Since 1949, Belgium and the Netherlands have both enjoyed a broad domestic consensus on national security policy and on their countries' roles within the Atlantic Alliance. Briefly, the main elements of the Belgian and Dutch security consensus can be seen as:

The Netherlands[1]
- The preeminence of NATO interests over other policy goals.
- The acceptance of U.S. leadership of the Alliance.
- The need for West German participation within NATO.
- An emphasis on strategic deterrence.

Belgium[2]
- Loyalty as an ally.
- The provision of adequate but "cost-effective" national security measures.
- Solidarity within the Alliance.
- An "influential role" for the smaller NATO powers in the Alliance decision-making process.
- The strengthening of Western Europe's voice within NATO.
- An emphasis on Belgium's role as a bridge-builder between East and West.

The Belgians and Dutch share several basic characteristics. By far the most important of these is the priority that the Low Countries have long placed on NATO and membership within the Atlantic Alliance. Both countries, in rejecting their old, prewar stands on (largely unarmed) neutrality, came to believe that their security effectively could be guaranteed only within a strong, cohesive military alliance. NATO interests, therefore, should take precedent over other policy goals, even national interests. In effect, these countries were asserting that there was no such thing as a national security policy, only Alliance security policy.

In conjunction, the Low Countries traditionally emphasized the need for a politically and militarily strong NATO, for a high degree of Alliance solidarity, and for continued Belgian and Dutch loyalty as an ally, in both word and deed. This, in turn, meant support for U.S. leadership within NATO and a conscious effort to cleave as closely as possible to the will of the United States when it came to security policy and defense doctrine. In particular, such a stance meant an acceptance not only of NATO nuclear doctrine (and the U.S. nuclear umbrella) but also a willingness to follow the U.S. lead on nuclear strategy, including the deployment of nuclear weapons on Belgian and Dutch soil and adherence to flexible response doctrine.

Where Belgian and Dutch security policy has differed, it has generally been at the margins. Even then, it was mainly a matter of degree. Belgium, for example, despite its emphasis on being a loyal ally, has generally attempted to play a more active and influential role within the Alliance, particularly when it came to promoting detente and arms control. At the same time, the Belgian approach in such endeavors was traditionally cautious and generally well confined within the NATO framework. Whereas Belgium sought to serve as a gentle catalyst for detente and arms control, it took pains not to get too far out ahead of the United

States in these areas.[3]

For their part, the Dutch usually have been more willing to play the part of a junior member within NATO and to take a more passive stance toward decision making within the Western Alliance. Throughout the first 20 years or so of NATO's existence, the Netherlands almost totally subordinated national goals to NATO and U.S. security policies. In fact, it was even argued that "national 'interest' [was] not a concept of much relevance to Dutch foreign policy," and that Dutch security policy was, for all practical purposes, virtually nonexistent.[4] During this period, therefore, few NATO initiatives originated from the Netherlands, and, on the whole, Dutch politicians generally saw the process of detente, arms control, and nuclear policy making as being largely the domain of the United States.

Overall, therefore, the Low Countries historically have placed a high priority on a strong, unified Western Alliance, led by the United States and ultimately backed up by the U.S. show of nuclear arms. Moreover, the security consensus in both countries cut across a broad swath of the domestic political spectrum, from the far Right to center Left and including a large portion of the general population, whereas the particulars of defense policy decision making were a matter left to these nations' political elites.

All this makes the changes in Belgian and Dutch security politics in recent years all the more dramatic. Whereas overall security policy—for example, defining one's security within the Alliance—in these countries perhaps has not changed much, the apparent decline of traditional consensus around certain important ingredients of security policy has been a crucial development. The old predictability NATO once enjoyed regarding Belgian and Dutch defense commitments has been in doubt for some time now, and what identifiable trends there have been lately are not encouraging.

Social, economic, and political factors can be seen to account for this shift in the Belgian and Dutch security consensus. The upheavals of the 1960s that engulfed the rest of Western Europe did not leave the Low Countries unaffected. In some ways, the effects of "postindustrialization" hit these two countries harder than others in the West. In turn, they have left their imprint on current Belgian and Dutch defense and security policies.

DEPILLARIZATION AND THE POLARIZATION OF THE POLITICAL PROCESS

Until about the mid-1960s, Belgian and Dutch society and politics were noteworthy for being centered around certain traditional institutions. In the Netherlands, these were called "pillars" (zuilen), and included in the church, the labor movement, and other ideological subsocieties.[5] Each country basically contained the same three main pillars: Christian (the Roman Catholic church in Belgium and both the Dutch Reformed and Catholic churches in the Netherlands), Socialist/Labor, and Liberal (comprising secular or nonreligious opponents to the Socialist bloc and, contrary to its name, occupying the right wing on the national political spectrum). As the term implies, these pillars formed the basis for the social and political life of these two countries. Not only political parties but trade unions, schools, newspapers, broadcasting, hospitals, and even soccer teams were organized along the lines of these pillars. If one was born into a Catholic family, for example, he or she would most likely attend a Catholic school, join a Catholic trade union, read a Catholic newspaper or listen to a Catholic-aligned radio station, and vote for a Catholic religious party. Ties to one's own pillar were very strong, and there might be only minimal contact with those members of other pillars. The different social groups were, as one person put it, "equal but separate."[6]

Interestingly, whereas this led to an extremely fragmented society, politics in the Low Countries were actually remarkably stable, largely because of the consensus-oriented nature of the political cultures of these two countries. The political elites of the three major pillars—who, in turn, dominated the political realm of their respective nations—were aware that the extreme factionalization of society would not allow for effective government if they could not come to some kind of accommodation among themselves.[7] Politics could never be "winner-take-all," and instead they would have to reconcile their differences if governance were to be a feasible proposition. Hence, consultation, negotiation, and compromise became key ingredients in Belgian and Dutch politics.[8]

The emphasis in Belgian and Netherlands politics has traditionally been on constructing broad alliances across the social and political spectrum for government policies. It was possible, for example, to construct coalition governments among the three major political groups (Christian Democrat, Socialist/Labor, and Liberal) with almost surprising fluidity. In addition, governing coalitions usually sought out opposition opinion and advice when making important decisions on legislation and national policy.

Not surprisingly, continuity was a major feature of this method of governing. Whatever the composition of the coalition in power, national policy tended to vary little from government to government. With such a high priority on the need for consensus and governability, government policy tended to revolve around a few broad, basic concerns that all the major parties could agree upon, with a particular emphasis on the preservation of the status quo. In particular, this included the continuation and expansion of the welfare state (with its benefits parceled out roughly proportionately to—and through—the three major pillars)[9], government subsidy of the domestic economy, and especially support for the Western alliance.

Beginning around the mid-1960s, however, this rather cozy system began to break down. Profound social changes undermined the pillars' traditional loyalties and, in turn, their role as harbingers of social identity. Postwar affluence, greater social and geographic mobility, and the "internationalization" of their culture (in particular, through the introduction and popularization of that great social homogenizer, television) weakened the old isolationism of the pillar system. A decline in church attendance, plus the gradual liberalization and secularization of society, undercut and reduced the influence of the confessional pillars. Meanwhile, the welfare state established a rival, state-run institution of education, health care, old age support, etc., running from cradle to grave that also helped weaken the influence of the traditional structures of society.

In Belgium the rise of regional/linguistic differences in the 1960s compounded these problems. By the late 1950s, the Dutch-speaking Flemish majority in the northern part of the country, which had historically been economically and politically subordinate to the French-speaking Walloon minority in the south, was on the ascendancy. This was due in no small part to the growth of services and new, high technology industry in the north, whereas Wallonia was left with declining coal and steel interests. Flanders expanded economically, but so did Flemish "nationalism" and the feeling that Belgian Francophones wielded a disproportionate influence in Brussels. This, in turn, prompted a Walloon counterresponse, and the 1960s witnessed the emergence of both Flemish and Walloon sectarian political parties.[10] Regional/linguistic centrifugal forces broke the traditional unitary political structure of the country; in its place arose a quasifederalist system, with a central government and a myriad of regional and linguistically based assemblies in Flanders, Wallonia, and Brussels. Even the three major political parties split along linguistic lines, with separate Dutch- and French-speaking Christian Democratic, Socialist, and Liberal parties.[11]

As the traditional pillars—and, in Belgium, the unitary model of government—began to weaken, a hybrid system, combining elements of the old structure with the emerging societal changes, has gradually formed to take its place. The most long-lasting effects of depillarization, however, are that the old system of consultative and consensual government has been gravely shaken and the spirit of compromise "partly abandoned."[12] In addition, the depillarization of politics has led to voter "dealignment," and party partisanship (e.g., a trade unionist voting Labor or Socialist, or an avid churchgoer voting for the Christian bloc) is no longer as strong or as automatic as it was previously. As a result, the Belgian and Dutch political systems are today much more unstable than before, and governing coalitions are much more fragile than in the 1950s and 1960s.

Therefore, the political process in both Belgium and the Netherlands has become increasingly polarized. Depillarization has led to a decline in voter allegiances and to a more volatile political environment. New political parties with few links to the old pillars have sprung up in both countries, such as the regional/linguistic parties in Belgium, the "Democrats '66" in the Netherlands (which was formed in protest to the Dutch system of accommodation politics), or the new Green movements.

Moreover, a more adversarial style of politics began to emerge in the late 1960s and early 1970s. The rise of the "New Left" within the Belgian Socialist party and particularly within the Dutch Labor party (PvdA) radicalized these moderate social democratic movements. Furthermore, the emphasis of the New Left on change and political confrontation made it more difficult for these parties to pursue consensus politics. This, in turn, aided the rise of the "nonconfessional" Right, and the Liberal parties in both Belgium and the Netherlands not only have grown stronger but have responded in kind to the increasing radicalism of the mainstream Left by adopting more rigid conservative principles. In Belgium this political polarization was further complicated by the schisms between the major parties along linguistic lines.

Economic Dislocation

As elsewhere throughout the Western world, the Low Countries were hard hit by the two OPEC oil shocks of the 1970s and the ensuing global recessions. In both Belgium and the Netherlands, economic conditions in the late 1970s and early 1980s deteriorated significantly compared to the booming 1950s and 1960s. Meager (or even negative) economic growth, coupled with rapidly rising unemployment (well into double digits by the early 1980s), inflation, and yawning government deficits plagued both countries. At the same time, taxes remained high and public spending on social services continued to rise, whereas organized labor's refusal to accept wage moderation, simply placed additional burdens on the public purse.

Draconian measures inaugurated in the early 1980s with the intention of reigning in government spending, cutting taxes and wages, lowering the deficit, and encouraging growth met with mixed success. Certainly the rise in public expenditures was largely halted, and inflation came down greatly. Moreover, the GNPs of both countries actually started to rise. However, unemployment still remains very high (11 percent in Belgium and 12 percent in the Netherlands, as of early 1990). In addition, given a general unwillingness to cut back much further on the welfare state, it is hard to see how the central governments of the Low Countries can hope to take more out of their budgets for social programs.[13]

EFFECT ON THE TRADITIONAL
SECURITY CONSENSUS

All these factors—social, political, and economic—have had at least some impact on the undermining of the longstanding security consensus within Belgium and the Netherlands. Societal depillarization (and, in Belgium, linguistic-based regionalism) has destabilized the traditional, elite-based process of decision making and governance. With the decline of these old institutions, establishments, norms, and processes, therefore, the political system has not only become more contentious but more unpredictable, whereas government policy making has in itself become much more rancorous.

Nowhere has this political polarization and more confrontational style been more strongly felt than in the recent debate over security policy. As a result of their shift to the Left, the defense policies of the Belgian Socialists and Dutch Laborites have become much more critical of NATO and U.S. security policy and of their own country's role within the Alliance. The process of dialogue, detente, and arms control, begun in the late 1960s, was wholeheartedly embraced by the PS/SP and PvdA in the Low Countries. When the Cold War appeared to reassert itself in the late 1970s/early 1980s, they often tended to blame Western (and particularly U.S.) actions. In turn, they took it upon themselves to try to reinvigorate detente and to press for better relations between East and West. As such, the Socialist and Labor groups became increasingly negative to NATO military programs, particularly nuclear, as it was felt that these would sour efforts at detente. In addition, they opposed higher defense spending and efforts to upgrade the Belgian and Dutch armed forces, calling instead upon the West to pursue new initiatives, including arms control, to reduce East–West tensions and improve bloc relations.

At the same time, the burgeoning peace movements injected a new actor in the security consensus process, complementing the growing polarization within the political arena. Not only did the peace movements introduce and bolster new security and defense concepts, they greatly increased the public's involvement in the domestic security debates in Belgium and the Netherlands.

This polarization and radicalization of security policy is best revealed in the rancorous debate over nuclear modernization in the late 1970s and early 1980s. Perhaps the most noticeable effect of political destabilization during this period, for example, was the breakdown of the broad consensus over nuclear weapons—first over plans to introduce enhanced radiation weapons (the neutron bomb) in Western Europe, and then over the decision to deploy new intermediate-range nuclear forces (INF). These programs, especially the INF dual-track decision, split the old Belgian and Dutch security consensus asunder. The

Socialist/Labor group generally steadfastly opposed deployment of cruise missiles on Belgian and Dutch soil,[14] whereas the Liberals were usually fully in favor of the dual-track decision. Sandwiched in the middle, the Christian parties were internally divided between a traditionally pro-NATO majority and a small but powerful pacifist section (largely influenced by church-run peace movements in these countries).

The internal debate over these new nuclear forces was unprecedented in the postwar history of the Low Countries. So damaged was the defense consensus on this issue that the governments of Belgium and the Netherlands were unable to secure final approval for the stationing of the missiles on their territory until the mid-1980s. The breakdown over nuclear policy soon spread to other areas of the security debate, particularly the funding of national defense and the acquisition of new conventional weaponry, such as new combat aircraft.

For its part, the severe economic situations of the Low Countries and the corresponding demand to reduce government expenditures have led to tremendous pressures to cut the budgets of the Belgian and Dutch armed forces. The political resistance to further pruning of social spending and the general reluctance to raise taxes, together with growing polarization over security, have made the defense budget a much more contentious item in central government planning and expenditures. Many have come to view defense cuts as a means to reduce government spending and lower the public sector deficit without further gutting favored social programs. At the very least, others argue, the military should share in the country's overall austerity situation.

Furthermore, military spending has become a touchstone of the widening and polarized debate over security policy. Obviously, where one stands on defense spending depends on where one sits on the security policy; with the collapse of traditional security consensus in these countries, however, the chairs are now farther apart. No longer are defense budgets passed with minimum of debate, and calls for increased defense spending, à la NATO's Long-Term Defense Plan, have met with stiff resistance. The battle over nuclear weapons or conventional modernization programs has also carried over into the debate over military expenditures, such as over the issue of infrastructure payments to support INF deployment.

These political and economic developments have made defense policy decision making a much more public and contentious issue than it was previously. In turn, it is more difficult to maintain the traditional consensus on security policy. With the widening of the security debate and with the defense budget coming under much closer scrutiny, both domestic defense policy and overall NATO doctrine became a more open process, subject to wider pressures from more disparate interests.

Conceptually, the public's and domestic elites' embrace of several principles of the traditional security consensus remains intact. Support for the Western Alliance remains high, as does the acceptance of an adequate national defense and the need to fulfill one's commitments to NATO. Even the idea of nuclear deterrence, especially strategic deterrence, is probably not as divisive an issue as is commonly thought. However, it can no longer be said that security policy in both Belgium and the Netherlands is still a low key affair worked out among largely like-minded political elites. The injection of new actors and new ideas into the debate has clearly shaken the old security consensus and is sure to shake it some more as the Low Countries attempt to deal with domestic and Alliance-wide security issues in the 1990s.

RECENT TRENDS IN BELGIAN AND DUTCH DEFENSE EFFORTS

Defense Spending

The government austerity programs inaugurated in both countries during the 1980s has meant some lean years for the Belgian and Dutch armed forces. After growing gradually but consistently throughout the 1970s, Belgian defense expenditures peaked in 1981; since then, military spending has fallen or stagnated. As a percentage of the national wealth, military spending has hovered around 3 percent of the GNP since 1965. In the late 1970s and early 1980s, this actually rose to around 3.3 percent. However, this has since dropped off; and by the late 1980s, defense spending amounted to roughly 2.7 percent of the nation's GNP. Throughout the 1980s, actual Dutch military spending grew only fitfully, at an average rate of less than 1 percent a year. From a peak in the mid-1970s, defense expenditures have slowly slipped from 3.5 percent of the Dutch GNP to around 3 percent today and from 11 percent of central government spending to around 9 percent.

Continuing budgetary constraints have meant that neither country has been able to keep up fully with its defense needs. These tight defense budgets have been exacerbated by rising personnel costs for the armed forces and by weapons inflation, which have tended to outstrip any increase in military spending. Manpower, for example, has consistently accounted for roughly half of the Belgian and Dutch defense budgets. High personnel costs are further compounded by the fact that the Dutch and Belgian uniformed personnel—even conscripts—are by law paid wages roughly comparable to their civilian counterparts, making them some of the best-paid soldiers in NATO; in addition, they also receive overtime and weekend pay. Save cutting manpower, it is difficult to visualize how these countries could extract further savings from the personnel budget. In addition, expenditures in real terms on equipment and weapons has risen over the past 20 years, even though the actual number of armaments procured has on average declined. Finally, the procurement budgets of these countries have tended lately to be dominated by a few "big ticket" items that have sucked up funds and left parts of the armed services underequipped. The result has been a squeeze on operations, with less money available to spend on readiness and response.

Belgian and Dutch Armed Forces

Throughout the postwar period, the Belgian approach to defense has centered around the principle of cost-effectiveness—in other words, for "providing the necessary security, although *at the lowest possible level*."[15] At the same time, the demand for expanded social spending limited the possibilities for growth in defense expenditures. Therefore, beginning in the 1960s and continuing up to the late 1970s, the emphasis in defense efforts shifted toward the creation of a smaller (and cheaper to operate) but more modern armed forces. The Belgian idea was to establish a "well-trained and well-equipped force that will cost us as little as possible and still be acceptable to our allies."[16] The size of the military was allowed to shrink—particularly in terms of manpower—while the armed forces were reorganized and outfitted with more up-to-date armaments.

The Belgian armed forces currently number roughly 92,000 troops (army, 68,000; air force, 19,500; navy, 4,500), plus a reserve force of over 180,000. As noted above, there has been a general decline in the strength of its armed forces since the late 1950s, when the Belgian military stood at around 110,000. Like most European countries, Belgium relies on national service (lasting 10 to 12 months, depending on whether the soldier serves in Germany). Interestingly, professional soldiers in the Belgian armed forces outnumber conscripts two-to-one, due to a conscious effort made in the 1970s to create an all-volunteer force. Rising personnel costs, however, soon caused this policy to be reversed and, as a result, Belgium is stuck with a hybrid (and expensive) system of both conscripts and a lot of professionals.

The major branches of the Belgian armed forces are its army and its air force. The navy consists of only a handful of surface combatants (four domestically designed and built frigates), although it does boast a high degree of proficiency in mine warfare, possessing 27 assorted minesweepers and mine countermeasures support ships. Belgium is also participating in the tripartite minehunters program (along with France and the Netherlands) and will ultimately take possession of 10 of these new mine warfare ships.

The primary function of the army is the First Belgian Corps along the NATO central front in western Germany, a critical position sandwiched between the German Third Corps in CENTAG and the First British Corps in NORTHAG. The army comprises two mechanized divisions, each with two active and one reserve brigades, plus a number of miscellaneous battalions (reconnaissance, fire-support, air defense, etc.). Only one division of about 25,000 troops, consisting of one armored and one mechanized brigade, is forwardly deployed in the Federal Republic. The remaining division and the first division's reserve brigade are based back in Belgium and would have to be moved forward some 200 kilometers to their defensive positions in wartime.

Belgian armor consists of 334 Leopard I main battle tanks, around 1,700 various infantry fighting vehicles and armored personnel carriers, and about 180 main artillery pieces (155mm and 203mm). Antitank capabilities include 80 West German *Jagdpanzerkanone* with 90mm guns and the Milan antitank guided missile (ATGM) system. The army also operates Belgium's air defense network and contributes to the NATO air defense belt in the Federal Republic. Besides various anti-aircraft guns, Belgium maintains six Improved Hawk SAM squadrons in northern Germany; it is also ordering the French-made Mistral short-range SAM (similar to the Stinger missile) while deactivating all its Nike missile air defense units.

The Belgian Air Force (BAF) has 144 assigned combat aircraft, grouped into four wings of two squadrons each. The entire BAF tactical air command is committed to NATO's 2nd Allied Tactical Air Force (2ATAF). The BAF has five fighter-bomber (FBA) squadrons (four of F-16s and one of Mirage 5s), two air defense squadrons with F-16s, and one tactical reconnaissance with Mirage 5s. In addition, the BAF operates one training squadron of Alpha Jets, which could be converted for armed reconnaissance or light air defense.

The Belgian armed forces suffer from a variety of shortcomings and problems, nearly all of which can be traced back to ongoing budgetary and funding constraints. As one Western security analyst so succinctly put it, Belgium's defense deficiencies stem not so much from a lack of commitment to NATO as from a lack of resources.[17] With only two brigades stationed in Germany (a third and fourth were withdrawn in the mid-1970s), and the remaining forces either far from their defensive positions in the Federal Republic and/or on reserve status. maldeployment is a consistent criticism of the army. Less than half of what is considered necessary to adequately cover the First Belgian Corps is in place in peacetime.[18] Training and readiness also have gaps, whereas live firings have been restricted and maintenance has suffered. Finally, Belgian reserve units are even more poorly equipped, manned, and trained.

However, the Belgians have their most serious problems in the area of new and sufficient numbers of weapons and equipment. The Belgian Army possesses

only enough tanks for one armored brigade; furthermore, it has no plans to procure the Leopard II or even more Leopard Is anytime in the near future. It is also
short of medium and self-propelled artillery and an antitank weapon with the
capability to penetrate the reactive armor on modern Soviet tanks. Ammunition
stocks are low, and the army has delayed for years the purchase of badly needed
transport and antitank helicopters. For its part, despite its procurement of the F-
16—a first-class, frontline warplane—the Belgian Air Force lacks modern air-
to-air and air-to-ground munitions to properly outfit the aircraft. Only two
squadrons of F-16s are equipped with the Sidewinder air-to-air missile, for
instance, and even then the BAF has very small stocks of AAMs. Plans to
acquire badly needed electronic warfare systems for its aircraft have been post-
poned for years. Finally, the BAF has no plans to replace its remaining, increasingly obsolete Mirages.

Even its critics are quick to point out that the Belgian military does rather
well with what little it is given. Belgium units perform well in exercises and
have demonstrated high standards in NATO competitions and tactical evaluations; the army and air force receive high marks from other NATO armed forces
for their tank gunnery and combat flying. Some munition shortages have been
rectified; for example, per gun ammunition stocks for Belgian 155mm artillery
are supposedly the highest in NORTHAG. In addition, there is a strong emphasis on modernizing and upgrading existing equipment. The Leopard tank and
antitank cannons have been retrofitted with laser rangefinders and digital fire-
control computers; the BAF's F-16s are due to undergo a midlife improvement
program to enable them to effectively use next-generation air-to-air and air-to-
ground munitions, such as AMRAAM.

Nevertheless, the Belgian armed forces continue to experience severe problems with regard to acquiring modern weaponry and maintaining adequate
stocks of munitions and war reserves. Despite its best efforts, the size and
strength of Belgian military have gradually but constantly shrunk, and there
exist serious deficiencies—or even absences—in certain areas of armaments.
Manpower problems, particularly with regard to in-place forces in Germany,
will continue to worry the rest of NATO.

Like the Belgians, the Dutch have long emphasized a smaller but more modern armed forces. In the early 1960s, the Netherlands embarked on a program of
rationalization of its military—what is termed "mechanization and motoriza-
tion." The army was reduced in size and transformed from a force that was
largely mobilization-based to one that was more combat-ready. Manpower was
allowed to decline and the intake of conscripts was reduced, whereas the military purchased additional tanks, artillery, and modern aircraft.

Dutch military manpower currently stands at about 107,000 (army, 67,000;

air force, 18,000; navy, 17,000; royal constabulary and central ministerial organization, 5,000). Reserves (mostly ground forces) add an additional 160,000 troops. Conscripts make up slightly less than half of all active duty personnel, and only one male in three of draft age is called up to do national service. Conscripts serve 14–16 months on active duty, after which they are placed on "short leave" for several months, when they are liable for immediate recall.

The Netherlands also operates a unique reserve system known as "Direct Intake into Mobilizable Units," or RIM, to use its Dutch acronym. RIM units are organized at the battalion level, with one RIM battalion matched with an active unit. Under this system, conscripts recently discharged from a particular active duty company are assigned en masse to a RIM company and are placed on stand-by readiness for the next several months. The Dutch argue that RIM greatly increases the readiness and cohesiveness of the army's reserve structure and helps retain conscript proficiency for twice the normal period of national service.

The Royal Netherlands Army (RNLA) is composed of two active and one reserve mechanized divisions, each with one armored and two mechanized brigades, plus an independent infantry brigade, for a total of 10 brigades in all. In actuality, the army is largely organized (and fights) at the brigade level. The main role of the RNLA within NATO is to defend its corps sector in western Germany as well as major lines of communication to the central front. Unfortunately, Dutch ground forces stationed in West Germany are woefully few. Only one "reinforced" armored brigade consisting of 5,500 troops, is permanently deployed in the First Netherlands Corps area. All other Dutch ground forces, including the corps headquarters, are stationed back in the Netherlands, roughly 350 kilometers from their wartime positions. Despite recurring pressures from NATO, the Dutch have consistently rejected proposals to forward-deploy an additional brigade in the Federal Republic. To aid rapid deployment to its defensive positions in Germany, the RNLA has procured about 480 railroad flatcars to move tanks and other armored vehicles to the front and has begun to construct storage depots in the Federal Republic for prepositioning fuel and ammunition.

Compared to Belgium, the RNLA comes across as a well-equipped fighting force. It fields more than 900 tanks, almost evenly divided between Leopard IIs and upgraded Leopard Is. It also possesses more than 2,600 armored vehicles, including 1,700 YPR-765s, a Dutch-built, modified version of the M-113 infantry fighting vehicle. The army has also completely modernized its artillery, the bulk of which is self-propelled. In addition, the RNLA is acquiring 22 Multiple-Launch Rocket Systems (MLRS). Major antitank weapons consist of Dragon and TOW ATGMs, with TOW-2 missiles on order. Army air defense includes Stinger manportable missile systems.

The Royal Netherlands Air Force (RNLAF) has 162 assigned combat aircraft subordinate to 2ATAF. The RNLAF has one squadron of NF-5s primarily tasked to a fighter-bomber-attack mission, two interceptor day fighter (IDF) squadrons of F-16s, one RF-16 tactical reconnaissance squadron, and five squadrons of F-16s assigned a "swingrole" function of both offensive (FBA) and defensive (IDF) air missions. The RNLAF also boasts a rather decent weapons package for its force of F-16s, including Sidewinder AIM-9L and AIM-9M AAMs, laser-guided munitions, and cluster bombs. Finally, the Netherlands operates both Patriot and Hawk SAM systems.

The Royal Netherlands Navy (RNLN) has a long and proud tradition, and the privileged position it occupies in Dutch defense is evident in the unusually large naval force that the Netherlands has for a country of its size. The RNLN consists of four destroyers, 11 frigates (plus several more in reserve), six submarines, 26 mine warfare vessels, a naval air arm, and a small marine unit.[19] The Netherlands also maintains an extensive shipbuilding industry and designs and builds its own submarines.

The Dutch armed forces have been called a "well thought out compromise between modernization and manpower."[20] For a small nation, the Netherlands endeavors to maintain a well-rounded, three-service military, and for the most part the Dutch have worked hard to live up to their Alliance defense commitments. They have purchased sophisticated weapons systems and kept their military standards and professionalism high. Indeed, the Dutch armed forces are a good example of the kind of security contribution a small nation can make to the Alliance.

Nevertheless, the Netherlands faces two serious problems, one that has persisted for years and another that is growing and promises only to worsen. The first is the continuing maldeployment of Dutch ground forces. With only one brigade forwardly deployed in Germany, timely reinforcement of the First Netherlands Corps is a critical factor. It could take several days to mobilize and deploy all necessary Dutch forces to the central front, making it likely that the First German Corps might have to defend part of the Dutch corps area. It has long been a major concern to NATO, therefore, what might happen should the RNLA fail to reach its defensive positions before the outbreak of any hostilities.

The second is the likely prospect of future budgetary constraints at a time when decisions will have to be made regarding extremely effective but expensive next-generation weapons systems and munitions. For instance, readiness and procurement have begun to suffer in places. Yet despite modest growth in the Dutch defense budget, funding remains tight. In addition, the existence of a rigid, if unofficial, spending ratio, whereby the army received roughly 50 percent of defense expenditures for the three services, and the navy and air force 25 percent each, often made it difficult for any particular branch of the military to temporarily receive more funds to cover certain contingencies (such as large procurement programs), forcing it to "rob Peter to pay Paul" within its own service budget. Purchases of the F-16, for example, absorbed the bulk of the RNLAF's procurement budget for several years, greatly limiting funds for buying munitions. Meanwhile, the rising cost of the F-16 forced the air force to stretch out aircraft purchases, delaying the reequipping of older squadrons. Moreover, due to long maritime traditions, spending on the RNLN has tended to be sacrosanct, which, in turn, has limited funding for the ground and air forces, where some have argued that it might be better spent.[21]

BELGIAN AND DUTCH SECURITY POLICY OVER THE NEAR TERM

The next few years promise to be volatile ones for the future direction of the security policy of the Low Countries, particularly regarding such issues as nuclear weapons, arms control, intra-Alliance relations, and Western relations with the East. Belgian and Dutch security policy over the near term will be most conditioned by four factors: (1) a continuing aversion to nuclear weapons, (2) the ongoing process of dramatic change in Eastern Europe (including the reunification of Germany) and the collapse of the Warsaw Pact, (3) continuing fiscal austerity, and (4) an increasing preoccupation with European integration and development.

By the late 1980s, although still largely accepting of strategic nuclear deterrence, it was readily apparent that a new consensus *largely negative to nuclear weapons* had replaced the old accord on flexible response in the Low Countries. For the most part, antinuclearism has now permeated nearly all sectors of society and nearly all parties, save perhaps the far Right. Furthermore, Belgium and the Netherlands, already predisposed toward improved East-West relations and a lowering of tensions between the two blocs, put great stock in the prospects for reform in Eastern Europe and the USSR. If Gorbachev can succeed in his attempt to restructure and even partly liberalize Soviet society, it would buttress Belgian and Dutch interest in pressing for expanded Western efforts at detente. In addition, German reunification, the collapse of the Warsaw Pact, and the fading of the Soviet threat has led many in the Low Countries to conclude that the Cold War is over and that the time is ripe for a dramatic reassessment of Western security policy.

At the same time, military expenditures in the Low Countries should remain tight. Despite the fact that prospects for an upturn in the Belgian and Dutch economies in the 1990s are good, pressures on their respective governments to economize on defense spending and/or shift budget resources to the civil sector should continue, particularly in the light of a dramatically altered European security environment. Dutch plans for 2 percent real annual increases in defense spending have been dropped, and a 1 percent real decline per annum has been projected instead. The Belgians have committed themselves to cutting at least 2 billion francs ($52 million), about 2 percent, from their defense budget from 1990 on.[22] In fact, one should not be surprised to see even more dramatic reductions in Belgian and Dutch military expenditures over the next several years. In addition, inflation in weapons systems should continue to rise faster than the national average, further pushing up the costs of weapons procurement. The combination of these two factors can only exacerbate a growing or already critical shortage of resources, and it is difficult to see the existing or emerging problems in the Belgian and Dutch defense efforts being resolved anytime soon. This, in turn, will likely increase the rivalry between the services for the ever scarcer defense francs or guilders. It should also mean having to continue to make difficult and often unpopular trade-offs between manpower, investments, and operations. Apart from any external political developments in Europe, therefore, both countries will come under growing economic pressures to keep their defense efforts and NATO commitments at the lowest possible level.

Belgium and Netherlands have already shown themselves to be strongly opposed to further NATO nuclear modernization, and, in contrast, the Low Countries are more and more unwilling to take on new additional nuclear responsibilities within the Alliance. Increasingly—particularly in light of the INF Treaty—they have opposed U.S.-led efforts to upgrade and replace NATO's short-range nuclear forces (SNF) and to develop systems designed to "compensate" for the loss of the Alliance's land-based INF. For example, Belgium's Center Left government, which came to power in 1988, was openly negative to the idea of a follow-on to Lance (FOTL), aligning itself with West Germany in attempting to defer or cancel the program outright. For its part, the Netherlands gave only grudging support to FOTL while also calling for further study and discussion before any final decision was made. Both countries strongly supported the U.S. eventual decision to cancel FOTL. Belgium and the Netherlands have also expanded their opposition to the modernization of other less visible theater nuclear forces, such as nuclear artillery shells and the tactical air-to-surface missile (TASM). Low Countries opposition to TASM is particularly significant, as this system is fast becoming NATO's "weapon of choice" for the preservation of the credibility of flexible response doctrine.

Along with a general reluctance to expand their nuclear commitments, so too are the Low Countries unlikely to take on added conventional duties. In fact, as the result of political reluctance and budgetary pressures, Belgian and Dutch conventional capabilities should continue to shrink and their armed forces become increasingly hollow. For one thing, the Low Countries forces should decline in size. Even before the negotiations on cutting conventional forces in Europe—the so-called CFE talks—opened, for example, there were plans to cut at least 10,000 troops, about 10 percent, from the Dutch armed forces over the next several years.[23] At the same time, current deficiencies in such areas as munitions, fuel, and certain armaments and weapon systems should become more pronounced, as earlier modernization programs are deferred, scaled back, or cancelled. Delays and stretch-outs, such as one has seen in the procurement of the F-16 fighter jet, combat helicopters, and warships, will most likely continue, whereas some items will be procured in less than adequate amounts to meet NATO standards of stock, such as AMRAAM. In addition, certain weapons and equipment, such as next-generation aircraft, modern main battle tanks, and high-tech air-to-ground munitions, simply won't be bought.

The next several years will probably see a reduced or changing role for the Low Countries armed forces within the Western Alliance, under the rubric of "mission specialization." For example, the Belgian and Dutch air contribution to NATO will be cut back, as their air forces age and as they disband aircraft squadrons and surface-to-air missile units without replacement. Their navies are also liable to shrink and certain duties dropped. Even these countries' continued commitment to NATO forward defense is in doubt. Belgium has proposed with-drawing all of its forces stationed in Germany, disbanding their units and selling or scrapping their equipment. The Netherlands, meanwhile, has already stated its intentions of pulling out 750 troops from Germany by 1992.[24] Instead, these countries will seek to limit and specialize their functions within the Alliance, dropping certain military duties in order to concentrate more fully on others. In addition, the Low Countries will likely give greater emphasis to their political and confidence-building roles, such as carrying out verification of arms control treaties.[25]

By far, Belgium and the Netherlands would much rather see a substantial transformation in Alliance security policy—and particularly further attempts at arms control, both nuclear and conventional, and at detente—over any major new weapons development and procurement programs. For one thing, arms control would provide a pretext to excuse the decline in Belgian and Dutch defense efforts; a CFE agreement, for example, would formalize in a treaty cuts in their armed forces that are already in the works. For another, improving East–West relations and, in particular, the collapse of the Warsaw Pact threat greatly back up Belgian and Dutch arguments that the Atlantic Alliance must respond to the changing security environment in Europe by rethinking its nuclear weapons doctrine, especially its position on tactical nuclear forces. For a variety of reasons, then, the Low Countries will continue to push arms control and detente over expensive, and politically volatile, arms modernization programs, and increasingly depend on recent changes in Europe to rationalize their shrinking defense efforts and NATO commitments.

Finally, one should expect to see growing Belgian and Dutch support for a stronger European voice within the West and for the "greater Europeanization of Europe's defense."[26] As the Warsaw Pact crumbles and the rationale for a highly integrated, transatlantic military alliance begins to falter, the Low Countries should, as will other West European nations, increasingly place priority on European interests and on European integration.

One important aspect of this "Europeanization of defense" is a growing pan-European effort to develop and produce weapons systems, both to make weapons procurement more cost efficient and to promote European defense industries. Another is for a more integrated and Eurocentric approach to defense, which can be seen through the revival of the West European Union. These developments not only promise to strengthen European coordination on defense efforts, but they will also allow for "a more faithful articulation of European interests"[27] within the Atlantic Alliance when it comes to defense and security concerns.

It should be noted that the Low Countries already cooperate with each other in a number of areas when it comes to defense. For example, joint training is currently a feature in both countries' air forces and navies, not only making more efficient use of training costs and equipment but also enhancing the standardization of two allied forces that operate a good deal of common equipment in the same area and using the same tactics. Procurement is another area where the Low Countries are increasingly working together, such as in the joint production and procurement of fighter aircraft, helicopters, and mine warfare vessels.

Its advocates argue that the trend toward the Europeanization of defense efforts will strengthen NATO and bolster European support for Alliance policies. At the same time, it is hard to believe that this will also not lead to a more independent-minded European wing within the Western Alliance, increasingly critical of the U.S. leadership of NATO and more prepared to advance its own agenda within the Alliance. Indeed, Western Europe appears to be coming much more self-assertive over what it desires of the Atlantic Alliance. Furthermore, this new assertiveness comes at a critical time, when the West is in the midst of a dramatic reexamination and reappraisal of its security policy. As a result, Alliance cohesion, its unity of purpose, and the traditional U.S. role in NATO will all be sorely tested over the next several years.

For example, the Low Countries, together with other European members of the Atlantic Alliance, should continue to put pressure on the United States and NATO to begin to radically rethink traditional nuclear policy. On the whole,

Belgium and the Netherlands would rather see the Alliance greatly deemphasize its role for nuclear weapons. Belgium, for example, has already called for a major review of NATO nuclear strategy and, furthermore, has stated its refusal to accept deployment of TASM on its soil until this review is completed. For its part, the Netherlands has allied itself with the Federal Republic in proposing the immediate removal of all nuclear artillery shells from Germany.[28]

The question of burden sharing should be another source of growing friction between the United States and NATO Europe. The Low Countries, particularly Belgium, have long been irked by U.S. and NATO criticisms that they were not pulling their weight within the Alliance. Whether these claims were legitimate or not is today irrelevant. The emerging geopolitical environment in Europe means that many old NATO responsibilities will be shed, rather than new ones added, and for the United States to continue to push the burden sharing issue will only further exacerbate splits within the Alliance.

CONCLUSION

Domestic Belgian and Dutch security attitudes and arising European commitments should offer increasing competition to traditional priorities for NATO and U.S. leadership. As one Dutch security analyst has put it, the Low Countries traditional priority for NATO is no longer unconditional.[29] Instead, a more independent and increasingly more critical stance toward the United States and longstanding Alliance security policy will likely assume its place, although it will almost certainly come in the guise of a pan-European stance.

At the same time, Belgium and the Netherlands are not likely to be major actors in any future NATO debate over strategy, doctrine, arms control, or Alliance relations with the East. As in the past, the Low Countries will be more "reactors" than initiators, although they may serve as important agents or allies for promoting (or resisting) change, such as in the current SNF debate. However, as schisms over certain aspects of NATO policy widen and intra-Alliance tensions possibly worsen, this catalytic role could turn out to be a significant part for these countries to play.

Moreover, the future course of Low Countries security policy will likely depend little upon which particular political groups are in power. Whereas Center Left governments (currently in power in both Belgium and the Netherlands) tend to be more predisposed toward arms control and detente, the shift in the national consensus in favor of a stronger Europillar, improved East-West relations, arms control, denuclearization, and restricting defense expenditures is so broad and so apparently complete that the Christian Democratic and even Liberal parties are finding it increasingly difficult to hold a more traditional NATO stance. This is particularly true when it comes to nuclear weapons. For example, in the Center Left government in Belgium, the Flemish Christian Democrats have come out in favor of the elimination of NATO SNF.

In addition, whereas continued or expanded change in Eastern Europe and the USSR will likely accelerate Belgian and Dutch disarmament and the contraction of their NATO responsibilities, it does not necessarily follow that a reversal of Soviet reforms and the resumption of a more hostile Soviet stance toward the West will result in a turnaround of Low Countries defense efforts. Many Belgians and Dutch (particularly those in the center and on the Right) might see this as a justification for calling for increased defense spending and an arms buildup, but it is also arguable, given the deep permeation of detentist and arms control sentiments together with the general reluctance to increase military expenditures, that just as many may agitate for increased efforts at rapprochement with the East. As many did in the early 1980s at the height of the INF dispute, they may call upon the West to take the initiative in "saving" detente, by proposing further arms control and confidence-building measures. They may even blame the West for spoiling detente, particularly if NATO and the United States do not take "sincere" steps to revive it. Rather than unify the Alliance, therefore, it is altogether possible that a renewed Soviet threat could further divide NATO.

Another possibility is the partial disengagement of the United States from Europe, either in the form of a shift in U.S. strategic interests or in the removal or reduction of U.S. troops in Germany. If such a disengagement were part of an effort to "Europeanize" NATO defense, it is still doubtful that the Low Countries would significantly increase their defense efforts or Alliance commitments, although they may welcome the opportunity to strengthen Western Europe's voice within NATO. A dramatic disengagement, particularly if it occurred in response to the denuclearization of Europe over the objections of the United States (leaving U.S. forces in Europe no longer protected under a tactical nuclear umbrella), would probably accelerate the collapse of NATO and possibly even the neutralization of the Low Countries, perhaps under the "protection" of a reunified Germany.

Such an extreme scenario is unlikely, but the transformation of Europe's security environment makes it certain that change in Belgian and Dutch security policy is unavoidable. Of course, attitudes in the Low Countries toward security, defense, and NATO issues were shifting significantly, if subtly, even before the recent developments in Europe. Now, however, this process promises to be both broadened to address security questions fundamental to the future of the Low Countries in the Alliance and greatly accelerated.

NOTES

1. Jan G. Siccama, "The Netherlands Depillarized: Security Policy in a New Domestic Context," pp. 119–126, in Gregory Flynn (ed.), *NATO's Northern Allies: The National Security Policies of Belgium, Denmark, the Netherlands, and Norway*, Rowman & Allanheld, Totowa, New Jersey, 1985.

2. Luc Reychler, "The Passive Constrained: Belgian Security Policy in the 1980s," pp. 6–8, in Flynn, *NATO's Northern Allies*.

3. Reychler, "Passive Constrained," p. 20.

4. Siccama, "Netherlands Depillarized," p. 117.

5. Siccama, "Netherlands Depillarized," pp. 134–135; Thomas R. Rochon, "Beyond Perfection" (the Netherlands), *Wilson Quarterly*, Spring 1987, pp. 56–58; John Fitzmaurice, "The Politics of Belgium and Denmark: A Comparative Perspective," *Government and Opposition*, Winter 1987, pp. 36–37.

6. Rochon, "Beyond Perfection," p. 56.

7. In Belgium the main religious party was the Social Christians, whereas in the Netherlands, up until the late 1970s, this pillar was occupied by three parties (one for the Catholic Church and one each for the two main denominations of the Dutch Reformed Church); in 1977 these parties merged to form the Christian Democratic Appeal (CDA). The Socialists were represented by the Belgian Socialist party and the Dutch Labor party (PvdA). In Belgium the Liberal political faction was known as the Party of Liberty and Progress; in the Netherlands it was called the People's Party for Freedom and Democracy (VVD).

8. Fitzmaurice, "Politics," pp. 44–45; William K. Domke, "The Netherlands: Strategy Options and Change," p. 283, in Catherine McArdle Kelleher and Gale A. Mattox (eds.), *Evolving European Defense Policies* (Lexington Books, 1987); Ken Gladdish, "The Dutch Political Parties and the May 1986 Elections," *Government and Opposition*, Summer 1986, pp. 321–324.

9. In the Netherlands, for example, religious organizations provide much of administrative structure for government welfare programs, such as schools and hospitals, running these services privately but receiving the lion's share of their operating funds from the state.

10. The main Flemish party is the *Volksunie* (VU); the primary Wallonian party is the *Rassemblement Wallon* (RW); in Brussels, there exists another Francophone party known as the *Front Democratique des Francophones* (FDF).

11. In Flanders the old Social Christian party now called itself the Christian Peoples party (CVP); it retained its original name in Wallonia (PSC, to use its French acronym for reasons of brevity and fairness, the combined Christian faction in Belgium is referred to throughout this chapter as the Christian Democrats). The Socialists split into the *Parti Socialiste* (PS) and the *Socialistische Partij* (SP). The Liberal faction broke into the *Partij voor Vrijheid en Vooruitgang* (PVV) in Flanders and the *Parti Reformateur Liberal* (PRL) in Wallonia.

12. Fitzmaurice, "Politics," p. 45.

13. In addition, the Low Countries have exceptionally "open" economies, meaning that they are extremely dependent upon foreign trade. Exports, for example, amount to over 70 percent of Begium's gross national product, and over 60 percent of the Netherlands. These countries must also import the lion's share of their energy supplies.

14. Interestingly, in Belgium the Walloon PS—although more radically inclined when it came to domestic policy—tended to be more moderate in its position regarding the missiles than was the SP, which was more influenced by both the Dutch and Flemish peace movements.

15. Reychler, "Passive Constrained," p. 7 (original in italics).

16. F. Govaerts, "Belgium, Holland and Luxembourg," p. 328, in O. De Raeymakers (ed.), *Small Powers in Alignment,* Leuven University Press, 1984 (quoted in Reychler, Leuven, Netherlands, 1985, p. 13).

17. Anthony H. Cordesman, *NATO's Central Region Forces: Capabilities/Challenges/Concepts,* Jane's, 1988, p. 176.

18. The Belgians hotly contest this criticism, arguing that their country maintains the highest proportion of troops per inhabitant in the Federal Republic (38 percent of its army is deployed in West Germany), that—unlike the Netherlands—its corps headquarters is situated in Germany, and that major weapons and equipment depots are established there. In fact, they insist that the "whole First Belgian Corps" can be on its forward defense positions within hours of the decision to deploy. It is unclear, however, whether this includes reserve forces (which could take up to a month to bring up to combat readiness) or how deployment might operate in light of wartime disruptions. See Cordesman, *NATO,* p. 179; and The Resources Strategy Project Team, *Belgium Within the Alliance: The Present and Future,* Center for Strategic and International Studies, Washington, DC, March 1988), pp. 25–26.

19. International Institute for Strategic Studies, *The Military Balance, 1989–1990,* Brassey's, 1989.

20. Cordesman, *NATO,* p. 132.

21. This fixed 2:1:1 budgeting ratio is now due to be dropped, with the intention of raising the army's share of defense spending in order to bolster the Netherlands' ability to defend its corps area.

22. MILAVNEWS, "Belgium," March 1989.

23. Cordesman, *NATO,* p. 115.

24. "Belgium Plans to Withdraw Its Troops from W. Germany," *Washington Post,* January 26, 1990; "European Media: Dutch Troop Withdrawal . . ." *Current News,* Early Bird edition (Department of Defense), January 26, 1990, p. 14.

25. "Verification: New Role for Dutch?" *Jane's Defense Weekly,* February 24, 1990, pp. 339–340.

26. Reychler, "Passive Constrained," p. 48.

27. Ibid., p. 49.

28. Pierre Lefevre, "Coeme Urges NATO Nuclear Strategy Change," *Le Soir,* April 7–8, 1990, reprinted in *FBIS-WEU-90-086,* May 3, 1990, pp. 4–5; "European Media: Belgium Missiles . . ." *Current News,* Early Bird edition (Department of Defense), May 8, 1990, p. 18; Robert Pear, "NATO Splits on Removing Nuclear Artillery from West Germany," *New York Times,* May 10, 1990.

29. Siccama, "Netherlands Depillarized," p. 157.

Chapter 8

Scandinavia

John Lund

Denmark and Norway hold an unusual position in NATO. Public support for NATO membership is very high and growing; indeed, public support has often been much higher than it is in the United States. Yet, undercurrents of neutralism have remained strong and have surfaced on several occasions. Both nations prohibit the permanent stationing of foreign troops or bases on their soil and neither permits nuclear weapons in peacetime. Relations between these nations and the United States has been generally very good. However, both countries have been the subject of American criticism over the last few years. Denmark has borne the brunt of American ire owing to the low level of Danish defense spending and the tendency of Denmark to object to NATO nuclear policies. Norway was attacked for failing to prevent the sale of advanced machinery to the Soviet Union by a partly state-owned arms manufacturer, allowing the Soviets to build quieter submarines. Furthermore, Norway was openly criticized in the report *Discriminate Deterrence* for allegedly obstructing American efforts to defend the region.[1]

For many years, the United States had adopted a low-profile policy toward the Scandinavian NATO nations, which well suited Denmark and Norway. These two nations pursued security policies that were adapted to their unique geopolitical situation. Security policy remained primarily the concern of a very small policy making elite. The few disagreements that arose over the years were handled quietly and at relatively low levels.

Beginning in the late 1970s, this situation gradually changed. The Soviets substantially expanded and modernized their forces on the Kola Peninsula. The United States Navy, especially in the 1980s under the leadership of John Lehman, focused new attention on the far north. The deployment of air- and sea-launched cruise missiles heightened concerns in Fenno-Scandinavia that the region would become a major arena in any superpower struggle. Meanwhile, the issues of the neutron bomb and deployment of the intermediate nuclear forces awakened substantial opposition within the Danish and Norwegian publics to NATO nuclear policy. In the process, security issues became more important in the domestic political debate and were no longer simply a matter for small elites.

The purpose of this chapter is to assess the prospects for Danish and Norwegian policies toward NATO through the mid-1990s, based on certain assumptions about the internal and external environments.[2] It sets forth explicitly the assumptions made, then assesses the likely course of Danish and Norwegian policies over the next several years. Next, plausible variations on these assumptions are pursued to determine what effects they might have.

The first part of this chapter provides key assumptions underlying this analysis. The following parts offer projections on the policies of Denmark and Norway, respectively, and follow a common outline:

- General political conditions, as a background for discussion of security policy.
- Specific issue areas, including arms control negotiations, changes in conventional forces, theater-based nuclear deterrence, economic issues, and the structure of NATO.
- Some variations on the assumptions of the likely case and how changes in these could affect the analysis, including electoral variations, Soviet policy, and policies of NATO and other nations.
- Conclusions.

KEY ASSUMPTIONS

The following assumptions have been used for the analysis of both Danish and Norwegian security policies. These assumptions are varied in the sections dealing with Denmark and Norway to show the sensitivity of national policies to these factors.

The Soviet Union and Eastern Europe

Soviet policy toward Europe—both East and West—remains the preeminent issue facing NATO. In the near term, Soviet policy will most likely proceed roughly as it has in the last few years under Gorbachev. Eastern Europe will continue to devolve rapidly away from Soviet control and communist rule, and multiparty democracies will emerge. This chapter assumes that the Warsaw Pact maintains its current membership but ceases to function as an effective military alliance. Soviet troops are withdrawn from Czechoslovakia and Hungary, with residual forces left elsewhere. Furthermore, the analysis assumes that the Baltic republics remain within the Soviet Union during a transition period to independence, without the central government resorting to armed intervention.

The next five years should witness real progress on certain East–West security and arms control issues, with a significant easing of tensions. A conventional arms agreement ("CFE I") will be reached featuring rough parity at lower levels in major army and air force weapon systems. Additional reductions are possible, and next five years will probably witness negotiations for reductions to as low as 50 percent of NATO's force level of 1989.

Regarding Fenno-Scandinavia, the Soviet Union will continue to pursue a policy of isolating regional security issues from the general European context. The Soviets will make diplomatic and military gestures toward the region, such as unilateral troops reduction in border areas or elimination of some nuclear forces, in an effort to gain easing of tensions and perhaps a regional agreement limiting military forces. The Soviets would like especially to see the region declared a nuclear-free zone.

Despite possible reductions in ground and short-range nuclear forces, one can expect the Soviet Union to continue to modernize its strategic and naval forces in and around the Kola Peninsula, increasing the military threat to the region. The Soviets continue to deploy their most modern air and naval forces to bases there. Even following major strategic or conventional arms control agreements, the Kola Peninsula will remain a vital strategic region for the Soviets.[3] This trend will be reinforced to the extent that the Soviet Union loses strategic depth in Central Europe and loses confidence in the stability of non-Russian republics.

This analysis assumes that Soviet gestures toward reduced tensions and apparent force reduction will be far more obvious to the general public than the modernization of forces on the Kola Peninsula. In this environment, we can expect diminishing public support in Denmark and Norway for increased defense spending or for modernized nuclear weapons in Europe.

U.S. Policy

The Bush administration can be expected to maintain a strong commitment to Europe. As part of this commitment, the United States will continue to uphold the policy of nuclear deterrence. This means that it will seek to push through modernization of both NATO's nuclear and conventional weapons, albeit under conditions substantially different from those of the 1980s. The United States will resist efforts to change the U.S. Navy's policy of not disclosing whether ships are carrying nuclear weapons. The administration will proceed with conventional arms control negotiations, resulting in an agreement that mandates a

slight reduction in American forces stationed in Europe. American defense budgets are assumed to decline in real terms. This will act to reduce American naval
presence in the far north.[4] Burden sharing, the effects of 1992, and the specter of
a economic Fortress Europa will reinforce this tendency.

The Nordic Connection

A central element of Danish and Norwegian security policy since World War II
has been the special influence of Finland and Sweden. Leaders throughout Scandinavia have described Nordic Europe as a unique region of low tensions and
low levels of military forces in an otherwise tense Europe. This special condition was threatened by the proximity of overwhelming Soviet military force.
The official stance of the Nordic states has been to maintain a balancing act
between reassuring the Soviets that the region would not be the source of any
military threat to Soviet interests and deterring Soviet aggression against themselves. However, Norway and Denmark recognized from their World War II
experience that they were absolutely dependent on external reinforcements to
successfully defend their territory if war did come. In pursuit of these conflicting
objectives, Denmark and Norway abandoned their traditional neutrality and
joined NATO, but they imposed upon themselves certain restraints on their
membership. Both countries prohibit foreign troops or bases on their territory in
peacetime (except during exercises), prohibit nuclear weapons, and restrict the
operations of allied forces in and around their territory during exercises.

In practice, the concerns on the part of Norway and Denmark to maintain a
situation of "low tensions" have given the Soviet Union some influence on
NATO policy. By placing pressure on Finland, the Soviet Union has been able
to redirect Norwegian and Danish policies.[5] This special pattern of influence and
relationship will remain an important factor in Danish and Norwegian security
policy. Both countries will continue to closely coordinate positions on a wide
range of security issues. The general public in each country will be influenced
by the debates in the other. Both countries will be affected by developments in
Sweden and Finland. Gorbachev's visit to Finland in October 1989 and his
announcement of some unilateral reductions in nuclear and conventional forces
had the potential to put place tremendous pressure on Denmark and Norway, but
his speech was quickly overshadowed by the events in East Germany. However,
additional gestures toward the region could force the Danish and Norwegian
governments to offer some concessions of their own.

One area that could have critical regional implications is the Soviet Baltic
republics. In particular, Finish and Swedish concerns about the situation in the
Soviet Baltic republics could potentially create pressures on Norway and Denmark.

This chapter assumes that the Baltic republics remain within the Soviet Union; however, if the Soviet Union were to offer autonomy or independence to these republics provided that a special regional defense agreement could be signed with Nordic Europe, the pressures on the Norwegian and Danish governments would be great.

Policies of Other NATO Members

Undoubtedly, the most important NATO country to watch in the coming five years is Germany. The events of late 1989 made full German reunification a near certainty. Even before the ouster of East German leader Honecker and the fall of the Berlin Wall, West Germany had become increasingly assertive in expressing its national views and interests in NATO and in Europe as a whole. For the purposes of the baseline analysis, this chapter assumes that a United Germany remains firmly within the Western Alliance and will attempt to assume a greater leadership role within Europe and the NATO Alliance. Germany will seek the complete withdrawal on all short-range nuclear systems but will avoid complete denuclearization by maintaining an airborne nuclear role.

The United Kingdom has played an important role in Danish and Norwegian security policy. It maintains an important commitment to send air and ground reinforcements to these two countries. The naval and air units based in Britain would also strongly contribute to defense of the northern region. The commander of the NATO northern region command is British. Norway and the U.K. have their own special relationship dating back to the British Expeditionary Force in Norway in 1940 and the wartime government in exile; the ties between Denmark and Britain is decidedly weaker. For these reasons, Britain has earned some say in Norwegian and Danish security affairs. In the baseline case, it is assumed that British elections in late 1991 or early 1992 return Margaret Thatcher or another Tory and that Britain maintains its current commitment to the region. Britain is assumed to resist moves toward rapid disarmament and substantial changes in existing security arrangements in the next five years.

The remaining NATO nations do not significantly affect either Denmark or Norway, at least individually. Until 1987, Canada maintained a commitment to reinforce northern Norway with a brigade of troops; in June of that year, Canada withdrew that commitment and subsequently has lost any real influence on Norwegian policy. The Netherlands and Belgium occasionally consult with Denmark and Norway as the "smaller NATO nation," but the only significant effect has been the decision to jointly build and procure the F-16. Otherwise, coordination between these nations has a minor impact. Neither Denmark nor Norway is strongly affected by the policies of France or the nations of the southern region, and this will almost certainly continue to be true.

This analysis assumes, for the base case, that the governments in place in 1990 are essentially retained throughout this period. This means that policies are largely dominated by center and right of center coalitions. If, in contrast, the next five years witness a resurgence of leftist governments elsewhere in Western Europe, especially Germany, then leftist tendencies in Nordic Europe will probably be strengthened.

Overall, it is assumed that current trends will lead to a more European and more political NATO. The European members of NATO will explore ways of pursuing "European" solutions to common problems and to gradually reduce reliance on (and thus the influence of) the United States. This will be a slow evolution, with no substantial damage to relations. However, this chapter also assumes that all major actors will seek to maintain some American presence in and commitment to Western Europe.

Economic Conditions

The European Community (EC) will move forward toward economic unification, but at a substantially slower pace than many Europeans now hope, as Western Europe tries to adjust to the changes in Eastern Europe. Denmark continues the process of integrating its economy more fully with other EC members, while Norway remains outside the EC. In fact, no extension of EC membership is expected in the next five years. Sometime during the early 1990s, Western Europe is assumed to experience an economic recession, resulting in even greater pressures to reduce defense budgets than is already true.

DANISH SECURITY POLICY: THE NEXT FIVE YEARS

Danish politics has been marked by considerable electoral instability. This trend is likely to continue. With proportional representation and multiparty system, no single party has been able to win a majority in the parliament, the Folketing, in recent decades. Furthermore, the consensus on security and other policy areas has been eroding continuously since World War II. The differences in the platforms of the various parties are so great that no government has been able to form a majority coalition since the early 1970s. Thus Denmark has been ruled by a succession of minority coalition governments with a new government typically forming every two to three years. The Danish political universe consists of several standard alliances of parties. On the Left, the Social Democratic party (SDP) and the Socialist People's party (SPP), and several smaller parties often vote as a bloc, called in Denmark the "socialist" parties, against the center and

Right, or "nonsocialist" parties. The SDP ruled Denmark throughout much of the postwar period and it remains the nation's largest party. Its platform resembles that of any other European SDPs, with particularly strong emphasis on Nordic cooperation and, recently, on antinuclear and "defensive defense" policies. The SPP, formerly a communist party, advocates left-wing socialism; it is strongly anti-NATO and anti-EC, favoring unilateral disarmament and nonalignment. The Left Socialist party is a Marxist-Leninist party that lost its parliamentary representation in 1987, due largely to internal factionalism. Common Cause is an extreme Left party that won four seats in 1987 but lost them in 1988. The Danish Communist party has never garnered enough votes to win representation in the Folketing, and the advent of *glasnost* and *perestroika* has led to growing internal strains in the party.

The SDP and SPP form the real socialist alternative, with the several small parties on the far Left having almost no influence. Yet after the 1988 elections, when SDP proved unable to win support for any coalition that included SPP, the SDP has moved more toward the center and the SPP has become increasingly isolated and ineffective in the Folketing.

On the extreme Right, the Progress party advocates a libertarian philosophy, at times pursuing its opposition to centralized government by voting against whatever majority is formed on a particular issue. However, the Progress party has generally supported nonsocialist over socialist coalitions when it comes to forming governments. It advocates abolition of the military and the diplomatic service. Its antiimmigration platform has led to charges that it is racist. Danish press reports in 1989 suggested that some members of the Progress party are moving toward accommodation with the mainstream nonsocialist parties. Ironically this move, although temporarily increasing its influence in the Folketing, may undermine the party's long-term appeal with the disaffected portions of the electorate who expect the party to be antiestablishment.

The conservative factions consist of the Conservative People's party and the Liberal party. Both support strong defense and NATO's nuclear policy (or at least oppose active antinuclear policies), as well as Danish membership in the EC. The Conservatives currently comprise the second largest party, but not by a large margin. In 1982 the Conservatives were able to form a government for the first time since 1929. At that point they had been in opposition for a decade. Prior to 1982, the Liberals had been the leaders of the center Right coalition, but their support has gradually eroded. Two more parties tend to be centrist or slightly right of center: the Center Democrats and the Christian People's party. Both parties generally support NATO and an adequate defense. Together, these four parties form the core of the nonsocialist power in the Folketing. Although they refuse to ally themselves with the Progress party, they must have its support if they hope to win a nonsocialist majority.

For the last several years, the balance of power in the Folketing has been held by the Radical Liberals or "Radicals." The Radical platform advocates a moderate to conservative economic policy, emphasizing the role of the individual and small enterprise in society; in foreign affairs it advocates pacifism. Until the late 1970s, the Radicals supported SDP governments, but increasing dissatisfaction with the leftist policies of the socialist coalitions has led the Radicals to switch support to the conservative nonsocialist parties. However, the Radicals refuse to support a government reliant upon the extremist Progress party, so after the 1985 election the Radicals withdrew support for either Left or Right coalitions. Only in 1988 did the Radical party enter into a coalition government with the Conservatives and Liberals, once it was assured that the Progress party would have no influence on government policies. Despite the Radicals support for the Conservative-led majority on domestic and economic policy, their pacifist beliefs allow a nongovernmental majority to form on a number of security issues, essentially antidefense and antinuclear. The Christian People's party and the Center Democrats have refused to join in a coalition with the Radicals, arguing that they are too leftist.[6]

Led by the Social Democrats and with Radical support, the socialist parties were able to win a series of 23 security policy votes from 1984 to 1988 against the Conservative-led government (see Fig. 8-1). These votes included the withholding of Denmark's contribution to NATO's infrastructure funding of the GLCM and Pershing II (1984) and opposing Danish participation in SDI research (1985). Conservative Prime Minister Paul Schluter was willing to accept these losses because of the high priority his government placed on economic policy. Schluter made clear in NATO forums that his government did not control Danish defense policy.

The turning point came in April 1988 when the SDP passed a resolution requiring the government to "remind" visiting warships of Denmark's ban on nuclear weapons. Schluter decided to make this vote a "vital element" of his government's policy (equivalent to a vote of confidence), arguing that the resolution placed at risk Denmark's full membership in NATO.[7] When the government lost the vote, Schluter called a general election.

The results of the 1988 election were inconclusive, with both the socialist and nonsocialist alignments losing seats and the right-wing Progress party gaining seven seats (see Fig. 8-2) After several weeks of negotiations, Paul Schluter formed a new minority government of Conservatives, Liberals, and Radical Liberals, with the support of the Center Democrats and Christian People's party, and implicitly the Progress party. This coalition is considered unstable and new elections could be called at any time. The coalition is held together less by any sense of conviction than by a lack of a good alternative. One apparent effect of the election so far, however, has been to halt the series of alternative security policy resolutions passed by the leftist parties.

SPECIFIC DANISH ISSUE AREAS

Conventional and Nuclear Arms Control Negotiations

Denmark is not a major player in arms control negotiations for either conventional or nuclear forces. However, the de facto security policy majority in the Follketing (the socialists plus Radical Liberals) has managed to voice its dissentions to aspects of NATO's arms control policies. For example, within NATO forums, they forced the government to oppose NATO's dual track decision on INF, both by inserting official footnotes to NATO documents and by withholding infrastructure funding. This security policy majority believes that Denmark should go further toward actively encouraging new arms control agreements in Europe.

A hardy perennial of Scandinavian politics is the Nordic Nuclear Free Zone (NNFZ).[8] Stated simply, a NNFZ would seek to formalize the nonnuclear status of the Nordic states and ban nuclear weapons from the Nordic area, usually defined as the territories of Norway, Denmark, Sweden, and Finland. The Conservative-led Danish government has been opposed to the proposal because, barring a major change in NATO policy, a NNFZ would be incompatible with Denmark's membership in the Alliance and could weaken deterrence. However, the SDP has been able to pass several initiatives forcing the government to work for the establishment of a NNFZ. A committee of civil servants has been formed to study the issue, and new parliamentary initiatives are occasionally offered. Gorbachev raised the issue of a NNFZ in his speech to the Finish parliament in October 1989, and pressure from Finland and Sweden could build again. If the Left can win a majority in a new election, the NNFZ would certainly be considered more seriously in Copenhagen. The fate of the NNFZ in Denmark rests largely with the Social Democrats. The SPP and the Radical Liberals would support the idea unconditionally. The Social Democrats have so far insisted that any zone be approved by NATO. If they change their stance, the NNFZ would have a majority in the Folketing.

Quantitative and Qualitative Changes in Conventional Forces

The Danish military has been widely regarded within NATO as inadequate to fulfill its obligations to the Alliance. As a result, NATO ministers chastised

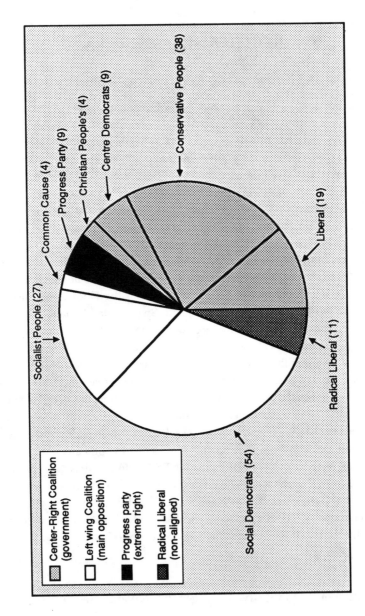

Figure 8-1   The Danish parliament: 1987.

Center-Right Coalition (government)

Left wing Coalition (main opposition)

Progress party (extreme right)

Radical Liberal (non-aligned)

Conservative People (38)

Centre Democrats (9)

Christian People's (4)

Progress Party (9)

Common Cause (4)

Socialist People (27)

Social Democrats (54)

Radical Liberal (11)

Liberal (19)

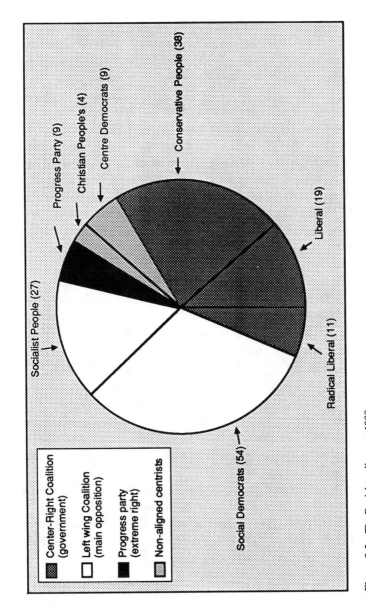

Figure 8-2 The Danish parliament: 1988.

Center-Right Coalition (government)

Left wing Coalition (main opposition)

Progress party (extreme right)

Non-aligned centrists

Socialist People (27)

Progress Party (9)

Christian People's (4)

Centre Democrats (9)

Conservative People (38)

Liberal (19)

Radical Liberal (11)

Social Democrats (54)

Denmark for its military weakness and low defense spending, as did both Lord Carrington and General Rogers individually, while the British threatened to withdraw their commitment to reinforce Denmark. Even before the stunning changes in Eastern Europe in late 1989, Danish political reality had effectively ruled out any major improvement in conventional forces in Denmark in the 1990s. The conventional arms control negotiations have undermined support for defense spending as people began to anticipate substantial reductions in Warsaw Pact forces.

The collapse of the Warsaw Pact as an effective, offensively oriented military alliance has resulted in the collapse of Danish support for military spending. The Conservatives have dropped calls for increased spending and instead are hoping to maintain existing levels. The Radical Liberals and socialist parties have been arguing for substantial defense cuts. In December 1989 the Danish Defense Commission published its recommendations for the Danish defense establishment for the 1990s, which offered a politically acceptable compromise. These recommendations, which foresee fairly significant force reductions, are apt to be the upper limit to Danish forces in the future. More likely, further reductions will be in store.

The principal that has guided Danish defense planning and procurement for the last few decades is the anti-invasion concept. With a small population and an exposed geographically position, Denmark believed that its resources would be best used by concentrating on defeating a Warsaw Pact invasion of Denmark. This concept is not new. However, in recent years some Danes have reinterpreted it in light of the idea of defensive defense. Whereas the military (including NATO) argues that anti-invasion defense works best by attacking invasion forces before they come close to Danish shores, many politicians now prefer a force structure that permits defense only in or very near Danish territory. By 1989 this preference had already begun to affect the structure and capabilities of the Danish military, accelerating in 1990 with the collapse of the Warsaw Pact as an effective military alliance.

The Danish Air Force is the healthiest of the services and forms the core of Danish defense. It recently completed a major modernization program with the acquisition of the F-16, which consumed most of the national military acquisition budget of the 1980s and left little for the army and navy. By the mid-1990s, the Drakens will be eliminated, partly under CFE reductions. The Danish Air Force hopes to procure some additional aircraft to replace one of the two squadrons of aging F-35 Drakens in the late 1990s.[9] However, even these plans may be dropped or substantially scaled down as a result of CFE and Soviet troop withdrawals. In any event, the Danish Air Force has been seriously constrained by a massive pilot shortage, which effectively grounds many of its planes. In addition, the capabilities of this very modern fleet of F-16s has been limited by the decision to restrict the air force to more "defensive" missions such as air defense and attacks on amphibious assaults. Even before the fall of the Berlin Wall, the air force had not been able to procure munitions that could be used to strike targets in Warsaw Pact territory (such as airbases or columns of vehicles). Now those missions will probably be dropped completely, especially given the relatively short combat radius of the Danish F-16s.

The Danish army and navy have fared much worse in recent years. Their equipment is terribly outdated, much of it from the late 1950s and early 1960s. Under the new Defense Commission guidelines, the army will eliminate some 35 to 40 of its tanks as part of CFE reductions, perhaps eliminating the very old M-41 or Centurions. The remaining Centurions are to be replaced with used German Leopard I tanks, as originally planned. The navy will lose the last of its major surface combat ships—two frigates—and two of its submarines will be modernized. The frigates will be replaced by smaller Standard Flex 300 craft and shore-based antishipping missile batteries, advancing the concept of a more "defensive defense."[10] It appears doubtful that even these limited modernization plans will now be fully implemented.

The condition of the Danish military could deteriorate further if the socialist parties gain greater support in a new election, assuming they do not revise their electoral platforms. The SDP has been toying with the idea of adopting a much stricter form of "defensive defense," having proposed to eliminate all submarines and major surface combatants from the navy, restricting the air force to home air defense, and eliminating what little armor the army possesses. The 1989 defense agreement takes several major steps in this direction. The SPP and Progress party would prefer to eliminate the military entirely. Such an extreme outcome is unlikely, but a greatly reduced military posture is quite possible, especially under a CFE regime. An intermediate and quite feasible approach would be to retire aging weapon systems (i.e., Draken aircraft, submarines, M-48 tanks) without replacement, probably under the guise of CFE.

Theater-Based Nuclear Deterrence

Like Norway, Denmark prohibits nuclear weapons on its soil in peacetime and would probably continue the ban in wartime. This policy was enunciated in 1959 when NATO first began its debate on theater nuclear forces. In recent years, some Danish political parties have become increasingly vocal in their opposition to NATO's nuclear policies. In May 1984 the SDP was able to force legislation stopping the Danish contribution to NATO's infrastructure funding for GLCM deployments. The far Left parties want Denmark to quit membership in NATO's Nuclear Planning Group (NPG), but the SDP and the nonsocialist parties prefer continued membership, albeit for different reasons. Prior to the

1990 NPG meeting, both the government and the socialists had supported Germany's opposition to modernization of theater nuclear forces until after 1992 and its call for immediate negotiations for the reductions of these weapons. Both groups applauded the NPG decision to cancel plans for a follow-on to Lance and to reduce substantially the stockpiles of nuclear artillery.

Danish concerns about nuclear weapons center on allied ships in Danish ports. The INF treaty has focused more attention on the issue because SLCMs on American ships could be seen as a "compensation" for systems removed under the treaty. This possibility has drawn attention within Denmark to the question of port calls by American ships. The issue came to a head in 1988. On April 14, the Social Democrats, after considerable internal conflict, managed to win support for a measure requiring that all visiting warships be "reminded " of Denmark's three-decade-old ban on nuclear weapons. The Conservative-led government of Paul Schluter decided to declare this matter a "vital element" of its security policy, resulting in a general election. The inconclusive election results meant that the issue remained unresolved. After some additional posturing,[11] the parties reached a compromise whereby allied ships were assumed to adhere to Denmark's policy, essentially the same stance as before. In the aftermath of these inconclusive results, the major parties in Denmark will probably avoid calling another election on nuclear issues.

Economic Issues

Burden sharing continues to be a major issue for Denmark within the Alliance. The country is often criticized for its low level of defense spending. Denmark never came close to reaching the NATO goal of 3 percent real growth in defense spending, despite the relatively low base from which it started and the wealth of the country. With Denmark's relatively high personnel costs (almost 60 percent of the defense budget), very little money is left for weapons acquisitions. Given that the parties have agreed to no real growth in defense spending over the next four years, we can expect that burden sharing will continue to be a point of contention between Denmark and its allies. Criticism comes not only from the United States, but also from the United Kingdom (with its commitment to reinforce Denmark) and Germany (which shares responsibility for defense of the Baltic approaches). However, such pressure tactics can merely reinforce the position of the more isolationist parties who tap into the Danish aversion to outside interference.[12]

Beyond these burden sharing issues, no real relationship exists between foreign trade and security issues in Denmark. Denmark has no major defense industry, and popular opinion does not provide much support for the little that exists. Denmark must import virtually all of its major weapons.

Within Denmark, the biggest economic question over the next few years—perhaps the biggest political question as well—will be how to adjust to the establishment of a unified internal market in the European Community at the end of 1992. The adjustments required will be considerable. The Danish tax burden is the highest in the EC, as is the per capita debt. Denmark will have the largest downward adjustment in value-added tax in all of the EC, resulting in a loss of revenues equal to 5 percent of Danish GNP. Adjustments will not be politically easy, because many people in Denmark still oppose membership in the EC; in fact Denmark has the highest proportion of public opposition of all the EC countries.

Structure of NATO

The Nordic members of NATO—Norway, Denmark, and Iceland—have sought to maintain a separate identity and sense of membership within the Alliance. They imposed certain limiting conditions on their membership, such as a ban on nuclear weapon or foreign bases on their territory. Beyond their commitment to this Nordic identity within NATO, the Danes have traditionally been quiet concerning shifting responsibilities within the Alliance.[13] The changes in Eastern Europe and the imminent reunification of Germany have made the Danes somewhat more vocal. The pro-defense parties emphasize the need to maintain NATO and a substantial American presence in Europe. In the past, moderates in all parties have resisted calls for a reduced American role in NATO, fearing that this would lessen commitment to the Atlanticist view and its emphasis on the northern flank, thus leading to a reduced commitment by the principal Atlantic powers—the United States and the United Kingdom—to reinforce Denmark. Now, the concern is more political and economic stability during the transition to a Europe without blocs. The left-wing parties favor a substantially reduced role for the United States within Europe, especially if it meant decreased reliance on nuclear weapons. However, they would not advocate increased ties to a "continental" pillar; instead, they would push for even greater emphasis on reductions in tensions and increased security discussions with the Nordic nations.

SOME VARIATIONS ON THE LIKELY CASE

Plausible Electoral Variations

Two important characteristics of contemporary Danish politics are (1) the multifaceted coalitions that form in the Folketing and (2) frequent elections. Almost all governments are formed on domestic issues, usually centered on key economic and social policies. Since 1981 the government has rarely enjoyed a majority on security policy, whereas the SDP has been able to pass a series of its own bills. In the future, a strong possibility would be that neither the pro-defense nor the antidefense alignments have a majority, with the Progress party (and perhaps other parties) voting against both sides. In such an event, security policy could reach an indefinite impasse. Such a condition virtually exists today. After the experience of 1988, no government is likely to call another election over security policy. However, elections will probably be required at some point in the next year or two given the basic instability of the current Folketing. From the point of view of the author, the most plausible electoral possibilities, in decreasing order of probability, would be the following.

Roughly like current conditions, with no coalition having a firm majority on any issue. This seems by far the most likely outcome. No changes are made in Danish security policy. The military continues to slowly deteriorate due to a freeze on defense spending. The 1989 Defense Commission recommendations remain in effect technically, but some addition reductions are made.

Resurgent Right and center coalition in new elections. The Conservatives are able to form a new center Right coalition without the Radical Liberals. The recommendations of the 1989 Defense Commission are realized. The military services modernize the forces left after CFE, with the air force upgrading its F-16s and the army acquiring new tanks. Denmark remains mute on nuclear issues within NATO.

Reestablishment of a centrist security consensus. The 1989 defense agreement proves to be a watershed in Danish security policy. The SDP moves back toward the center on security policy, whereas the traditionally pro-defense parties compromise on certain aspects of defense policy. All parties agree that Denmark should maintain the force structure established in the 1989 agreement unless modified by a CFE agreement, and they agree to modernize forces as needed. Training and readiness are improved. Certain "offensive" missions are prohibited (a blue-water navy and rear area attacks by the air force), but all remaining missions are adequately funded. This consensus remains even if governments change on other issues.

Resurgent Left/pacifist coalition in new elections. The SDP moves to the Left and reconciles its differences with the Socialist People's Party. The SDP with the support of the SSP, and perhaps the Radical Liberals, forms a majority government after new elections. The new government is committed to enforcing Denmark's ban on nuclear weapons and to establishing a thoroughly "defensive defense." Visiting warships are monitored for nuclear weapons. The remnants of the blue-water navy are eliminated, plans to replace the Draken fighter are cancelled, and the F-16 is limited to an air defense role. Within NATO, the Danish government opposes nuclear modernization (specifically TASM) and pushes for greater reductions in the conventional arms control talks.

Soviet Policy

The baseline analysis assumed a continuation of Soviet policy roughly as it has proceeded in the last couple years. It assumes that Soviet forces are completely withdrawn from Hungary and Czechoslovakia, with substantial reductions in Poland and Bulgaria. Germany is united, but some Soviet troops remain in the territory of the former German Democratic Republic during a transition period. In this environment, the Danish public finds less and less justification for increases in defense spending and for accepting nuclear weapons in Europe.

Two alternative Soviet behaviors could change these attitudes and the assessments above:

Complete and rapid withdrawal of Soviet forces from Eastern Europe. If the Soviet Union entirely withdrew its forces in Eastern Europe, support for defense spending in Denmark would probably collapse. If the Soviets allowed the Baltic republics to establish their independence, then most Danes would have difficulty perceiving any imminent threat from the Soviet Union. The socialists and Radical Liberals would likely argue that NATO was the vestige of "old thinking" and that Denmark must take moral leadership in creating a new Europe. The result wold be an accelerated dismantling of the Danish military, and possibly its virtual elimination.

Revival of Soviet reactionism. If the Soviet Union resumed an openly hostile attitude toward reform in Eastern Europe, Danish attitudes would change toward greater support for defense spending. This could also occur if the Soviets crush the independence movements in the Baltic republics. The more pro-defense parties would argue that they were correct all along, that a leopard cannot change its spots, and that Denmark must not repeat the mistakes of the 1930s when Denmark unilaterally disarmed.

Traditionally, Danish attitudes have not been highly sensitive to modest changes in Soviet behavior. Yet, this era is far from traditional, and Soviet actions could have a profound influence on public opinion and the security consensus. Given the narrow balance of power in the Folketing, even a small shift in attitudes could result in large shifts in policy.

Policies of Other NATO Members

On the whole Denmark is not greatly influenced by the actions and comments of allied nations (with the notable exception of Norway), but some Danish parties are responsive to actions in allied countries. The SDP maintains close contact with its West German counterpart, the SPD, and often follows its lead on security policy matters. The formation of an SPD government in West Germany could be expected to significantly influence the SDP in Denmark. A more widespread resurgence of socialist parties in the West could certainly help the SPD. On the other side, the nonsocialist defense-oriented parties have been concerned about the growing negative image of Denmark within the Alliance and are sensitive to what the major Alliance members say; in their minds, this partly justified calling elections after the Conservative government lost the vote concerning port calls. Also, a strong showing in Eastern Europe by Christian Democrats and conservative parties might help bolster the standing of center Right parties.

Certain policy changes by allied nations could affect Danish policy. The baseline projection above assumed that allied country countries pursue policies roughly in line with current behavior. Some plausible alternative policies include:

Norway bans port calls by ships carrying nuclear weapons. In this event, one would expect Denmark to follow suit. Similarly, if Norway should object to American naval deployments or strategies in the Norwegian Sea (for instance, deployment of vessels carrying nuclear-armed SLCMs), Denmark would undoubtedly support the Norwegian position.

A united Germany declares its neutrality. This action would lead to a collapse of NATO as we now know it. Denmark would probably opt for neutrality or an alignment with its Nordic neighbors if possible.

Great Britain withdraws its commitment to reinforce Denmark. Such an action could become a political issue in Denmark. The Socialist People's party and Radical Liberals might use this as an argument to withdraw from NATO rather than succumb to pressure from outside powers. The nonsocialist parties would attempt to strengthen Danish defense and perhaps seek an offsetting commitment from the United States.

America substantially disengages from Europe. Disengagement can come in the form of shifting emphasis away from Europe toward the Pacific or elsewhere, or in the form of decreasing troops strengths for budgetary or arms control reasons. The results could be similar to the above case. However, if the result were merely a "Europeanization" of NATO's defense, Denmark would probably remain within the Alliance but without increasing its defense spending.

CONCLUSIONS ABOUT THE FUTURE
OF DANISH SECURITY POLICY

The most likely course for Danish security policy over the next few years is a steady decline in military capabilities, beyond any treaty-imposed reductions, and substantial opposition to deployment of TASM and SLCM. The current absence of a strong majority, either for or against improved defenses, will result in compromises that fail to do anything. On more symbolic questions involving arms control and nuclear weapons, the antinuclear majority in the Folketing will continue to pass resolutions that make clear their objections. Otherwise, barring a major shift in representation in the Folketing, the next few years will be marked by inaction, or reaction to external events, in the security sphere.

NORWEGIAN SECURITY POLICY: THE NEXT FIVE YEARS

Norway has enjoyed considerably greater electoral stability than has Denmark. Like Denmark, Norway has a multiparty system, with the members of the parliament, the Storting, being elected by proportional representation. However, the Storting is not subject to dissolution; if the government loses a vote of confidence, the next largest party that is not in the current government is asked to form a new one. Members of the Storting serve for a full four-year term. This single fact makes the Norwegian political environment far more stable than Denmark's because all parties realize that they must live with the makeup of the parliament for its full term. Changes of government in midterm are relatively rare, having occurred only four times in the postwar period (1963, 1971, 1972, and 1986), twice over the controversial proposal for Norway to join the EC.

The Socialist Parties

The Labor party has dominated Norwegian political life for the last half century. Labor has led the government for 48 of the last 59 years and has since 1927 continually held the largest number of seats in the Storting. After almost five years out of power in the early 1980s, Labor, revived for a time under the leadership of Gro Harlem Brundtland, who survived and governed better than most observers in Norway expected. From 1986 to 1989, Brundtland headed a minority Labor government with the de facto support of the center and Christian People's parties in the center and the Socialist Left Party on the Left. The party suffered a major setback in the 1989 elections when it lost eight of its 72 seats. It now sits in opposition.

Labor's policies resemble those of the other Scandinavian SPDs, although perhaps more centrist than they on defense issues. Labor has organized and nurture Norway's security and foreign policy consensus in the postwar period. Although a minority within the party tends to be anti-NATO, the leadership and the majority of the membership remain firmly committed to Alliance. Moderate Laborites, including the leadership, tend to be Atlanticists, whereas the left wing tends to be more Nordic and somewhat anti-American. However, the moderate's pro-NATO stance does not translate into support for maintaining defense spending; the Labor government has reduced manpower levels and has slowed growth rates for military spending.

In foreign economic policy, the party leadership seems to favor seeking membership in the EC, but a poll in early 1989 indicated that the Labor rank-and-file was split roughly 30-30-40 among those in favor, opposed, and undecided. Because of this internal division, the Labor leadership sought to keep the question of membership in the EC off the political agenda in the 1989 election. However, by early 1990 as a result of the vast changes occurring in Europe, sentiment within Labor had shifted strongly toward membership. It now seems likely that Labor will eventually support Norwegian membership in the European Community, probably sometime in the mid-1990s.

The Left in Norway holds a much weaker position than other Scandinavian nations. The Socialist Left party, a former coalition of far Left socialist and communist parties, maintains a platform that is anti-EC, anti-NATO, and antinuclear. The party gained considerable support and influence during the late 1970s and early 1980s in the wake of the debates over the neutron bomb and deployment of Pershing II and ground-launched cruise missiles. When the centrist parties in the parliament began to support the Labor government in the mid-1980s, the influence of the SLP declined sharply. In response, the party slightly moderated it position on a variety of issues. The Socialist Left was able to capitalize on dissatisfaction with Labor in 1989 election, and it increased its representation from six to 17 seats. In recent years, it has de-emphasized its anti-NATO stance but has increased its opposition to anything involving nuclear weapons. The party would favor the establishment of a Nordic Nuclear-Free Zone. Several small communist parties have been unable to garner more than 0.2 percent of the vote and do not hold any seats in the Storting.

The Nonsocialist Parties

The nonsocialist coalition is led by the Conservative party, the oldest in Norway. The Conservatives favor a strong defense, including NATO's use of nuclear weapons if necessary, and overwhelmingly favor entry into the EC. In the early 1980s, they enjoyed an upwell of popular support, increasing their representation in 1981 from 44 to 53 seats and allowing them to form a minority government under Kare Willoch (Fig. 8-3). For a time it appeared that the Conservatives would surpass Labor as the nation's largest party. However, their support has been diminishing. In 1985 they lost three seats and their coalition lost two seats overall. They managed to form a minority government with the

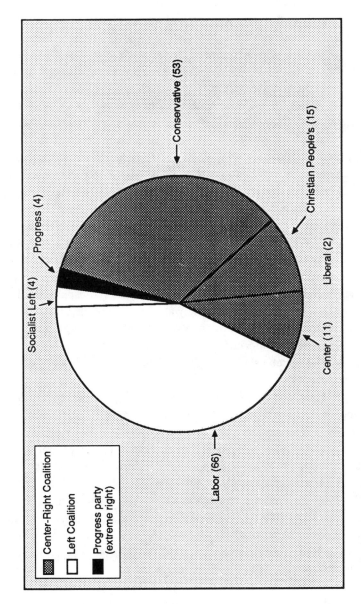

Figure 8-3 The Norwegian parliament: 1981–85.

Conservative (53)

Christian People's (15)

Liberal (2)

Center (11)

Labor (66)

Socialist Left (4)

Progress (4)

- Center-Right Coalition
- Left Coalition
- Progress party (extreme right)

support of the Progress party, but the government was forced to resign the following year when the Progress party withdrew its support. In the 1989 election, the Conservatives suffered a dramatic decline, losing 13 of their 50 seats. Despite this large loss, the party was able to form another minority government with the support of the revived Progress party.

Three other parties, primarily rural, help form the mainstream nonsocialist alternative. The Christian's People party, also known as the Christian Democratic party, advocates conservative policies with particular emphasis on antiabortion legislation and increased trade with developing countries. The party almost always votes with the Conservatives on domestic issues, but some members tend to be pacifist and antinuclear. The Christian Democrats currently hold 14 seats after losing two seats in the 1989 elections. The Center party, formerly the Agrarian party and still referred to as Agrarians, emphasized ecological issues and shorter work weeks, generally adopting a moderate, nonsocialist stance. It currently holds 11 seats, having lost one seat in 1989. After the collapse of the nonsocialist government in 1986, the Agrarians and the Conservatives had been feuding; the Conservatives opposed increased subsidies to farmers, renewing the old urban/rural split in Norwegian politics. They managed to put aside their differences to form a new government, but the stability of the grouping is uncertain at best. The Liberal party stresses ecological issues and philosophically liberal economic policies, two stances increasingly at odds. One of the oldest parties in Norway, it had gradually lost its votes to various splinter groups until it completely lost its representation in the Storting in 1985. All three parties overwhelmingly oppose membership in the EC, with the Center Democrats being the most vocal opponents.

The Progress party is a right-wing group, formerly known by the official tongue-tying title "Anders Lange's Party for a Strong Reduction in Taxes, Rates, and Public Intervention." The Progress party advocates a platform very similar to Jean-Marie LePen's National Front in France, offering simplistic solutions to the nation's problems and appealing to Norway's latent xenophobia. The party favors a strong defense, but not necessarily closer ties to NATO.

Until the 1989 election, the Progress party was the smallest in the Storting, having only two seats after the 1985 election;[14] however, those two seats held the balance of power. After the 1985 election, the socialist parties held 77 seats and the other nonsocialists 78 seats. At first the Progress party supported a Conservative-led government, but in April 1986 it withdrew that support over a proposed gas tax increase, and a new Labor-led government was formed. Oddly enough, a socialist government was kept in power for three years with the assistance of an extreme antisocialist party.

The Progress party was by far the biggest winner in 1989. It gained 20 addi-

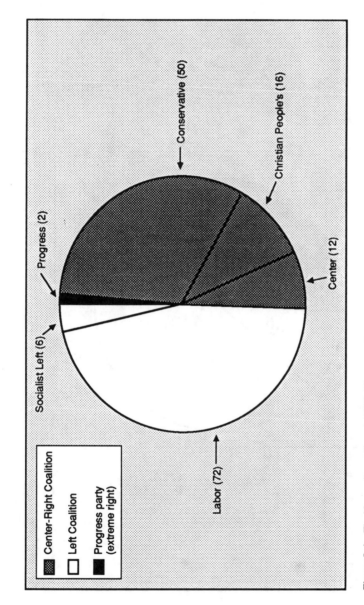

Figure 8-4 The Norwegian parliment: 1985–89.

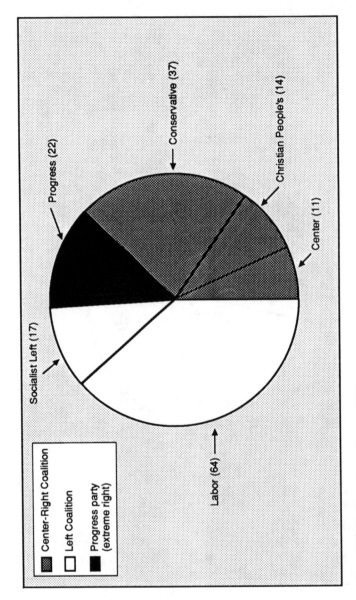

Figure 8-5 The Norwegian parliament: 1989.

Conservative (37)

Christian People's (14)

Progress (22)

Center (11)

Socialist Left (17)

Labor (64)

Center-Right Coalition

Left Coalition

Progress party
(extreme right)

tional seats for a total of 22, or 13 percent of the Storting. The party can no longer be considered a small fringe group. In almost any scenario, it will have a major it not decisive say in who governs. The centrist parties may begin to chafe at the need to appease the Progress party. The Conservatives will be torn between keeping their coalition partners happy and not losing the support of Progress. The Labor party cannot hope to do much better, needing the support of the Socialist Left if it is ever to form a government, but also probably needing the centrist parties as well.

The outlook until the election in 1993 will be a period of unprecedented instability, or at least inaction, in Norwegian politics. The mainstream parties have both lost credibility, whereas the extremists have gained a growing voice. Although the Norwegian constitution will limit the degree of governmental instability, the prospects for divisive and damaging political maneuvering remains.

SPECIFIC NORWEGIAN ISSUE AREAS

In 1989 the Norwegian parliament established a new Defense Commission tasked with reviewing the full range of security defense policies. It will make recommendations on the future force structure and policy of Norway's military forces. Coming at this juncture in history, this report promises to be the single most important defense document since Norway joined NATO and established its base policy. The commission will most likely adopt a fairly moderate, Atlanticist-oriented position. Still, it could suggest major changes in the size and structure of Norway's standing forces, in Norway's agreements with its allies on reinforcement commitments, and on prepositioning of equipment. This analysis assumes a more moderate outcome.

Conventional and Nuclear Arms Control Negotiations

Norway has maintained a low profile on arms control matters, taking a back seat to the major NATO members, except when it involves the Nordic region. Former Defense Minister Johan Horgen Holst has been very effective in convincing a majority of Norwegian policy makers on the need to balance reassurance (that Norway will not allow its territory to used for aggression against Soviet interests) and deterrence (of Soviet attacks). Many Norwegian statements and documents had included Holst-inspired rhetoric even before he became defense minister.[15] Norway will generally support nuclear arms control, either strategic or theater, as long as it maintains this balancing act. Norway would object to any arms control agreement that made the Kola Peninsula[16] or Norwegian Sea an area of increased military activity or importance, such as if ICBMs were eliminated and greater emphasis was placed on SLBMs and SLCMs. In conventional arms reduction talks, Norway will emphasize the need to include Soviet forces on the Kola Peninsula and in the Leningrad Military District. In particular, Norway will want assurances that forces withdrawn from Central Europe will not be simply redeployed into the Soviet Union. Norway may go so far as to hold up an agreement until it received such assurances. Norway can be expected to support agreements reducing the potential for superpower confrontations in the Norwegian Sea provided that such agreements did not significantly hinder the ability of NATO to reinforce Norway in crisis. This will be a difficult tightrope to walk.

As stated in the section on Denmark, the Nordic Nuclear-Free Zone (NNFZ) has been a recurrent idea in Nordic affairs. The Norwegian government has shown only lukewarm interest in the proposal because, without a major change in NATO policy, a NNFZ would be incompatible with Norway's membership in the Alliance and could weaken deterrence. However, the concept was reintroduced into the political debate by a Labor politician and former ambassador, and the idea has won support among leftist groups in Labor and forms part of the platform of the Socialist Left party. The Labor party has made "consideration" of a NNFZ part of their platform, but the leadership has attempted to mute interest in the concept. Interest fell off in the late 1980s, but could be revived by Gorbachev's speech to the Finnish parliament in October 1989. If a Labor-Left Socialist government is formed, the NNFZ could once again climb to the top of the national agenda.

Quantitative and Qualitative Changes in Conventional Forces

The Norwegian government will probably not seek any major changes in conventional forces during the next several years. Slight reductions will probably be introduced, but the continued strong Soviet military presence on the Kola Peninsula will make Norwegian leadership hesitant to reduce forces too rapidly. In terms of equipment, the Norwegian military should be in moderately good condition if all currently planned programs go through. The air force recently completed a major modernization program with the acquisition of the F-16, which consumed most of the national military acquisition budget of the 1980s. The air force will receive the Penguin Mk III antishipping missile, which is essential for the F-16s' mission of interdiction of amphibious assaults. The army is currently undergoing a modest modernization program consisting of the acquisition of more antitank missiles, oversnow vehicles, and some older tanks and armored personnel carriers from the United States. The navy is retiring a few submarines and modernizing the remainder. It remains unclear which forces would be cut or which modernization programs cancelled if required by CFE or by budget restrictions.

Manpower remains the biggest problem for the Norwegian military. In Norway, labor laws apply to the military, ensuring a minimum wage, limiting soldiers to a 38-hour work week, providing time-and-a-half for overtime, and so on. This helped to raise manpower costs to 50 percent of the defense budget in the early 1980s, although more recently the government has brought this figure down to 40 percent. Despite real growth rates of 3 percent in defense spending, the military has had to eliminate hundreds of positions; the 1990 budget alone calls for a reduction 450 positions out of a total strength of 35,000. More seriously, military has been forced to reduce the refresher training by a third for its reserves. With a population base of only 4 million, Norway must rely heavily on mobilization for its defense. In the event of war, the army would mushroom from 19,000 to 100,000 in less than a week. Thus any reduction in the readiness of reserves gravely diminishes Norwegian capabilities.[17] But not only the mobilization forces are affected: the air force has been unable to retain enough pilots for all its planes. For the last several years it has been able to maintain only some 50 pilots for its 67 F-16s. Similar problems exist for technicians in all the services.

From 1986 to 19889, the Labor government attempted to limit the growth of defense expenditures by reducing manpower and increasing "efficiency," the dominant buzz word in the defense debate. The Labor government was not able to secure a majority for its proposals, with a centrist Right bloc winning more money for defense. The new government should be able to maintain levels of defense spending close to the levels of the late 1980s. The Progress party, contrary to its general libertarian line, favors more spending on defense. This can be explained in part by their interest in reducing reliance on outside powers (i.e., NATO) to defend Norway, and in part by their feeling that the money can come from reduced expenditures in the social sector.

Norway has been able to maintain real growth in defense spending due largely to the government revenues from oil production, which allowed a substantial modernization program in the 1980s, given the small population of Norway. If the price of oil should fall or if an accident should cripple Norwegian drilling platforms, government revenues would be hurt substantially and the military modernization programs would most likely be reduced.

Theater-Based Nuclear Deterrence

Norway prohibits nuclear weapons on its soil in peacetime and would probably continue the ban at least in the early stages of any conflict. Norway explicitly reserves the right to permit the deployment of nuclear weapons on its soil whenever it sees fit. This policy was first enunciated in 1959 and has been periodically reaffirmed or strengthened over the years. More recently, in 1986 the government refused to allow a U.S. F-111 to refuel in Norway since the aircraft was nuclear capable. Despite these occasional disagreements. Norwegian governments of both the Left and Right have continued to support NATO's nuclear strategy.[18] At the same time, the Norwegian government has not been supporting the proposal to modernize NATO's medium-range nuclear weapons.

The main Norwegian concern involving nuclear weapons centers on allied ships, particularly SLCMs on American vessels operating in and around Norwegian territory. This issue will undoubtedly gain greater prominence as NATO comes to rely more heavily on SLCM. The leftist parties and some elements of the Labor party would like to ban port calls by ships carrying nuclear weapons. Currently, the Norwegian government merely informs all governments of its ban on nuclear weapons, and it "expects" everyone to abide by its policy. The INF Treaty has renewed interest in the question of port calls the issue, since the use of SLCMs on American ships could be used as a "compensation" for systems removed under the treaty. So far the Labor party has been able to keep the issue from becoming part of the party platform, although some local party chapters (including Oslo and Bergen) have called for a more active ban.

Whereas the Labor party has not wanted to make port calls an issue, it has been concerned with the possibility that deployments of SLCMs in the Norwegian Sea would increase tensions in the area. Johan Holst has urged NATO and the United States to proceed cautiously and to avoid a "Mediterraneanization" of the Norwegian Sea, where large numbers of American and Soviet vessels would be in constant proximity to each other. At the same time, Holst has reaffirmed Norway's commitment to a regular, but moderate size, American presence in the Norwegian Sea.

Economic Issues

In security policy, the most troubling economic issue for Norway in the late 1980s had been the Toshiba–Kongsberg scandal. In the winter of 1986–1987, the U.S. government presented evidence to the Norwegian government that the Kongsberg Weapon Factory—state-owned and heavily subsidized—along with Toshiba in Japan had been exporting highly sophisticated computers and cutting equipment to the Soviet Union, which allowed the Soviets to build far more quiet submarines. The estimated damage in terms of additional antisubmarine warfare capability needed was measured in the billions of dollars. This scandal led to efforts in the U.S. Congress to ban imports of weapons built by Kongsberg. Such a ban would have virtually crippled the Norwegian arms industries since Kongsberg relies on sales to the U.S. military, in particular for the Penguin missile, the primary antiship missile of both the navy and air force. Norwegian officials have worked hard to thwart a ban, with success. Yet, the government faced a dilemma: if it wishes to avoid a ban, it must show—to the satisfaction of the U.S. Congress—that measures have been taken to punish the individuals responsible, but if it wishes to maintain the support at home, it cannot appear to be caving in to American pressures. Although now largely in the past, the Kongsberg affair remains an example of the sort of nasty problem that can arise in Norwegian-American relations.

A major question for Norway in the next five years will be how to respond to the creation of a unified market in the EC at the end of 1992. Norway is unlikely to apply for membership any time soon, that is to say, before the late 1990s. Norwegians remember how divisive the question of membership was in the early 1970s, and they are wary of repeating that episode. Still, the issue will not go away. Depending on how the unified market develops, Norway may find itself being pushed toward closer ties with either the United States and Canada, or with the neutral states of Sweden and Finland. Either possibility holds problems for Norway's concept of itself and its security.

Structure of NATO

Within NATO Norwegian officials have emphasized two aspects of identity: the Nordic and the Atlantic. From the beginning of the Alliance, Norway has stressed the special nature of the Nordic members of NATO: itself, Denmark and Iceland. These states have maintained a separate identity and sense of membership within the Alliance, and they have imposed the well-known limitations on their membership. The Norwegians in particular stressed the importance of the so-called Nordic Balance: the pattern of security relationships in the far north involving Norway, Denmark, and Iceland on one side, the Soviet Union on the other, and neutrals Sweden and Finland in the center. The need to operate within the conditions of this relationship fundamentally shaped Norwegian security policy.

At the same time, Norway has always emphasized that it is an Atlantic nation. Prior to World War II, Norwegian security relied on the implicit guarantee of the primary Atlantic naval power—Britain—to protect freedom of the seas and Norwegian independence. From the beginning, Norway has emphasized the Atlantic nature of NATO. Norway's closest allies have been the North Atlantic powers: the United States, United Kingdom, and Canada. Even the Netherlands, with its sizable navy, holds an important place in Norwegian security. Traditionally, Norway remained somewhat aloof from continental affairs. It had no historical ties to France and it kept Germany at a distance. Norwegian defense has been oriented northward toward Finnmark rather than southward toward Denmark, Germany, and the Baltic Sea.

However, Norwegian policy elites are changing their attitudes toward the relative isolation from "Europe"—for example, the continent—and about its preferred distribution of responsibilities within NATO. During 1988, Norwegian policy makers began to speak increasingly of the "European" aspects of Norwegian policy. Papers are being issued by the various ministries on the role of Norway in Europe. The Storting has been debating the impact 1992 and has been toying with the idea of holding a new referendum on membership in the EC. The Defense Ministry is more thoroughly considering defenses of south Norway and the Baltic, and it is increasing security discussions with Germany.[19] Norwegian officials speak of their need to understand the European context of the security debate between East and West. This emphasis would shift back northward if the Soviets pull out completely from East Germany, Poland, and the Baltic republics.

One cannot predict where this debate will end; the Norwegians themselves do not know. It seems likely that, at minimum, Norway will move toward greater economic and security cooperation with the continental West European nations and will place relatively less emphasis on relations with the United States and the United Kingdom. German–Norwegian relations will become more important in both the economic and the military spheres. The outcome of the EC question could strongly influence these tendencies one way or the other.

Abstract and Symbolic Issues

Norwegian officials are very concerned that NATO understand its views of the world. Since the 1960s, Norwegian officials used the concept of the Nordic Balance to explain this view. This term was used to explain a perceived pattern of relationships in Nordic Europe whereby (stated very simply):

- Restraint by Nordic NATO states in peacetime results in lower tensions in the region, allows Finland to maintain its independence from Moscow, and reduces the risk of war.
- The implicit threat that Norway would permit U.S. bases and even nuclear weapons in Norway acts to restrain the Soviet Union in crisis.

Norwegians, even high level officials, refer to themselves and the other Nordic peoples as being caught by the accident geography between the two superpowers. Although Norwegians feel much stronger affinity to the West than to the East, many still view NATO as more a marriage of convenience than of passion.[20]

Recently, the term Nordic Balance has fallen into disfavor, because the word "balance" was misleading. Instead, Norwegians now speak of the Nordic area as a "region of low tensions" and describe Norwegian security policy as a combination of deterrence of the Soviet Union through conventional defense and rapid reinforcement, and reassurance of the Soviet Union—and indirectly Sweden and Finland—that Norwegian territory will not be used for aggression against Soviet interests. This requires maintaining a fine balance between Norwegian sovereignty and avoiding actions that might provoke the Soviet Union. Norway will continue to stress the importance of its "base policy"—the prohibition against foreign bases in Norway—in its relations with both the United States and USSR. It will insist on freedom of the seas in the water around Norway, but will also strive to limit the "Mediterraneanization" of the Norwegian Sea and to avoid U.S.–USSR confrontations in both the Norwegian and Barents seas. At the same time it will seek to have the widest possible commitment from NATO to reinforce NATO in crisis and war.

Another important symbol in Norwegian security policy is the image of "flags." The term "flag" is shorthand to refer to a nation, specifically a NATO ally. The Norwegian political goal for allied reinforcements is to have as many flags involved as possible. Similarly in the Norwegian Sea, Holst has been speaking increasingly of the need to get more allied flags in NATO patrols and to rely less on American ships. The point is to let the Soviet Union know that an attack on Norway is an attack on NATO while limiting the potential for superpower clashes in the region. Thus when Canada withdrew its commitment to reinforce Norway, the Norwegians viewed the action as a major blow, less for the loss of military capability (which was marginal at best) but for the loss of an important symbol. Similarly, Norwegian officials were rather uninterested in American or British forces as compensation, as both countries were already adequately represented and additional American forces could be counterproductive.

SOME VARIATIONS ON THE LIKELY CASE

Plausible Electoral Variations

The 1989 elections have largely bounded the plausible alternative future governments. The current Storting will sit until September 1993.

The most likely course over the next few years would be for the Conservatives to rule for two to three years with Progress party support, then fall to a Labor-Socialist Left government. Since all parties realize that they must live with each other until 1993, they will be reluctant to rock the boat excessively. The Conservative government will avoid controversial positions in an effort to keep its coalition in power. However, at some point we can expect that this balancing act will fail and that Labor will be asked to form a government. Under this scenario, difficult decisions are avoided on a variety of issues, and the government will be willing to tolerate losses on some votes rather than give up control. This could mean that a situation on defense issues similar to Denmark from 1984 to 1988 could emerge in Norway.

A nasty alternative future would arise if the Progress party fails to offer stable support to any coalition. Under this scenario, governmental control and coalitions will change several times over the next four years, with potentially wild shifts in policy (at least by Norwegian standards). Security and foreign policy could become unpredictable.

Another possibility would be for the eventual formation of a Labor–Center–Christian Democrat majority coalition. This combination seems unlikely in 1990, but if several years of relying on the Progress party becomes intolerable, the centrist parties might prefer alignment with Labor than either a Labor-Socialist Left coalition or continuation of the current government.

Soviet Policy

Norwegian security policy remains very sensitive to both American and Soviet security policy, both as it relates specifically to Europe as well as the overall Soviet–American strategic balance. A number of plausible changes in Soviet behavior or in relations between superpowers could affect the projections made in this chapter.

A START agreement reduces ICBMs disproportionately more than sea-based systems. Situated next to the Kola Peninsula, Norway is highly sensitive to any increase in Soviet reliance on SSBNs. If the United States and Soviet Union signed a strategic arms accord that led to a relatively greater Soviet reliance on SLBMs—even if SLBMs were reduced—the Soviet Union would probably place even greater emphasis on protecting its SSBN fleet. Similarly, if the B-1, B-2, and cruise missile are not reduced or eliminated, the importance of air defense in the far north will grow. These situations would probably result in an increased Soviet military presence on the Kola Peninsula and an increased Soviet determination to deny NATO use of Norway's northern airbases in wartime. Any major increase in Soviet conventional military forces in the region could undermine Norwegian security and defense policy.

Increased assertiveness of Soviet naval strategy in the far north. From the mid-1960s through the mid-1980s, Soviet naval deployments and exercises in the Norwegian Sea increased enormously, causing Norway to seek greater reinforcement commitments from its allies. Since 1985, Soviet naval activity dropped off significantly. Yet, in early 1989 the Soviets deployed two major warships to the Kola Peninsula: an aircraft carrier and a new type of missile cruiser, the largest ship in the Soviet fleet. Norwegian and NATO officials are still uncertain what this all means, but they are coming to conclude that the Soviet maritime threat is less than they once thought. However, if Soviet Northern Fleet resumes a more active profile in the Norwegian Sea, the Norwegian public may become more willing to accept American naval deployments in the region. This possibility may grow as the Soviet Union loses its strategic depth in central Europe.

Reduction in Soviet military forces in the far north. The converse of the two previous cases holds as well: if Soviet conventional forces on the Kola Peninsula are reduced, Norwegian threat projections will decrease. Support would grow for defense spending would fall and calls for a smaller American presence in the region would increase. Reductions in forces in Central Europe would have some influence on public opinion, but far less an elite opinion.

One change not mentioned is internal change in the Soviet Union. In the opinion of this author, Norwegian policy is not terribly sensitive to changes in internal Soviet behavior per se, but only insofar as it affects external behavior. Norwegian policy has changed at the margins over the years, but the basic tenets of Norway's policies laid down in 1948 have held consistently through many changes in the Soviet Union. The events of late 1989 certainly have helped to reduce tensions in Europe, as has a more open Soviet society and a more Western approach to diplomacy would help relations. Yet, if Soviet forces on the Kola remained unchanged in strength or doctrine, Norwegian policy on security would probably remain largely unchanged. The Norwegians may even protest if they feel that reductions in tensions elsewhere in Europe are not being reflected in the far north.

Policies of the NATO Allies

Being absolutely dependent on external reinforcements for its defense, Norway will remain sensitive to the policies and actions of its allies. Of all these countries, the United States has the greatest impact. Possible changes in American policy that would affect Norway include the following.

Increased assertiveness of U.S. naval strategy in the far north. Norway has been very cautious and concerned about the more forward maritime strategy pursued by the U.S. Navy since the early 1980s. Norwegian officials feel they can live with the current level of activity, albeit with some reservations, particularly concerning possible wartime plans to attack Soviet SSBNs during conventional operations. However, any further increase could result in a public and elite backlash against American policies and an effort to distance Norway from American actions. A more assertive American posture could come in the form of a more isolationist approach (à la *Discriminate Deterrence*), or increased deployments of SCLM-armed vessels, or increased deployments of carrier task forces. However, these options will not be realistic in a period of severe budget constraints.

Substantially reduced American military commitment to Europe. Any reduction in the American commitment of forces to Europe, whether driven by arms control or fiscal constraint, would be felt in Norway. Even less visible American actions could have important repercussions there. For example, a reduction in the number of USAF wings might mean that fewer units were available to reinforce Europe, or the reliance on more USAF reserve or air national guard units might mean that the reinforcement schedule would have to be extended. The loss or delay of even one unit committed to Norway would result in a strong reaction from the government. All other things being equal, Norway would likely seek greater commitments from the U.K. and or perhaps Germany to compensate for any loss.

Of the remaining NATO countries, Denmark holds the greatest potential to directly influence Norwegian security policy. If Denmark should take the lead on some issues—for instance, an effective ban on nuclear-armed ships, or official approval of a NNFZ—Norway would undoubtedly be pressed to follow. The security affairs majority in the Storting have tended to be somewhat more cautious on these matters than their counterparts in the Danish Folketing. Still, the pressures to follow the Danish example could prove to be irresistible.

A change in British policy involving the northern region would be strongly felt in Norway. British reinforcements hold an important place in Norwegian security policy: they provide powerful forces to the defense of North Norway without the potential destabilizing effect (in Norwegian eyes) of American forces so close to the Soviet Union.[21] Norway could not easily compensate, politically or militarily, for a reduction or elimination of this British commitment. Such a change would force Norway to reconsider the basis of its security policy.

Germany remains the biggest wild card in Norwegian policy. Norwegian attitudes toward German reunification seem mixed, but are becoming more accepting. Norwegians are eager to see reduced tensions in Europe and are pleased to the extent that German unification helps to achieve this goal. At some point, however, Norway would need to see a reduction in tensions and forces in the far north, not simply in Central Europe. Since the far north involves Soviet territory and Central Europe does not, the issues involved will be fundamentally different. The latter area would, of course, be the major concern for the Germans; the former would be much lesser concern. Norway could find itself facing the question of whether to follow Germany's lead to resist so as not to be left behind in its own security interests.

CONCLUSIONS ABOUT THE FUTURE
OF NORWEGIAN SECURITY POLICY

Norwegian politics is entering a period of unprecedented instability and divisiveness—at least by Norwegian standards. The forces of instability will always be held in check in Norwegian national politics by the constitutional prohibition against dissolving the Storting and by the Norwegian preference for calm deliberate debate. Still, the next several years could witness previously unknown turmoil in Norwegian politics. In this environment, Norwegian security policy and its relations with the United States and NATO, hitherto consistent, could become more unpredictable.

POLICY RECOMMENDATIONS
FOR SCANDINAVIAN NATO

The rapidity of change in Europe at the end of the 1980s makes any attempt to predict the course of events for the early 1990s extraordinarily difficult. Security issues that seemed major concerns a few months ago have been overshadowed by even bigger events. Yet, despite these qualifications, one can make some meaningful statements about the future of Danish and Norwegian security policies and their effect on the United States.

Perhaps the most important point to keep in mind is that despite all the political changes in Europe that have occurred or appear on the horizon, geography has not changed. The United States will remain a maritime power, and Norwegian and Danish territory control major portions of the sealanes. Even if NATO as we now know it were to disappear, the United States would be driven to seek some security arrangement with these countries. Therefore, the United States should take special care in managing its relations with these nations, especially in issues involving naval forces and naval arms control despite any other changes that occur in Europe. Another key and related point involves the importance of intra-Nordic relations to Denmark and Norway. As the military threat to Europe appears to decrease and the rationale for the NATO Alliance appears to some people to diminish, the appeal of "Nordic" solutions to security issues can be expected to grow in the region. The United States should not underestimate the potential appeal of a regional agreement that addresses the security concerns of the Nordic countries but locks out the United States and the rest of the NATO Alliance. If the feeling grows that NATO is superfluous, the probability of regional agreements that exclude United States will grow.

NOTES

1. The report stated in part: "Defense of the northern region is dependent to a decisive degree on rapid reinforcement from the United States and the rest of NATO; yet, the increased restrictions on U.S. and NATO activities in Norway limit our ability to bring force to bear quickly in defense of the region." *Discriminate Deterrence,* Report of Commission on Integrated Long-Term Strategy, Fred C. Ikle and Albert Wohlstetter, cochairmen, The Commission on Integrated Long-term Strategy, Washington, DC, January 1988, pp. 67–68.

2. This analysis relies extensively on translations of Danish and Norwegian articles as they appear in reports of the Foreign Broadcast Information Service's Daily Report for Western Europe. Unless otherwise noted, information concerning Norway and Denmark comes from those FBIS reports.

3. See "Norway: Defense Minister: Military Threat Remains," *FBIS-WEU-89-236,* December 11, 1989, p. 15; "Norway: Defense Chief Warns Against Weakening Northern Forces," *FBIS-WEU-89-240,* December 15, 1989, p. 23; "Norway: Military Expert on Soviet Forces in North," *FBIS-WEU-89-241,* December 18, 1989, p. 19; John Lund, *Don't Rock the Boat: Reinforcing Norway in Crisis and War* (Santa Monica: The RAND Corporation, R-3725-RC, July 1989), pp. 1–3, 33–34. In 1989 alone, the Soviets deployed a new aircraft carrier, a new class of missile cruisers, and a new class of attack submarines. In the late 1980s, the Soviets built a new base for its Typhoon SSBNs only 50 kilometers from the Norwegian border.

4. The United States does not base any forces in Denmark or Norway because both countries have banned the presence of foreign troops or bases on their territory. Therefore, U.S. naval forces become the principal means by which American military presence is felt in the northern region of NATO in peacetime.

5. For more discussion of this in the case of Norway, see Lund, *Don't Rock the Boat,* pp. 16–23.

6. For more information on the traditional role of the Radicals in the making of Danish defense policy, see Erline Bjol, "Denmark: Between Scandinavia and Europe," *International Affairs,* Vol. 62, No. 4, Autumn 1986.

7. Clive Archer, "Denmark: The Bomb and the Ballot," *The World Today,* August-September 1988; also David Fouquet, "Denmark Sets a Tough Nuclear Test," *Jane's Defense Weekly,* May 7, 1988. Schluter cited British statements to the effect that Britain could no bnger maintain its commitment to reinforce Denmark if the resolution passed.

8. For more on the NNFZ, see Richard A. Bitzinger, *Competing Security Doctrines and a Nordic Nuclear-Free Zone* (Santa Monica: The RAND Corporation, P-7502, November 1988).

9. Although no decision has been made, the most likely choice to replace the Drakens will be to buy or lease from the U.S. Air Force some older F-16As, the model that Denmark has already procured.

10. Hans Haekkerup, the SDP defense negotiator, referred to this as an important change in Danish defense "in a more defensive direction." Conservative negotiator Connie Hedegaard dismissed this interpretation as "really inconceivable nonsense." Despite the Conservatives' objections, the fact remains that replacing all major surface combatants with shore-based missiles has been a major element of the defensive defense proposals, and therefore can be seen as a victory for its advocates.

11. One example of this postelection action came in late June when an American destroyer visited the Danish port of Aalborg. When the government failed to send a letter to the captain reminding him of Denmark's ban on nuclear weapons, the leaders of the SDP, SSP, and Communist party attempted to deliver the message themselves. They were unsuccessful, and other parties accused the group of attempting to pursue an independent foreign policy.

12. This aversion to external pressure became evident in the 1988 election, when the socialist parties chose to campaign against the government's pro-NATO platform under the slogan "Denmark decides itself."

13. The low level of Danish defense spending and the resulting criticisms from the NATO allies has greatly weakened Denmark's voice in NATO fora.

14. At the local level, the Progress party had fared much better; it has gotten the third largest number of votes nationwide.

15. See Norway, Royal Ministry of Defense, 1983. Although this document was written under a Conservative-led government, many of the concepts and phrases describing Norwegian policy reflect Holst's worldview. Of course, many Norwegians hold a more traditional view of the Soviet threat, but the dominant viewpoint has tended to come closer to Holst's formulation. For some discussion of the views of Holst contrasted with the Conservatives, see Lund, *Don't Rock the Boat*, pp. 24–25.

16. The Kola Peninsula of the Soviet Union is home base for two-thirds of the Soviet ballistic missile submarine fleet and would form the first line of air defense against American bombers and cruise missiles launched toward the European Soviet heartland.

17. To make matters worse, the most critical region militarily, Finnmark which borders the Soviet Union, has been experiencing massive depopulation, almost entirely among the youngest cohorts. This evaporation of the mobilization base may eventually force Norway to increase the size of the standing army.

18. However, if a Nordic Nuclear-Free Zone were to be declared, Norway and NATO would face a major crisis.

19. The shift in focus can already be seen in one area: in 1987 Canada withdrew its commitment to provide reinforcements to Norway, and Germany is assuming part of that responsibility. Germany will commit an artillery battalion to Norway. Norwegian officials also reported having spoken to France about committing reinforcements, but France showed no interest.

20. For detailed discussion of Norwegian security attitudes, see Lund, *Don't Rock the Boat*, 1989.

21. For an in-depth treatment of the question of reinforcements in Norwegian policy, see Lund, *Don't Rock the Boat*, 1989.

Chapter 9

Conclusion

Robert A. Levine

This chapter applies the fundamental factors analyzed in the seven national and regional chapters to the rapid changes beginning in 1989 and accelerating into the 1990s. The chapter has three sections. The first includes brief prognoses for the most likely courses and possible variations for major European and Western nations. It is followed by some general premises about what these mean for U.S. policy and Western policy in general, and, finally, by some prescriptions for the United States at this time of turmoil in NATO and the West.

THE KEY PLAYERS: INTO THE 1990s

This section takes up very briefly the key players in the future of Europe in the order that Chapter 1 suggested would govern European events. First come the Soviet Union and the rest of the Eastern bloc; it is clear that the rapid changes here are initiating events in both East and West Europe. Second is the Federal Republic of Germany, which as simply Germany, is taking over from the United States the role of prime initiator within NATO. Then come the United States (which is treated cursorily because the purposes of the chapter—and ultimately of the book—is to make recommendations on what U.S. policy *should* be, rather than treating it with a set of premises as for the other nations), France, the United Kingdom, and other members of NATO, north and south. The last two groups are given lighter treatment because they are followers in determining the security course of the West. Finally, a brief discussion covers impacts from outside of Europe or the United States.

The Soviet Union

The most probable course for the Soviet Union over the next several years seems increasingly to be in the direction of ethnic crumbling and economic col-

255

lapse. Much less probable, however, is that this will lead to a renewed purposeful military threat to Western Europe. Neither the USSR as such nor some Russian or Slavic-Federation successor is likely to be in either militarily or economic shape to renew any variety of the old threat; nor would even a military government that came into being in order to halt the crumbling be in position to make the sharp turn back to external aggression. Military governments seldom possess the solutions to economic problems, and the economic/military erosion of the Russian center as well as the Soviet Union has already gone too far.

None of this suggests, however, that such developments will do away with all military dangers. Crumbling and collapse may well lead to anarchy and civil war; and anarchy and civil war in a nation or set of warring entities that retain not only large armies but major megatonnage must be a source of concern.

Possible variations are:

- Stabilization, under Gorbachev or a successor, of the Soviet Union, a looser federation of most of the member republics, or at least a new set of successor states, most of which are not at war with another. Even the strongest version (the stabilization and economic bottoming out of a federation containing most of what has been the USSR), however, would be extremely unlikely within a relevant time period to recreate the kind of military threat the West perceived through the Brezhnev period, or an economy that could support such a threat.
- A government—military or other—that attempted to use military power to hold onto the Soviet Union republics trying to secede, reconquer such republics, or even reestablish hegemony over some erstwhile members of the Warsaw Pact. One variation here might be the cessation or slowing down of agreed Soviet force withdrawals from what was East Germany. Developments of this nature would raise military and other issues for NATO, but even they could not recreate the old threat of massive military aggression against member nations of NATO.

Eastern Nations

The most likely political course is continued rapid internal liberalization in every WP nation. Economically, these nations will muddle through at worst; perhaps better than muddling through in a year or two in Hungary, Czechoslovakia, or even Poland. Military relations with the Soviet Union will atrophy as Soviet troops withdraw; and political relations will move toward Finlandization, but economic ties will be difficult to break quickly, thus perhaps inhibiting internal development.

Possible variations are:

- Renewed Soviet political or economic pressures.
- Economic disaster in Poland or elsewhere.
- Strong and illiberal nationalism in one or more of the nations, leading to conflicts with the others, or perhaps with the Soviet Union or the West.
- Yugoslav disintegration.
- Economic disaster in the East leading to massive waves of migration, inundating the West.

The United States

Because this chapter intends to make the recommendations for U.S. policy, most of what might be premises for other nations become policy variables assumed to be adoptable by American decision makers of they accept the recommendations. The one exception is in the one area where the electorate is likely to push the decision makers: budget pressures on defense and other expenditures will remain very strong, strong enough that unless events reverse themselves, it may be very difficult to maintain forces in Europe above a level of the 100,000 or so troops.

Possible variations are:

- The pressures will be so strong that the administration and/or the Congress will force unilateral withdrawals to levels substantially below 100,000.

Germany

Germany has been reunified within NATO, and the most likely possibilities for the new nation are positive, for both Germans and the rest of the West. On this most probable course, Soviet troops will leave the former German Democratic Republic on schedule, by the end of 1994. Economically, the reconstruction of the former GDR will be steady, although perhaps at times difficult and slow; and the German-centered economic, and ultimately political, integration of Western Europe will also move apace, although also with difficulties and lags. Internal German politics will be consistent with these gradual improvements: the governing coalition may change in the federal election of the mid-1990s, but no new government will take radical new directions in security or other aspects of external policy. Given that U.S. and other foreign troop levels in Germany will be dropping radically anyhow, the pressure for complete withdrawal of foreign troops or even nuclear weapons will not be great. Germany is likely to take a more active international role outside of Europe as well as inside, but given the other probable developments, this role will be largely in concert with the United States as well as Germany's European allies.

Possible variations are:

- A slowdown or even a complete halt in the withdrawal of Soviet troops from eastern Germany. As suggested in the Soviet discussion, this is unlikely, but it is not completely impossible. A successor regime to Gorbachev, for example, might try to use such tactics as blackmail to force the Germans to supply larger subsidies.
- More likely would be major difficulties in the economic reconstruction of the East. West Germany has been extremely prosperous, and there is little doubt that it can and will reconstruct the smaller eastern territories. But the enormity of the task has become more apparent as it has begun. The structure of public and private capital goods in the East is obsolete at best, and needs complete replacements at worst; both are overlaid with the need to solve horrendous environmental problems. Reconstruction will take immense flows of financing for all sorts of capital goods and for correction of the surrounding problems; incentives for private financing will require some degree of solution to the dilemma of low worker productivity in eastern Germany (due primarily to the poor capital stock) and the need for high wages to prevent unrest and renewed migration to the west. Unrest may occur; burdens on western taxpayers almost certainly will occur. Although the job almost surely will be done, it may be done with much more difficulty and less dispatch than postulated in the most likely scenario.
- West European economic and political integration may also be slower and more difficult than postulated. Some of the obstacles may be German, particularly if reconstruction does run into major problems. Others may stem from Germany's partners. It is even possible that current directions will reverse, with centrifugal forces in Europe overwhelming those pushing toward economic and political integration; Europe could return to a state of mutually suspicious nationalisms. The last is least likely, however, because an integrated West European economy is already in being; in any case, an exacerbation of mutual suspicions into actual hostilities seems impossible, at least for Western Europe. Slowdowns of integration without a change of direction is much the more likely contingency.
- Difficulties in either the reconstruction of eastern Germany or the integration of Western Europe could have important implications for German politics. The least likely difficulty is that politics will move to an extreme of

either the Right or the Left. More possible, however, would be a less extreme government that would nonetheless reevaluate both security and other aspects of Germany's international posture. That could lead, for example, to a request for removal of U.S. troops from German soil, and thus to the effective end of NATO; it could lead to a sharp deceleration of at least the political aspects of European integration; it could lead to a marked increase in national assertiveness in international arenas; it could even lead to a German nuclear-weapons program, although not within the near term. (The next federal election, which could lead to the more radical of these turns, is not likely to take place before 1994 or 1995.)

France

Steady as she goes, at least until the election of a new assembly in 1993, and probably until the presidential election of 1995. France will participate, for both Alliance and budgetary reasons, in the SNF talks likely to follow CFE and in future rounds of CFE. France will pursue openings to the East, among other reasons to compete with the FRG and avoid a German political or economic monopoly; it will maintain its policy of keeping the FRG tied to the West through EC deepening.

Possible variations are:

• So subtle as to be difficult to detect. They are likely to be in response to variations elsewhere in the West or perhaps the East, rather than internally generated.

United Kingdom

The most likely course until the 1991–1992 election and perhaps after it, will be a continuation of the current one: cautious verbal encouragement of Soviet and other East bloc change; budget limited but otherwise substantial defense effort, including both nuclear and European conventional components; stand-offishness from the EC (and the continent as a whole), which *de facto* apparently comes close to the broadening position, at least in eschewing deepening, although perhaps not in encouraging the Austrian application.

The most likely variation is:

• The replacement of Major, after the election, by Kinnock. Although Labour has moved away from unilateral nuclear or other disarmament, a

Labour government would undertake major efforts to accelerate CFE and nuclear negotiations, and a near-term vision of a new Europe with very low levels of armaments. Labour's view of the economics of new Europe would likely be more open than Thatcher's was, but how open, politically as well as economically, is not clear, nor is the party's picture of an appropriate Germany. A Labour government in Britain together with an SPD-led government in the FRG would certainly mean a very different NATO from now.

Other Northern NATO

The Low Countries and the Scandinavian members are likely to be motivated by: budgetary pressure; hopes for continued movement toward real detente; hopes for continued liberalization in the Soviet Union and the rest of the East; and, perhaps overridingly, desired movement toward European integration to which they see deepening as the best path. In military and political, as well as economic matters, however, they necessarily remain followers.

Other Southern NATO

Italy is an economic player, both in trying to deepen EC and in actual and potential participation is assistance to the East while developing markets there. In the last respect, Italian attention is focused on the southern Balkans. In defense and political matters, however, Italy remains a follower. The same is true of Spain and Portugal. Although all three of the West Mediterranean members of NATO are concerned with security matters around their sea other than East/West conflicts, they have no clear view of NATO being the appropriate vehicle. Greece and Turkey are concerned with each other, and Turkey with its large armed forces and its immediate proximity to the Soviet Union is concerned with the CFE process, although it is too dependent upon the other members of NATO to sabotage an agreement. With the exception of Turkey, which is not a member of the EC, the other Mediterranean nations tend to advocate deepening.

Possible variations are:

- Turkey is not a member of EC but has applied. The general attitude of current members, broadeners as well as deepeners, is Austria maybe, Turkey no—with the differentiation based on racial, religious, and cultural factors as well as economic and political ones. Should this eventuate in the admission of Austria without Turkey, and particularly if Austria were followed by liberalized ex-members of the Soviet bloc, that would be taken by Turkey as invidious in the extreme. It could lead to Turkish disruption within NATO, or even Turkish departure, which would have major negative implications for the Western position in the Middle East as well as the Mediterranean.

Out of Area

The most likely scenario is that Europe will remain Europe-centered. As put in the introduction to this book, "NATO policy has always been inwardly directed—toward maintaining the internal coherence of the Alliance." While the Iraqi invasion of Kuwait, and the Western response, cannot leave NATO unchanged, the most probable result will be a loose decision on the part of the Alliance to take cognizance of such future possibilities, but without being able to come to any political agreement to add an explicit mission or to make any very concrete advance preparation.

Possible variations are:

- The Middle Eastern events of 1990–1991 acting as a catalyst to recast NATO into a much more outwardly directed Alliance, in which the explicit mission has added as a major feature the expression of the Atlantic community's interests and policies in the rest of the world, with a military posture to match.
- The Middle East catalyzing not NATO unity, but disunity. An American perception of Europe once more laying the burdens of fighting and paying on poor old "Uncle Sap," and/or a European fear of precipitate U.S. action dragging the world into war could magnify many-fold the kind of tensions that arose over the 1986 American raid on Libya. In the absence of a Soviet threat still feared by the Alliance, such tensions could have a far more lasting negative effect on NATO.
- Migration into Europe from the South. Unlike the waves of migration that might stem from economic collapse in the East, migration to Europe from the Arab and other countries of Africa has been continuing at a gradual pace for some time. It has already caused political problems in France and some parts of Italy; acceleration, predicted by some, could make it into a major source of difficulties both for European integration, as it crosses borders opened by EC agreements, and for European security.

PREMISES FOR U.S. POLICY

From these analysis—the structure built in the introductory chapter, the fundamentals in the national chapters, and the applications immediately above—a number of generalizations can be drawn, as premises for American policy toward NATO, and toward Europe as a whole.

- *Things are changing rapidly*—at a rate unprecedented since the end of World War II. Exactly how they will change in the future is extremely uncertain.
- *Time takes time.* That is, even matters that have started rapidly will take time to develop dimensions and directions. Key examples are:
  —The collapse of the Communist governments in the key bastions of the GDR and Czechoslovakia occurred over a period of weeks; the working out of their internal and external direction will take several years.
  —Even after the Soviet Union has converted to a workable economic system, it will take years for that system to recover enough to provide decent (i.e., Western) standards of living for most citizens—and they are still far from having converted.
  —Agreement in principle for the START talks took two years; for the CFE talks, a few months. The START talks have continued for many years; the CFE talks completed in 1990, will be many years in implementation. Aside from the sheer mass of equipment to be dismantled, Soviet difficulties in restationing or demobilizing large numbers of troops departing from Germany has become increasingly apparent.
  —EC integration is similarly on its own schedule, difficult to accelerate.
  —Elections will take place in the U.K. in 1991 or 1992, in the United States in 1992, and again in Germany in 1994 or 1995. Until the elections, the governments now in place will remain in place. However, there is no guarantee of continuation of current policies after the elections.
- *Changes may be positive or negative*, opportunities or dangers; and at a time of such rapid movement it is very difficult to predict which.
- The major change that is predictable because it has already taken place, however, is that there is essentially a *zero chance of the kind of massive Warsaw Pact invasion of the West that has provided the canonical threat for NATO planning for almost 40 years*. This may or may not be new; the writer suggested that it was the case 25 years ago.[1] But whether or not true earlier, it is true today because of the Soviet economic collapse and military retrenchment. Perhaps this type of military threat will revive some

day, but on a time schedule that will permit response by a West that is in any case likely to continue to be guarded by nuclear deterrence.

- The last premise does not imply, however, that any military conflict in Europe, or even military conflict with East/West overtones, is impossible for all time. But any East/West combat is far more likely to stem from chaos or miscalculation than any deliberate governmental action.

- Nuclear weapons are going to continue to exist. The United States and the Soviet Union, and most probably France and Britain, will continue to possess them, not to mention China. No matter what the explicit nuclear postures of these nations, what McGeorge Bundy has called "the bomb in the background" will therefore continue to play a role in Europe. Nuclear possibilities do not provide any major current danger, but they remain a fact of life.

From all of these stem one general premise, the most important of them all:

- For the near future in any case, *dangers are more salient for policy than opportunities*. This is not a pessimistic statement: the opportunities seem substantially more likely to occur; but the dangers, based mainly on variations from the relatively optimistic "most likely" scenarios outlined above, would provide major difficulties if they were to occur. This can be seen by listing dangers and opportunities at this time of rapid transition: the key dangers, particularly the first ones, are very short run; the key opportunities need to work themselves out. Policy ought, of course, to strive to seize the opportunities while avoiding the dangers, but it would be naive in the extreme to claim that opportunity-seizure and danger-avoidance cannot clash.

  Dangers:
  —Soviet economic collapse or national unraveling. Shortages of food, fuel, and energy could bring about economic collapse at any time; in any case, nobody predicts short-term economic improvement. National problems in the Baltic and Muslim republics are equally far from solution.
  —Change of political regime or direction in the Soviet Union. Based in substantial measure on the previous danger, this could reverse the basis for all of favorable developments of 1989 and the perceived opportunities for the future as well.
  —Ditto for other East bloc nations.
  —Internecine warfare among East bloc nations; Balkanization of the Balkans. This might be contained without drawing the Soviet Union back in; it might not.
  —Pressure, perhaps from the streets of eastern Germany, to remove the

Soviet presence at a rate not acceptable to the Soviet Union. A less likely
concomitant of this could be a Soviet view that the West is responsible.
—Reassertion of Soviet control in bloc nations, by the current Soviet regime or future one; or simply a slowdown of Soviet withdrawal.
—A clumsy assertion of German national power, likelier in the economic
than the political or military realms.
—Weakening of the West because of premature, probably budget-driven,
drawdowns of U.S. or other NATO forces. As will be discussed, "premature" is defined here to mean as out in advance of mutual agreement
among NATO nations.

Opportunities:
—Steady progress toward institutionalization of the internal reforms in the
Eastern nations.
—Withdrawal of Soviet troops to the Soviet Union itself, and substantial
demobilization.
—Achievement of a militarily stable Europe at a very low level of arma-
ments.
—Major cost saving for the United States and other Western nations.
—An economically integrating Western Europe reaching out to the East.

These opporunitites are by no means trivial. The contention, however, is that
most of them are coming anyhow, and that a conscious effort for U.S. or Western policy to accelerate them would run the major liabilities of hitting the dangers first.

GENERAL RECOMMENDATIONS FOR U.S. POLICY

The analysis of NATO's member nations as well as the Warsaw Pact, and the
premises for U.S. European policy come together into a system that is interrelated as well as being long and complex. The models by which they interrelate
are not simple ones. How a particular American position—a CFE proposal or
interpretation, a unilateral step toward force reduction, or a "vision"—for example, would affect the Soviet Union, the countries of the bloc, our allies both col-
lectively and individually, and the economics and politics as well as the military
postures of Europe cannot be calculated simply if at all.

Paradoxically, however, the complexity itself may lead to a certain simplicity. We cannot solve the multivariate equations, and in particular we cannot
anticipate outcomes over time; the world is much richer than our models, and
the models are untested, particularly for kinds of changes now taking place. We
should therefore eschew intricate political strategies.

The recommendations here are thus based on a contrasting sort of simplicity. The general philosophy informing all of them stresses the final premise above: In Europe today dangers are more salient for policy than opportunities. from this one can arrive at the central recommendation that begins medicine's Hippocratic oath: *First, do no harm.*

All else follows:

- *Emphasize the short run.* If a decision that must or should be made now is likely to lead to a favorable outcome (as evaluated by the normative premises above or other norms) soon, then don't worry too much about where it leads eventually. One has to be a lot more certain than is really possible about what will happen "eventually," to give up the bird in hand. For example, U.S. reluctance to trade two-digit numbers of U.S. missiles for four-digit numbers of Soviet, out of fear of the "slippery slope" to the full denuclearization of West Europe seemed misplaced at best.
- *Preserve NATO.* In spite of all the changes in Europe, NATO remains important to the United States for three reasons:

  —Things change. Although the discussion above indicates a very low like-lihood of a Soviet return to the clear threats of Stalinism even if the Soviet Union should build an economy that can support both military might and consumer staisfaction (which is going to take a very long time anyhow), it is still within the realm of possibility that a future turn, including possible near turns discussed above, will revive some sort of Soviet-induced military/political danger to Western Europe.

  —The very shifts that have relegated a coordinated attack by massed armies of the Warsaw Pact to a remote consideration outside the ken of real security planning conjure up potential new threats, for example, stemming from the Balkans, that make it undesirable for the West to simply declare peace throughout Europe and dismantle the Atlantic security apparatus.

  —NATO remains much the most important transatlantic *political link*, not to be given up lightly until others are much firmer.
- *Promote a friendly EC.* It has been asserted that stability is the priority U.S. interest in Europe, and Europe is going to be most stable with an integrat-ing West, perhaps extending integration to the East. In addition, a prosper-ous Europe is important for maintaining prosperity in the United States. EC is thus important to the United States, but an unfriendly EC—or one per-ceived by the American electorate as unfriendly—could lead away from mutual prosperity, mutual security, and stability. The operating principle for the United States, then, is to promote EC, but not be afraid to oppose tendencies toward European autarchy.

• *Make European policy in consideration of the views and interests of all of our European allies, including but not limited to Germans.* Germany will be the dominant nation in Western Europe in security terms, and in all of Europe economically. The temptation in the United States will be to deal with the boss. But even economically, Germany will be less than half of the West. The other nations will have at least the capability of disruption. In our quest for stability and continued Western cohesion, European fears are as relevant as are German strengths.

The final recommendation is the most positive, the most radical, and probably the most important of the entire set.

• *Assist the nations of the East, including the nations in what is now the Soviet Union, to move toward political democracy and economic integration. What is needed is a U.S./EC/Japanese program recognizably analogous to the European Recovery Plane of 1948, usually known as the Marshall Plan.* The importance lies not in the analogy but in the facts. The greatest dangers to West European and transatlantic stability and prosperity come from the East, as they have for the past 45 years. Now, however, the dangers stem not from deliberate military aggression by the Warsaw Pact, but from political instability and economic collapse throughout the territory that composed the Pact, including the Soviet Union.

The West cannot do everything. It can offer little but counsel and mediation with regard to the national and ethnic conflicts in the Soviet Union or elsewhere; if the USSR is going to split into sets of constituent parts, it will do so, and any Western intervention would make things worse. But no new configuration in the East is going to solve the problems that stem from 45 years of perverse economics and politics. Here is where the West may be able to assist. Whatever the Marshall Plan did in detail, in broad outline it provided a structure for mutual planning among the United States, which was then the single "have" nation, and the several "have-nots," supported by resources from the United States. Now both haves and the have-nots are more numerous, but the needs are the same: planning, cooperation, and resources, together with pedagogical input on capitalist economics and institutions. Germany will take care of its own, but perhaps a new effort can be learned from the German reconstruction already underway, and reach out to the rest of the East including the Soviet Union or its successor confederations or states. These remain the most important to Western security, because even if USSR breaks into many parts, what remains will still retain the largest populations, the strongest military forces, and the most dangerous weapons.

In an ultimate sense, the goal for some or perhaps all of the Eastern nations may be membership in the EC, as they complete their democratic reconstruction. The time that it will take removes it from the frame of this study, however; and its desirability is outside the frame of a normative discussion of U.S. policy.

European security, however, remains well within the American frame of reference. Europe today is undergoing its most rapid changes in the almost half-century since the end of World War II and the beginning of the Cold War. The North Atlantic Treaty Organization must change with it. When European security is assured, NATO can go out of business, and perhaps the United States can go home militarily. But if the Alliance falls to pieces before security is certain, or if economic or other disaster substitutes a new forms of insecurity for those of the East/West confrontation, then all of the bright opportunities that seem apparent for the last decade of the twentieth century may be lost.

NOTE

1. In 1965, Norman Jones and I wrote this in an unpublished paper. Relevant portions are quoted in Robert A. Levine, *Public Planning: Failure and Redirection* (New York: Basic Books, 1972), pp. 121–122.

Index

ABM Treaty, 178
ASMP, 131, 162
ATBM programs, 183
ATGM systems (*see* Antitank guided missile
    systems)
AWACS aircraft, 180
Achille Lauro hijacking, 175, 176
Adenauer, Konrad, 39, 63
Agrarian party (Norway), 238
Air-to-ground missiles, 20, 24
Air-to-surface missiles (ASMP), 131, 162
Allen, Richard, 14
Allensbach Institute, 89
Alliance (*see* NATO)
Allied Command Europe Mobile Force, 149
Andreotti, Giulio, 173, 174, 185, 187
Andropov, Yuri, 154
Anglo–French nuclear cooperation, 162
Anti-Americanism, in Germany, 88, 92
Antiballistic missile (ABM) treaty, 178
Anticommunism, in German reunification, 39,
    41, 42
Anti-German feeling in Europe, 86, 87
Antitactical ballistic missile (ATBM) pro-
    grams, 183
Antitank guided missile (ATGM) systems:
    Dragon, 207
    Milan, 205
    TOW, 207
Arms control, 9, 78, 79
    British attitude to, 149–150, 162–163
    Denmark and, 225, 232
    French role, 131–133
    and German defense systems, 83
    Italy and, 177–179
    Low Countries' support of, 211
    and NATO, 149–150, 225
    naval forces' inclusion in, 171
    in 1990s, 259
    and Norway, 241–242

    and the Soviet Union, 150
    United States' role in, 219–220
    (*See also* CFE; INF; START)
Aspin, Les, 14
Atlantic Alliance (*see* NATO)
Austria, and EC, 11, 260–261

Baker, James, 14, 15, 96
Balcerowicz, Leszek, 57
Balkanization, of Europe, 3
Balkans, instability of, 175
Baltic republics, 23, 219, 221, 233
Bank for Reconstruction and Development, 52
Bankruptcy, in GDR, 53
BAOR (*see* British Army of the Rhine)
Basic Law (Art. 23), as instrument of German
    Reunification, 35, 101, 103
Belgium:
    air force, 204–206
    armed forces, 204–206, 216
    army, 204–206
    defense of Germany, 195, 205
    defense spending, 201–204, 209–210
    and FOTL, 210
    linguistic political split, 199
    NATO role, 195–197, 201–203, 205–206,
        210–214
    navy, 204
    nuclear policy, 158–159, 196, 210, 211,
        213, 214
    polarization of political system, 200–202
    security policy, 195–216
    and the United States, 195–197, 201–202
    Walloon sector, 199
    (*See also* Low Countries)
Berlin:
    as new capital of Germany, 80
    Western troops in, 80
Bevin, Ernest, 141

Birth rate, European trends in, 34
Brandt, Willy, 40, 41, 72, 100, 104
Brezhnev, Leonid, 16, 20
British Army of the Rhine (BAOR), 147–148
Brundtland, Gro Harlem, 235
Brzezinski, Zbigniew, 14
Bulgaria, economy of, 59
Burden sharing, as source of friction between
    the United States and Europe, 171,
    173, 186, 213, 230
Bush, George:
    administrative appointees, 14–15
    and CFE, 7, 132
    cabinet's attitude to Gorbachev, 22
    and Eastern Europe, 11
    German public opinion of, 88
    and 1989 NATO summit, 159, 160

CDU (*see* Christian Democratic Union)
CFE agreements, 7, 9, 19, 80, 81, 262
    and British defense cuts, 165
    French attitude to, 125, 131–133, 135
    and Low Countries, 211
    and Scandinavia, 219, 228, 229, 232, 243
    (*See also* Arms control)
CSCE process
    and East Europe, 86, 88
    function of, 19, 64–65, 69–71, 80, 141–
    142, 161
    and Mediterranean, 185
    United States' attitude to, 97
Campaign for Nuclear Disarmament, 152
Canada, relations with Norway, 221, 245,
    247
Canning, George, 141
Carrington, Lord, 228
Carter, Jimmy, 154
Catholic Church, in Italy, 175, 177
Center Democratic party (Denmark), 223,
    224
Center party (Norway), 238, 248
Cheney, Richard, 2–3, 14, 15
Chevenement, Jean-Pierre, 108, 121, 135
Chirac, Jacques, 117, 121, 124–126
Christian Democratic Union (Germany), 16,
    19, 36–40, 41, 42
    and German foreign policy, 64, 68, 72, 77,
    233
Christian Democratic party (Italy), 173–175,
    177, 187, 188

Christian Democratic party (Norway), 238,
    248
Christian People's party (Denmark), 223, 224
Christian People's party (Norway), 235, 238
Churchill, Sir Winston, 143
Cold War:
    French attitude to, 111–112
    Low Countries' attitude to, 201, 209
    United States' attitude to, 21–22
Committee for Security and Defense, 117
Common Cause party (Denmark), 223
Communism:
    collapse of:
        in Eastern Europe, 31, 47, 84, 87, 97
        in GDR, 36, 44–45
        and German foreign policy, 60, 61, 72,
        87
    effect of on GDR, 45–46
Communist party (Denmark), 223
Communist party (France), 123, 124
Communist party (Italy) (PCI), 173–175, 178,
    183, 185, 187–188, 191
Conference on Security and Cooperation in
    Europe (*see* CSCE)
Conservative party (Great Britain), 25, 150,
    154–55, 162–163
Conservative party (Norway), 236, 238, 241
Conservative People's party (Denmark), 223–
    225, 232
Conventional Forces in Europe agreements
    (*see* CFE agreements)
Council for Mutual Economic Assistance
    (CMEA), 44
Craxi, Bettino, 173, 174, 177
Cruise missiles, 115, 116, 153, 202, 236
Czechoslovakia, economy of, 59, 256

De Gaulle, Charles, 111–115, 118, 119, 123,
    127
    (*See also* Gaullists)
de Maiziere, Lothar, 39
De Muta, Ciciaco, 187
Defense spending:
    in France, 120–123
    in Great Britain, 146, 155, 163–165
    in Italy, 179–182, 186, 190, 191
    in Low Countries, 201–204, 208–210
    in Scandinavia, 217, 228, 230, 233, 236,
    243, 249
    in the United States, 22, 28, 171, 228, 257

Democracy, assimilation of in GDR, 46, 47, 98
Democratic party (United States), 19
Demographics, of united Germany, 34
Denmark:
  air force, 228–229
  anti-invastion concept of defense, 228–229
  armed forces, 225, 228
  and arms control, 225, 232
  army, 229
  ban on foreign bases, 220, 252
  burden sharing issue, 230
  Danish Defense Commission, 228, 229, 232
  defense spending, 217, 228, 230, 233
  and EC, 222, 223, 231
  economy of, 230–231
  and Germany, 230, 233–234
  and Great Britain, 221, 228, 230, 231
  and INF treaty, 225
  and NATO, 19, 217–218, 220–221, 224, 225, 228, 230, 231
  navy, 229
  and Norway, 233–234, 250
  nuclear policy, 217, 218, 223–224, 229–230, 232, 234–235
  nuclear port calls issue, 219, 224, 230, 234
  political system, 222–227, 231–232
  and SDI research, 224
  and Soviet Union, 233
  and United States, 217, 230, 234
  and Warsaw Pact collapse, 228
  (*See also* Scandinavia)
Detente:
  British search for, 143–144, 149
  CSCE as vehicle for, 65
  European desire for, 173
  Italian attitude to, 186–187
  Low Countries' interest in, 201, 209, 214
  1980s vs. 1970s, 155
  United States' attitude to, 21–22
Disarmament, 7, 9, 21
  French attitude to, 129, 132–133
  and Genscher's new European order, 69
  unilateral vs. multilateral in Britain, 150–151
Dislocation, problems of in German reunification, 53
Drakens aircraft, 228, 229, 232

EC:
  and Austria, 11, 260–261
  and Denmark, 222, 223, 231
  and EFTA countries, 67, 68
  and Eastern Europe, 11–12, 57, 60–61, 66–70, 86–88
    investment in, 105
  and European integration, 65–66, 84–85
  and France, 126–127
  free trade commitment of, 56, 58, 59
  GDR integration into, 53
  and German reunification, 32–33, 53, 56, 58–60, 70, 88
  German role in, 16–17, 32, 66–68, 87–89, 92
  immigration policy of, 34
  and Italy, 169, 177, 183–184
  and Norway, 222, 235, 236, 238, 245, 246
  and NATO, 66
  as pan-European institution, 67
  and protectionism, 27, 183–184, 191
  scenarios of development in 1990s, 9, 11, 19, 259–261
  security role in Europe, 88, 172
  and Soviet Union, 86–87
  summit, July 1989, 128
  and Turkey, 260–261
  and the United States, 20, 59, 96, 171
EEC (*see* EC)
EFTA (European Free Trade Association) 67, 68
ENI, 175, 176, 188
ERW, 130, 133, 136, 201, 218, 236
Eagleburger, Lawrence, 14
East German Federation of Free Democrats (GDR), 43
East Germany (*see* Germany, GDR)
East–West conflict, diminishing threat from, 262–263
Eastern Europe:
  and EC, 11–12, 57, 60–61, 66–70, 86–88, 105
  economy of, 11, 56–57, 59, 84, 256–258
  emigration from, 34, 49, 88, 99, 257
  French attitude toward, 127–129
  German role in reconstruction, 85–87, 96
  instability in, 66, 81, 84
  Italian economic interests in, 187, 188, 190
  market economies in, 48
  reform in, 69, 71–72

Eastern Europe, reform in (*Cont.*):
    and British foreign policy, 141, 144,
      159, 161
    and Low Countries, 209
    and NATO, 1–2, 7, 8, 11, 18, 160
    and short-range nuclear weapons, 159
    scenarios of change in, 23–24, 256–257
    Soviet withdrawal, 171, 258
    United States' role in reconstruction, 96–
      97, 266
Elysée Treaty (1963), 117
Enhanced radiation weapons (ERW), 130,
    133, 136, 201, 218, 236
Ente Nazionale Idrocarburi (ENI), 175, 176,
    188
Euromissile debate, 173, 177
Europe:
    balance of power in, 145, 157
    Balkanization of, 3
    denuclearization of, 129, 214
    economic and monetary union (EMU),
      127, 128
      (*See also* Europe, integration of)
    integration of, 20, 56, 65–67, 75, 159,
      257, 258
      and defense planning, 83, 212, 214
      (*See also* European defense cooper-
        ation)
      Franco–German axis of, 133, 137
      French support of, 126–128
      German role, 47, 73, 84–85, 183
      and Low Countries, 209
      as NATO alternative, 70
      and protectionism, 183–184
      and the United States, 183–184
European Central Bank, 56
European Community (*see* EC)
European Coal and Steel Community, 111
European Commission, 127
European Council, 128
European Defense Community, 111, 142
European defense cooperation:
    British attitude to, 142
    Italian attitude to, 172, 184–185, 190
    and NATO, 163
    and United States' role in Europe, 185
European Economic Community (*see* EC)
European Fighter Aircraft (EFA), 180
European Free Trade Association (EFTA), 67,
    68
European Monetary System, 115
European Recovery Program (ERP), 52

European Single Act, 34, 60, 66, 83
European Supreme Commander (SACEUR) of
    NATO, 24, 117, 149

FDP, 36, 37, 43
FOTL (*see* Follow-on to Lance)
FRG (*see* Germany)
F-16 aircraft:
    in Italy, 178, 186
    in Low Countries, 205, 206, 208, 209,
      211
    in Scandinavia, 221, 228–229, 232, 242,
      243
Falklands War, 148
Federal Republic of Germany (*see* Germany)
Fiat, 176, 188, 193
Finland:
    and NNFZ, 225
    neutrality of, 220
    and Soviet Union, 220–221, 242, 246–247
Flemish Christian Democrats, 214
Flemish nationalism, in Belgium, 199
Flexible response strategy, of NATO, 3, 8, 78,
    79, 146, 147, 182, 209
Foch, 131
Follow-on to Lance (FOTL), 7, 158, 182
    cancellation of, 210, 230
Force d'action rapide (FAR), 117, 138, 180
Force de frappe, 112, 113, 123, 126, 129,
    131
    (*See also* France, nuclear policy)
Forza d'Intervento Rapido (FIR), 176, 180
France:
    airborne nuclear weapons, 131
    aircraft carriers, 131
    air-to-surface missiles, 131
    armed forces, 78, 121–122, 129–131,
      135–136
    and arms control, 131–133
    army:
      budget constraints on, 135
      cooperation with NATO, 134–135
      reorganization, 115–118, 134
      Clemenceau (aircraft carrier), 131
    De Gaulle's influence on, 111–115, 118,
      119, 123
    defense spending, 120–123
    and detente, 173
    and disarmament movement, 125, 129
    and EC, 126–127
    and Eastern Europe, 59, 127–129

and European integration, 67, 126–128,
133, 160
and German relationship:
current, 84–85, 108, 127, 136–137
in 1940–1960s, 111–113, 126
shift in 1970–1980s, 114, 117, 118
and German reunification, 119, 126, 127
and Great Britain, 162
independent nuclear force, 162
and NATO, 5–7, 112–114, 116–118, 126,
131, 134–135
nuclear policy of, 112, 113, 115–118,
122–125, 127–133, 136
Ostpolitik of, 128–129
political opinion on foreign defense policy,
123–126
political system consensus, 125–126
power of presidency, 125
and Reykjavik summit, 115
scenarios for development in 1990s, 19,
25, 259
security policy of, 111–139
and the Soviet Union, 111–114, 118–120,
124–126, 132
and the United States, 112–116, 118, 119,
146
Franco–German brigade, 117
Franco–German cooperation, on defense, 111,
117, 136–137, 172, 185, 190
Franco–German Treaty of 1963, 111, 117
Free Democratic party (Germany), 36, 37, 43
Free-fall nuclear bombs, 147
Free-market economies, shift to in Eastern
Europe, 48
Free trade, EC commitment to, 56, 58, 59

GDR (*see* Germany, GDR)
Gaullists, and French defense policy, 123–126,
128, 137
(*See also* De Gaulle, Charles)
Genscher, Hans-Dietrich, 38, 43, 47, 63, 68–
72, 77, 107
German Democratic Republic (*see* Germany,
GDR)
German mark, 35–36, 56
German Unity Fund, 51, 105
Germany:
anti-Americanism in, 88, 92
armed forces, 76–83, 94, 108
budget deficit, 58
and CFE negotiations, 132

defense planning, 76–83
democracy guaranteed by NATO, 62
demography of, 34
and Denmark, 230, 233–234
and detente, 173
domestic issue preoccupation, 84
EC role of, 32, 66–68, 87–89, 92
and Eastern Europe reconstruction, 59,
66–68, 85–88, 96, 99–100
East–West political and cultural differences
in, 45–46
economy of, 16, 17, 32–35, 48, 49, 53–56
and European integration, 47, 65–67, 73,
84–85, 128, 183
foreign policy of, 60–61, 75–77, 84–97,
100–103
and French relationship:
current, 84–85, 108, 127, 136–137
in 1940–1960s, 111–113, 126
shift in 1970–1980s, 114, 117, 118,
136–137
GDR:
anticommunism in, 39
budget deficit in, 51–52
communism in, 36, 44–46
democracy in, 98
economy of, 32–33, 42, 49–50, 53–55
integration of, 84
investment in, 52, 55, 105
military forces in, 3, 77, 80, 94
modernization costs in, 49–50
nationalism of, 44
nuclear weapons in, 80
Poland and Hungary's role in collapse
of, 85
political state of, 42, 45–46
public opinion polls in, 92, 94
SPD sympathy in, 41
social security system in, 51, 52
Soviet withdrawal from, 79–81
as traditional German society, 44
United States' military presence in, 92
wage development in, 55
GNP growth in, 48, 49, 53–55
Genscher's idea of its role in new order in
Europe, 68–71
immigration from East, 34, 49, 88, 99,
257
and Low Countries' role in, 195, 205,
207, 211
and NATO:
commitment to, 24–25, 64

Germany, and NATO (*Cont.*):
    as initiator in, 1, 4–8, 11, 255
    military presence in, 60, 77–80, 89,
        91–96, 147–148, 195, 205, 207,
        211
    public opinion polls on, 89, 92, 94
    special relationship with, 134
  nationalism in, 46–48, 84, 88
  and neutrality, 62–63, 89, 92, 94, 115,
    190
  and Norway, 245, 246, 250
  nuclear policy of, 6–7, 78–80, 116, 158–
    159, 213, 221, 230
  Ostpolitik of, 40–41, 71–72, 85, 114
  and Persian Gulf crisis, 76
  political parties in, 17, 19, 36–48, 71–74
  population of, 32
  public opinion polls in, 88–95
  reunification of, 3, 15, 31–109
    armed forces role in, 77
    Basic Law (Art 23) as instrument of,
      35, 101, 103
    British attitude to, 144
    as capitalist economy, 51
    consensus of German people on, 74
    as a democracy, 35
    EC impact on, 56, 58–59
    economic factors in, 48–59, 86, 106
    economic impact on Eastern Europe,
      56–57
    effects of, 97–103
    and European integration, 60, 128, 183
    and exchange rate, 35–36, 51
    foreign policy issues of, 60–76, 101–
      103
    four phase plan for economic unity,
      51
    and France, 119
    and German nationalism, 46–48, 99
    and Italy, 183
    Kohl's role in, 36, 38–39
    and Low Countries, 209
    and NATO role of Germany, 4, 20, 60,
      62–65, 78, 79, 134, 159, 221,
      234
    and nuclear deterrence, 78
    and political system, 35–48, 97, 99
    privatization issue, 52, 105
    SPD policy toward, 41–42, 71–72
    Soviet attitude toward, 61, 74
    and the United States, 102–103
    world economic impact, 58

  scenarios for future development of, 9–
    11, 16–18, 24–25, 257–259
  and short-range nuclear forces, 6–7,
    133, 158–159
  social welfare system, 34
  telecommunications industry, 50, 105
  and the Soviet Union, 35–36, 86–87,
    89, 90, 92, 94, 97, 114
  and the United States, 58, 84, 88, 96–
    97, 102
Giscard, Valery, 115, 120, 123, 130
Glasnost, 128
  (*See also* Soviet Union, reforms in)
Glotz, Peter, 42, 74
Gorbachev, Mikhail:
  and arms control, 150
  British view of, 153, 154, 156
  and Finland, 220, 242
  and France, 118–120
  and German reunification, 61, 80–81
  Italian reaction to reforms, 186–187, 190
  and Low Countries, 209
  and NNFZ, 225
  reforms of, 1–2, 6, 16, 18, 69, 170–171
  United States' attitude to, 15, 21, 22
Gorizia Gap, as factor in Italian defense pol-
    icy, 176
Gramm–Rudman Act, 26
Great Britain:
  arms control, 149–150
  air force, 164–165
  army, 164–165
  and balance of power in Europe, 145, 157
  Conservative party, 25, 150, 154–155,
    162–163
  defense policy, 141–167
  defense spending, 146, 155, 164–165
  and disarmament, 144–147, 150–151
  dissent tradition in foreign policy, 152
  and Denmark, 221, 228, 230, 231, 234
  and detente, 143–144, 149, 172
  and EC, 25
  and Eastern European revolutions, 141,
    144, 159, 161
  equilateralism in public opinion, 153
  and FOTL, 7
  Foreign Office and Soviet Union, 156
  foreign policy formulation in, 144, 152
  French nuclear cooperation, 162
  and German defense, 147
  and Gorbachev, 153, 154, 156
  and INF, 150, 154

independent nuclear deterrent, 147, 162
Labour party, 25, 144, 146–147, 150–151,
154–155, 163, 260
military presence in Germany, 147, 164–
165
Ministry of Defence, 151–152, 156
and NATO:
military contribution to, 147–149, 164
role in, 5, 6, 25, 141–142, 145–146,
164
naval forces, 148–149, 164–165
and Norway, 221, 245–247, 250
nuclear policy, 142–143, 146–147, 151,
157–159
in 1990s, 162, 259–260
public opinion on, 154
out-of-area participation with United
States, 146
Parliament's role in foreign policy, 151–
152
peace movement in, 150, 152
and post war system in Europe, 141
public knowledge of defense issues, 152
public opinion:
on nuclear weapons, 154
of the Soviet Union, 152, 153–155
of the United States, 153, 154
scenarios of development in 1990s, 19,
25–26, 259–260
short-range nuclear forces, 158–159
and the Soviet Union, 141, 144, 145, 147,
153–157, 161
and the United States, 141–143, 146, 148,
153, 154, 162
White Papers on Defense
1986, 146
1989, 149, 157
Greece, 260
Greens, 43, 92, 93
Guadeloupe summit of 1979, 183
Gulag effect, 114
Gysi, Gregor, 43

Hades missiles, 116, 130, 132, 133, 136
Haig, Alexander, 14
Harmel Report of 1967, 78, 83
Haussmann, Helmut, 57, 105, 106
Hawk SAM systems, 205, 208
Healy, Denis, 147
Holst, Johan Horgen, 241–242, 244, 247

Howe, Sir Geoffrey, 156
Hungary, 23, 57, 59, 85, 256

INF agreement of 1987, 6–7, 8
and Denmark, 225
and France, 114
and Great Britain, 150, 153, 154, 158
and Italy, 178
and nuclear port calls issue, 230, 244
INF deployment, debate over, 201–202, 210,
218
Iceland, role in NATO, 231
Ikle, Fred, 14
Immigration:
into Germany, 34, 49, 88, 99, 257
into Italy, 175, 261
Inflation:
in Germany, 49
and NATO, 26–27
Inter-continental ballistic missiles (ICBM), 157
Intermediate Nuclear Forces (*see* INF)
Iraq, invasion of Kuwait, 10, 15, 17–19, 27,
261
Israel, American airlift to (1973), 181
Italy:
air force capability, 180
armed forces, 174, 179–180, 192, 193
and arms control, 177–179
army, 179
and Balkan unrest, 175
budget and trade deficits, 174
and burden sharing issue, 186
defense industry, 184
defense policy, 169–193
defense spending, 179–182, 186, 190, 191
defense white paper (1985), 176
demilitarization of Europe, 179
demographic trends, 174
denuclearization of, 185
and detente, 186–187
domestic terrorism in, 191
and EC, 169, 183–184
and Eastern Europe, 59, 186–188, 190
economy of, 174, 176, 188, 190–191
and European defense cooperation, 172,
184–185
FIR force, 176, 180
and F-16 transfer, 178, 186
and Franco–German defense cooperation,
185

Italy (*Cont.*):
  foreign policy's place in political scene in, 173
  and German reunification, 183
  Gorizia Gap as factor in defense policy, 176
  and Guadeloupe summit, 183
  and INF agreement, 178
  in Lebanon multinational force, 176
  and Libya, 175, 176, 190
  and Malta agreements, 176
  Mediterranean emphasis of foreign policy, 175–177, 179–181, 189
  Middle East involvement, 175–176
  migration from North Africa, 175
  and NATO, 6, 169–170, 173–174, 176–177, 181–182, 187, 189, 191
  Naval Air Arm Bill, 179
  navy, 179–180
  and North Africa, 175, 176
  nuclear policy, 177–178, 182, 183
  oil imports dependence, 174–176, 180, 186, 190–191, 192
  out-of-area contribution to defense, 186
  peace movement in, 177–178
  political parties in, 173–175, 177–178
  and SDI, 183
  scenarios for development in 1990s, 191, 260
  Soviet Union and Eastern Europe relations, 186–188, 190
  trade:
    with Soviet Union, 188
    with United States, 184
  and the United States, 172, 173, 178, 181, 184
  and United States' bases in, 181–182
  and Yugoslavia, 175, 189

Japan:
  American investment in, 58
  and protectionism in Europe, 184
Joint Defense Council, 136

King, Tom, 164
Kinnock, Neil, 260
Kissinger, Henry, 14
Kohl, Helmut:
  defense of united Germany, 77, 80–81
  and Eastern European aid, 68
  and European integration, 65–68, 128
  and France, 85, 133
  and German membership in NATO, 63–65, 133
  and German role in Persian Gulf, 76
  and role in reunification, 36, 38–39, 41, 42, 46, 47, 59, 103, 104
  and SNF modernization, 133
Kola Peninsula, 217, 219, 242, 248–249, 253
Kuwait, invasion of, 10, 15, 17–19, 27, 261
  (*See also* Persian Gulf crisis)

Labor party (Netherlands), 200
Labor party (Norway), 235, 236, 238, 241–244, 247, 248
Labour party (Great Britain):
  and arms control, 163, 260
  and disarmament, 144, 150–151
  flexibility in post Cold War Europe, 163
  MP's attitudes:
    to nuclear deterrent, 154–155
    to the Soviet Union, 154
  nuclear policy, 25, 146–147, 151
  and peace movement, 150
LaFontaine, Oskar, 41–42, 73
Lagorio, Lelio, 178
Lampedusa, Libyan attack on, 175, 176
Lance short-range missiles, 20, 147
Lebanon, multinational force in, 176
Left, political parties of:
  and Eastern Europe revolutions, 73–74
  German, 43
  Italian, 187–188, 191
  of Low Countries, 200–201
  of Scandinavia, 223, 236
  and United States' military presence, 92, 93
Left Socialist party (Denmark), 223
Lehman, John, 217
Leopard tanks, 205–207, 229
Liberal parties, in Low Countries, 200
Liberal party (Denmark), 223, 224
Liberal party (Italy), 173, 182
Liberal party (Norway), 238
Libya:
  ballistic missiles in, 183
  bombing of, 185, 261
  and Italy, 175, 176, 190
London Declaration (1990), 78, 80, 81

Low Countries:
    antinuclearism as new consensus in, 209
    armed forces' cuts, 202, 210–211
    arms control, 211, 213–214
    and Cold War, 201
    cruise missile deployment, 202
    defense cooperation, 212
    defense spending, 201–204
    depillarization of society, 199–200
    and detente, 201, 209, 214
    and East European reform, 209
    economy of, 200, 202, 215
    and European integration, 209
    and German reunification, 209
    INF deployment debate in, 201–202
    NATO commitments of, 210, 211
    and neutrality, 196
    nuclear debate in, 201–202, 213–214
    peace movements in, 201
    political parties in, 198, 215, 216
    Scandinavian relations, 221
    scenarios for development in 1990s, 260
    social and political organization, 197–200
    and Soviet Union threat, 214
    unemployment in, 200
    withdrawal of forces from Germany, 211
    (*See also* Belgium; Netherlands)

M-41 tanks, 229
Macmillan, Harold, 144
Malta, Italian agreements with, 176
Marshall Plan, 266
Mattei, Enrico, 176
Mediterranean:
    defense initiatives in, 172
    European defense cooperation in, 185
    Italy's interests in, 170, 175–176, 179–
        181, 189, 190
    Soviet presence in, 171
    United States' presence, 171, 186
Middle East:
    impact on Europe, 10
    Italy's involvement in, 175–176, 190
Migration:
    to Germany from East, 34, 49, 88, 99,
        257
    to Italy from North Africa, 175, 261
Military Program Law (France):
    1983, 120–121
    1989 review, 121–122
Mirage planes, 122, 131, 205, 206

Mistral SAM system, 205
Mitterrand, Francois, 7, 19
    anticommunism of, 114
    and arms cuts, 121, 132, 135
    change in defense policy in 1980s, 124–
        126
    and EC, 134
    and European arms cooperation, 136
    and Europe as a security force, 128
    and European integration, 127
    foreign policy of, 116, 118
    and German relationship to NATO, 134
    nuclear policy of, 123, 130–133
    and the Soviet Union, 124
Monetary system, of Europe, 56
Monetary union, of East and West Germany,
    50–51
Monetary union, of Europe (*see* Europe, inte-
    gration of)
Moscow Treaty, between Germany and Soviet
    Union, 114
Multiple Launch Rocket Systems (MLRS),
    207

NNFZ, 225, 236, 242, 250
NATO:
    arms control policies, 149–150, 225
    Belgian contribution to, 195–197, 201–
        203, 205–206, 210–214
    and Britain, 141–142, 146–149, 164
    burden sharing question in, 213, 220
    conventionalization of strategic policy, 182
    CSCE as complement to, 64–65
    Denmark's contribution to, 224, 225, 228,
        230
    EC as alternative to, 66
    East–West confrontation strategy of, 81
    and East–West trade interests, 188
    and Eastern European changes, 8, 11
    and Eastern Europe, 8, 11
    economic constraints on, 17, 20, 26, 28
    erosion of structure of, 84
    and European defense cooperation, 163
    and European integration, 70
    Europeanization of, 212–213, 234
    flow of power in, 4–8
    French attitude to, 112–114, 116–117,
        126, 131, 134–135
    GDR relation to, 80
    German admission to, 111
    German commitment to, 24–25, 36, 62, 88

NATO (*Cont.*):
  and German defense, 77–80, 108
  German public opinion polls on, 89, 92, 94
  and German reunification, 61, 63, 74, 221, 234
  German role in, 60, 62–65, 68–71, 74
  Iceland's role in, 231
  importance of, 3, 11, 160, 161, 265
  Italy's role in, 169–170, 173–174, 181–182, 187, 189, 191
  and Kuwait invasion, 18
  Long-Term Defense Plan, 202
  and Mediterranean policy, 176
  military presence in Europe, 20, 115, 159
  military strategy MC 14/3, 78, 83
  and NNFZ, 225
  Netherlands' contribution to, 195–197, 201–203, 207–208, 210–214
  new role of, 128
  Norwegian role in, 235–236, 244–249
  nuclear modernization, 116–117, 133, 210, 219, 230, 232, 244
  nuclear policy:
    of deterrence, 78–79, 115
    of flexible response, 3, 8, 78–79, 146–147, 182, 209
    opposition to, 217, 218, 229, 230
  and nuclear threat of Soviet disintegration, 23
  and out-of-area response issue, 15, 146, 186, 261
  Scandinavian countries' role in, 217–218, 220–221, 231
    (*See also* Denmark; Norway)
  scenarios for future development, 15, 18, 20, 22, 24–25, 255–261
  short-range nuclear forces (SNF), 133, 158–159, 210, 213–214
  strategy reformulation, 64, 78, 79
  summits:
    1989, 127–128, 132, 159, 160
    1990, 64, 72
  Turkey's role in, 260–261
  United States' role in, 14–15, 20, 27–29, 212–214, 255
  Warsaw Pact's military superiority over, 156, 157
NATO Military Committee, 176
NATO Nuclear Planning Group (NPG), 229–230

National Socialism, legacy of in Germany, 76, 98–99, 100
Nationalism:
  Eastern European, 74, 99, 258–259
  German, 46–48, 84, 88
Naziism, legacy of in Germany, 76, 98–99, 100
Netherlands:
  air force, 207–208
  armed forces, 206–209
  army, 206–208
  defense spending, 201–204, 208–210
  and FOTL, 210
  and German defense, 195, 207
  and INF treaty, 7
  and NATO, 195–197, 201–203, 207, 208, 210–214
  navy, 208, 209
  and Norway, 245
  nuclear policy, 196, 210, 211, 213–214
  polarization of political system, 200–202
  RIM units in armed forces, 207
  security policy of, 195–216
  and the United States, 195–197, 201–202
  (*See also* Low Countries)
Neutrality:
  German attitudes toward, 62–63, 89, 92, 94, 115, 190
  Low Countries' rejection of, 196
  in Scandinavia, 217
Neutron bombs, 130, 133, 136, 201, 218, 236
Nordic Balance, Norwegian policy of in NATO, 245, 246–247
Nordic Nuclear Free Zone (NNFZ), 225, 236, 242, 250
North Africa, Italian interest in, 175, 176
North Atlantic Treaty Organization (*see* NATO)
Northedge, Fred, 144
Norway:
  air force, 242, 243
  armed forces, 242–243
  and arms control, 241–242
  arms industries, 217, 244–245
  army, 243
  Atlantic policy of, 245–246
  ban on foreign bases, 220, 247, 252
  and CFE, 243
  and Canada, 221, 245, 247
  Defense Commission, 241
  defense spending, 236, 243, 249
  and Denmark, 233–234, 250

and EC, 222, 235, 236, 238, 245, 246
economy of, 244–245
flag issue in NATO, 247
and Germany, 245, 246, 250
and Great Britain, 221, 234, 245–247, 250
and NATO, 217–218, 220–221, 231, 235–236, 245–247, 248–249
and NNFZ, 242, 250
navy, 242–243
and Netherlands, 245
nuclear policy, 218, 236, 243–244
and nuclear port calls issue, 244
and oil production, 243
political system of, 235–241, 247–248
and START agreement, 248–249
and the Soviet Union, 217, 242, 244–249
and the United States, 217, 245–249
(*See also* Scandinavia)
Norwegian Sea, superpower confrontation in, 242, 244, 247, 249
Nott, Sir John, 148, 165
Nuclear deterrence:
French attitude toward, 115, 118, 126, 130, 162
Healy's policy of, 147
Italian support of, 182
as NATO strategy, 78–79, 115
Reykjavik's impact on national systems of, 158
United States' commitment to, 14, 17, 18, 96, 219
Nuclear disarmament, British Labour party and, 144, 150–151
Nuclear gravity bombs, 20, 24
Nuclear Planning Group (NPG), of NATO, 229–230
Nuclear weapons:
Anglo–French cooperation, 162
British MPs' attitude toward, 154–155
British policy on, 142–143, 146–147, 151, 157–158
British public opinion on, 153, 154
CFE limitation of, 132, 133
continuing threat of, 263
Denmark's policy, 229–230, 232, 234–235
French policy on, 112–113, 116–117, 122–125, 129, 136
German policy on, 38, 136, 221
Italian policy on, 177–178, 182–183
Low Countries' policy on, 196, 201–202, 209–211, 213–214
Norwegian policy on, 236, 243–244

opposition to, 25, 152, 217, 218, 229–230
(*See also* Arms control; Disarmament)
in post-Cold War Europe, 62, 162
short-range (*see* Short-range nuclear forces)
Soviet disintegration danger, 22–23, 96, 256
Nunn, Sam, 14

Obsolescence, in GDR industry, 50
Oil:
Italian dependence on, 174–176, 180, 186, 190–191, 192
Norwegian, 243
price increase in, 58
Options for Change study, 164
Organization for Economic Cooperation and Development (OECD), 55
Ostpolitik:
French, 128–129
German, 40–41, 71–72, 85, 114
Western, 96

PCI, 173–175, 178, 183, 185, 187–188, 191
Party of Democratic Socialism (PDS) (GDR), 43
Patriot missile systems, 180, 208
Peace movement:
in Great Britain, 150, 152
in Italy, 177
in Low Countries, 201
Penguin missiles, 245
Perestroika, 128
(*See also* Soviet Union, reforms in)
Perle, Richard, 14
Pershing missiles, 115, 116, 236
Persian Gulf crisis, 76, 83, 165
(*See also* Kuwait, invasion of)
Plateau d'Albion, 130
Pluton missiles, 116, 130
Pohl, Gerhard, 50
Poland:
aid to, 24
armed forces of, 78
economy of, 57, 59
embargo dispute in NATO, 188
emigration from, 49, 109
Germany gratitude to, 85
and NATO strategy, 20
scenario for development of, 256

Polaris missiles, 162
Pompidou, Georges, 115
Portugal, 56, 67, 260
Privatization, problem of in GDR, 52, 105
Progress party (Denmark), 223, 224, 229, 232
Progress party (Norway), 238, 241, 243, 247, 248
Prosperity, as theme in German reunification, 39
Protectionism, 27, 183–184, 191
Public opinion:
    in Germany, 88–95
    in Great Britian, 153–154

RAF in Germany, 148
Radical Liberal party (Denmark), 224, 225, 228, 232–234
Rafale fighter aircraft, 122
Rassamblement pour la Republique (RPR), 124
Reagan, Ronald:
    appointees of, 14
    arms reduction policy, 157
    British public opinion of, 154
    denuclearization ideas of, 143
    economic program of, 58
    and Soviet Union, 115, 152
Republican party (Italy), 173, 182
Reykjavik summit, 1, 115, 157–158, 178
Rocard, Michel, 121
Ruehe, Volker, 38–40, 77, 108

S-3 missiles, 130–131
S-4 missiles, 121, 122, 130, 131
SACEUR (European Supreme Commander of NATO), 24, 117, 149
SDI research, 115, 143, 178, 183, 224
SED, 38, 39, 42, 44, 71
SLCMs, 230, 244, 248
SNF (*see* Short-range nuclear forces)
SNLE, 130
SPD (*see* Social Democratic Party)
START treaties, 133, 158, 162, 248, 249
Scandinavia:
    defense policy of, 217–253
    and Low Countries, 221
    neutralism in, 217
    scenario for development in 1990s, 260
    and Soviet Union, 218–221
    (*See also* Denmark; Norway)

Schluter, Paul, 224, 230
Schmidt, Helmut, 100, 115
Schroeder, Patricia, 28
Schwarz, Hans Peter, 100
Scowcroft, Brent, 14
Sea-launched cruise missiles (SLCM), 230, 244, 248
Short-range nuclear forces (SNF):
    German policy on, 221
    NATO debate on, 7, 79, 127–128, 133, 158–159, 210, 213–214
    United States' modernization of, 171
Shultz, George, 29
Siberian gas pipeline, 188
Sigonella incident, 181, 185
Social Democratic party (SPD) (Germany), 17, 25, 77
    and EC, 73
    and Eastern European revolutions, 71–74
    and European integration, 73
    and NATO, 72
    Ostpolitik of, 40–41, 71–72
    and reunification, 36–42, 71–72
    and Soviet Union, 72–73
    and United States' military presence, 92, 93
Social Democratic party (SDP) (Denmark), 222–225, 229, 232, 233
Social Democratic party (Italy), 173
Social security system, in GDR, 51, 52
Socialism, future of in Eastern Europe, 74
Socialist Left party (Norway), 235, 236, 241, 242, 247, 248
Socialist party (France), 123, 124
Socialist party (PSI) (Italy), 173–175, 177, 178, 187, 191
Socialist People's party (Denmark), 222–223, 225, 229, 232, 234
Socialist Unity party (SED) (GDR), 38, 39, 42–44, 71
Sousmarins nucleaires lanceurs d'engins (SNLE), 130
Soviet–German agreement of 1990, 81
Soviet Union:
    Afghanistan, invasion of, 114
    anti-German feeling in, 87
    and arms control, 150
    British attitude to, 141, 144, 145, 147, 155–157
    CSCE role of, 65
    and Denmark, 233

and Eastern Europe, 11, 61, 79, 80, 97, 171
emigration from, 34
and Finland, 220–221, 246–247
and France, 111–114, 118–120, 124–126
GDR withdrawal of, 81, 258
and Germany, 35–36, 63, 86–87, 94, 114
  military threat to, 60, 62
and INF treaty, 6
improving relation with Western Europe, 170
and Italy, 187–188, 190
and Low Countries, 214
Mediterranean fleet, 171
military presence in Kola Peninsula, 217, 219, 242, 248–249, 253
as military threat to Europe, 16, 65, 66, 76–78, 81, 89, 90, 92, 96, 157, 256
navy in far North, 244, 248–249
and Norway, 242, 246–249
Norwegian arm sales to, 217
nuclear power of, 3, 114
nuclear threat in disintegration, 22–23, 96, 256
possible disintegration of, 22–23, 60, 84, 86–87, 96
possible return to militarism of, 21–22
Reagan/Thatcher hard-line approach to, 152
reforms in, 9, 10, 16, 18, 21–22, 69, 118–120, 156, 161
and Scandinavia, 218–221, 233, 242, 246–249
scenarios of development in 1990s, 16, 255–256
and Sweden, 247
and United States, 21–23, 64, 75, 96, 152
Spadolini, Giovanni, 176
Spain, 56, 67, 177, 178, 260
Stinger missiles, 205, 207
Stolpe, Manfred, 45
Stoltenberg, Gerhard, 64, 78–79
Strategic Defense Initiative (SDI), 115, 143, 178, 183, 224
Submarines, French nuclear, 130
Summits:
  EC (July 1989), 128
  Guadeloupe (1979), 183
  Moscow (1989), 153
  NATO (1989), 127, 132, 159

NATO (1990), 78, 80, 81
Reykjavik, 1, 115, 157–158, 178
Suez Crisis, 112
Sweden, 220, 225, 247

Tactical air-to-surface missiles (TASM), 210, 213, 214
Telecommunications industry, in Germany, 50, 105
Telschik, Horst, 67, 85
Thatcher, Margaret, 5, 25
  and arms control, 157
  and European economic unity, 128
  and INF, 150, 158
  and Soviet Union, 152, 155
  and United States' presence in Europe, 163
Todd, Ron, 151
Tornado weapon system, 147
Toshiba–Konigsberg scandal, 244–245
Trade:
  East–West, 188
  protectionism, 27, 183–184, 191
  of Soviet Union and Italy, 188
  United States' with Europe, 97, 171, 183–184
Trident weapon systems, 153, 155, 162, 163
Turkey, 11, 260–261

USSR (*see* Soviet Union)
Unemployment:
  in Germany, 49, 53, 54, 106
  in Low Countries, 200
United Nations, German military participation in, 70
United Kingdom (*see* Great Britain)
United States:
  airlift to Israel (1973), 181
  and arms control, 219–220
  and Baltic republics, 23
  bases in Italy, 181–182
  and British desire to involve it in Europe, 141–143, 146, 148
  British public opinion of, 153, 154
  British strategic differences with, 143
  British technological and stategic dependence on, 143, 162
  budget deficit, 58, 115
  burden sharing as source of friction with Europe, 171, 173, 186, 213, 220
  and CFE, 132

United States (*Cont.*):
    defense spending of, 22, 28, 171, 220, 257
    and Denmark, 217, 230, 234
    and detente, 172
    and EC, 20, 58–59, 96
    and Eastern Europe, 96–97, 266
    and European defense cooperation, 163,
        185
    and European integration, 70
    European role of, 13–29, 88, 128, 149,
        171, 190, 219, 231
        recommendations for, 264–267
    and FOTL, 7, 210
    F-16 base in Italy, 178
    foreign capital dependence of, 58
    and France, 112–116, 118, 119, 146
    and Germany, 15, 24–25, 32, 41, 58, 84,
        88, 96–98, 102–103
    and INF treaty, 6–7
    and Italy, 172, 173, 178, 181
    and Libyan bombing, 185, 261
    and Low Countries, 195–197, 201–202
    military presence in Europe, 14, 17–20,
        22, 24–25, 65–66, 159–160, 163,
        257
        German attitude toward, 89, 91–96
    NATO role of, 14–15, 20, 27–29, 212–
        214, 255
    navy, 171, 186, 190, 217, 219, 244, 249–
        250
    and Norway, 217, 245–249
    and nuclear deterrent, 157–158
    and nuclear forces in Europe, 113, 158–
        159
    and nuclear port calls issue, 219, 224,
        230, 234, 244
    and nuclear threat of Soviet disintegration,
        23
    and out-of-area conflicts, 15, 146, 186
    short-range nuclear force modernization,
        171
    and Soviet Union, 21–23, 64, 75, 96, 149,
        152
    and Toshiba–Konigsberg scandal, 244–245
    trade relations with Europe, 97, 171, 183–
        184

Voigt, Karsten, 73

Wage development, in GDR, 55
Warsaw Pact:
    collapse of, 1–2, 72, 159, 209, 228
    liberalization of in 1990s, 256–257
    and NATO, 4, 156, 157
    as Soviet instrument, 44
    (*See also* Eastern Europe)
Weinberger, Caspar, 14, 29
West, as role model for Eastern Europe, 61,
    74, 98
West Germany (*see* Germany)
Western European Union (WEU), 118, 142,
    185, 212
White Papers on Defence (Great Britain),
    151–152
    1986, 146
    1989, 149, 157
    1990, 161, 162
Willoch, Kare, 236, 238
Wolfowitz, Paul, 14

Yugoslavia, 175, 189, 257

Zanone, Valerio, 176, 177, 180

About the Contributors

Ronald D. Asmus has been an associate political scientist at RAND since 1988. He has conducted research on the political, economic, and military trends in Germany and their impact on European security. Ron served as an advisor for German affairs on several RAND projects dealing with defense and arms control issues. During 1988 and 1989, he published analyses of West Germany's *Ostpolitik*. He is currently focusing on the issues surrounding German unification.

Ron spent 1986–1987 as a research associate at the West Berlin Institute of International Relations, and for five years before that he was a senior research analyst for Radio Free Europe/Radio Liberty. He received his B.A. (1979) in political science from the University of Wisconsin, Madison. He received his M.A. (1981) in Soviet/East European studies, and his Ph.D. (1990) in European studies from the School of Advanced International Studies at Johns Hopkins University.

Richard A. Bitzinger is an international policy analyst at RAND, specializing in NATO and European security issues. Previous to joining RAND, he was Program Coordinator for the UCLA Center for International and Strategic Affairs, as well as Associate Director of the Center's Nordic Security Project. He received his M.A. from the Monterey Institute of International Affairs and is currently in the Ph.D. program at UCLA.

Gregory Flynn is a Senior Associate at the Carnegie Endowment for International Peace in Washington, D.C. and formerly Deputy Director of the Atlantic Institute for International Affairs in Paris, where he resided from 1976–1987. Dr. Flynn is author and editor of numerous works on European security and East–West issues, including *The West and the Soviet Union: Politics and Policy*, *NATO's Northern Allies*, *Public Images of Western Security*, and *The Public and Atlantic Defense*.

Ian Lesser is a staff member of the International Policy Department of RAND, specializing in European and Mediterranean affairs. Prior to joining RAND he was a Senior Fellow in International Security Affairs at the Center for Strategic and International Studies, and has also been a Senior Fellow of the Atlantic Council and a staff consultant at International Energy Associates in Washington, D.C. A graduate of the University of Pennsylvania and the Fletcher School of Law and Diplomacy, he received his doctorate from St. Antony's College, Oxford.

Robert A. Levine, a senior economist at RAND, is the author of *The Arms Debate* (1962) and *Still the Arms Debate* (1989), analyses of the positions policy makers and specialists advanced on nuclear policy, military policy, and arms control. Dr. Levine's work has recently focused on issues of national security policy and arms control; he was the director of RAND's National Security Strategies Program, in the Project AIR FORCE Division, from 1987–1989. Dr. Levine has also planned, supervised, and conducted policy analyses on U.S. domestic issues.

Affiliated with RAND since 1957, Dr. Levine has at numerous points in his career served in government (as Deputy Director of the Congressional Budget Office and as Chief of Research and Plans, Office of Economic Opportunity), academe, and for other research institutions (among them the Harvard Center for International Affairs, the Urban Institute, and the System Development Corporation).

Dr. Levine received his B.A. (1950) and M.A. (1951) from Harvard University, and his Ph.D. (1968) from Yale University. He is a member of the Institute for Strategic Studies and the American Economic Association, has published four books and numerous scholarly articles.

John Lund is an International Policy Analyst with the RAND Corporation. A specialist in applying a multidisciplinary approach to issues of international security, he received his Ph.D. from the RAND Graduate School for Policy Studies (1987), his M.A. from Columbia University's School of International and Public Affairs (1984) in international security, and his B.A. from Saint Joseph's University (1982) in international relations and in economics.

Since coming to RAND in 1984, Dr. Lund has worked extensively on West European military, economic, and political affairs. He has authored over a dozen RAND publications, including works on Nordic security; NATO air forces, procurement plans, and budgets; NATO theater nuclear forces; and Soviet international finance. He analyzed Nordic security policies and defense capabilities as a consultant to the President's Commission on Integrated Long-term Strategy. He has recently directed projects assessing the airlift operations in Desert Shield and examining the deployability of the United States Air Force in contingencies.

In 1988 Dr. Lund worked on assignment for RAND to the Headquarters United States Air Forces in Europe, Ramstein Air Force Base, West Germany. He is a member of the International Institute for Strategic Studies.

Phil Williams is Professor of International Security at the Graduate School of Public and International Affairs, University of Pittsburgh and Director of Research at the University's Ridgway Center. He is author of *Crisis Management, The Senate and US Troops in Europe,* co-author of *Superpower Detente,* of *Contemporary Strategy,* and co-editor of *Superpower Competition and Crisis Prevention in the Third World,* and of *Superpower Politics.*